Backcountry
Pilot

THE SOUTHWEST CENTER SERIES

Backcountry Pilot

Flying Adventures with Ike Russell

Edited by Thomas Bowen

THE UNIVERSITY OF ARIZONA PRESS
TUCSON

The University of Arizona Press
© 2002 The Arizona Board of Regents
All rights reserved

www.uapress.arizona.edu

First paperback printing 2010
ISBN 978-0-8165-2938-4 (pbk. : alk. paper)

Library of Congress Cataloging-in-Publication Data
Backcountry pilot : flying adventures with Ike Russell / edited by Thomas Bowen
   p. cm.
  ISBN 0-8165-2179-4 (cloth)
  1. Russell, Ike, 1916–1980. 2. Bush pilots—United States—Biography. 3. Bush
flying—Southwest, New—Anecdotes. 4. Bush flying—Mexico—Anecdotes.
I. Bowen, Thomas, 1942–

TL540. R874 B33 2002
629.13′092—dc21
[B]

                                2001052247

15 14 13 12 11 10   7 6 5 4 3 2

Photo of Ike Russell on page v by Thomas Bowen, March 1967.

The airplane is a means,
not an end... a means
of getting away from
towns and their bookkeeping
and coming to grips with reality.

Antoine de Saint-Exupéry

CONTENTS

PREFACE

When people get together around Tucson, there is a good chance that somebody will say, "That reminds me of the time I flew with Ike Russell . . . ."
One story tends to beget another, and pretty soon people will be laughing
and shaking their heads at the outrageous adventures that unfolded for those
fortunate enough to have flown with the legendary Ike Russell.

Ike's exploits have been famous for decades, and there is an entire corpus
of anecdotes about him that are known far and wide. They have become the
stuff of regional folklore, for stories about Ike are often told by people who
never met him, much less flew with him, and one may well hear quite different versions of some of his better-known escapades.

This volume brings together a wide range of anecdotes and reminiscences
about flying the backcountry with Ike, written by the individuals who actually
lived the experiences. Many describe the great adventures that have become
enshrined in folklore as classic "Ike Russell stories," in all their hair-raising and
hilarious splendor. But not all the narratives in this collection tell of audacious
exploits and gut-wrenching close calls. Many of Ike's flights—and indeed some
of his most important flying—did not result in high drama or riotous incidents, but nonetheless had far-reaching impact on the lives of a great many
people. It is hard to overstate Ike's contribution to scholarship and knowledge by flying scientists and scholars of all kinds to remote field locations
that could not otherwise have been investigated. Nor do most people realize
that he played an important role in improving the health of the Seri Indians
by flying medicines to them over a period of many years. Ike contributed to
the well-being of countless ordinary people, many of them isolated Mexican
villagers and ranchers, by bringing them goods that were otherwise virtually
unobtainable—even such essentials as shoes—and by giving rides to people
who needed medical attention or who simply wanted to visit distant relatives.

Ike was far more than just a highly skilled bush pilot; he was an extraordi-
nary human being. His towering intellect, encyclopedic knowledge, nonjudg-
mental appreciation of others, his fundamental humility, and his irrepressible
humor profoundly affected those around him. And all this from a man in
poor health who lived with almost constant pain and chronic fatigue. The
stories in this volume may tell of wild adventures and wonderful experiences,
but they are also loving portraits of a man with rare personal gifts who often
inspired the best in those whose lives he touched.

For the most part, this book is a work of oral history that makes little use
of the written record. This is true even of the biographical sketch that ends

the book, which was prepared chiefly from interviews with Ike's family and close friends. The most important written sources have been Ike's notebooks and pilot logs. Even these, however, have proved to be of limited utility, for Ike was not a good record-keeper. His later logs, particularly, are not always trustworthy and in a few instances are clearly in error.

Most of the stories in this volume were written entirely from memory. A few contributors had field notes or journals to fall back on, and everyone was encouraged to check their recollections against written records wherever possible. But it is important to bear in mind that even the most recent flights with Ike took place more than 20 years ago, and some occurred over half a century ago. As every contributor was painfully aware, memories over this span of time are far from perfect, especially for details. Time has an insidious way of winnowing out certain particulars and embellishing or idealizing others. One of the results is that overlapping stories sometimes relate the same events quite differently. Cross-checking with external sources has enabled some discrepancies to be resolved, but in other instances there seems to be no way of reconciling the inconsistencies. Of course, it may be that differing accounts are equally "correct" and merely reflect different perspectives on the same events.

In recognition of the fallibility of memory, nearly every contributor hedged his or her narrative with such phrases as, "I think what happened was . . . ." and "To the best of my recollection . . . ." Because equivocation is the kiss of death to a good story, most of these admirably honest declarations of uncertainty have been editorially deleted. Since this practice amounts to bending the truth a bit in the interest of narrative flow, the reader should be aware that some of the details in these anecdotes are not as certain as they may seem. But even with these caveats, it is safe to say that these recollections about flying with Ike are fundamentally reliable, and one might even characterize them as "authoritative" accounts. To be sure, they are told as stories, not scientific reports, but coming from personal experience, they are probably as close to what really happened as we are ever likely to get.

It is a tribute to Ike that this book materialized at all, for many of the contributors gladly took time out from busy schedules to be a part of this enterprise. Nor would it ever have come to pass without the wholehearted and enthusiastic support of Ike's immediate family—his widow Jean Russell and their sons Luke, Bob, and Dave Russell. These four remarkable and gracious people gave freely of their knowledge and memories of Ike, and working with them has been both a privilege and a pleasure that I shall long cherish.

Many people besides Ike's family and the authors of the stories contributed information about Ike, and I particularly thank Ward Davidson, Bill Hansen, Carolyn Hastings, Loyd Hopper, Randolph and Julia Jenks, Peggy Larson, Becky Moser, Pat Patterson, Kate Reeve, Barbara Straub, Bob Straub, Kate

PREFACE xiii

Straub, Jay and Patty Thomas, and Richard White. I am indebted to Jeff Bowen for guidance on technical aspects of airplanes and flight, to Barbara Jardee for preparing transcripts of taped interviews, and to Adela Hice and Lupita Cruz for logistical support in Tucson. I thank also Nancy Ford for spotting so many of my errors, Ann Wagner for helping correct the proofs, Paul Mirocha for the excellent maps, Bill Benoit for his fine design work, and Yvonne Reineke for deftly coordinating the production process. Marty Brace helped enormously with the editing of the manuscript, and I am deeply grateful for her keen eye, insightful comments, and sage advice. And finally, I wish to thank Joe Wilder, Director of the University of Arizona Southwest Center, for his unflagging support and good cheer throughout the duration of this project.

T. B.

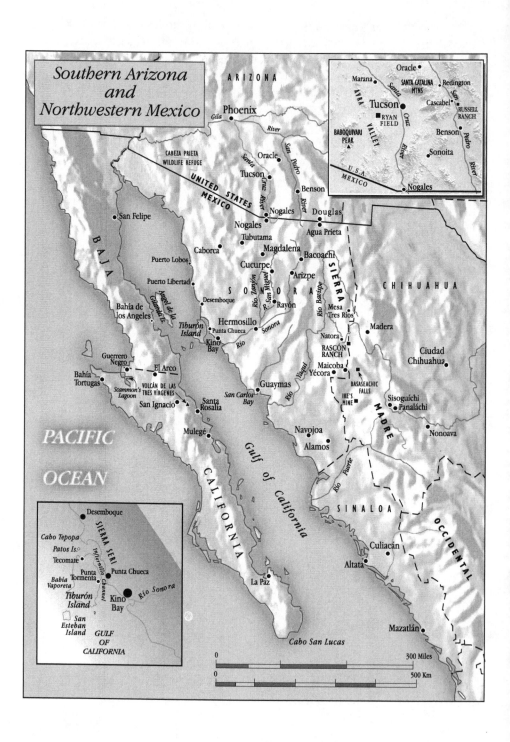

Southern Arizona
and
Northwestern Mexico

ARIZONA

Phoenix
Gila   *River*

CABEZA PRIETA
WILDLIFE REFUGE

UNITED STATES
MEXICO

Oracle
Santa
Cruz
River
Tucson
Benson
San Pedro River

San Felipe

Nogales

Nogales
Tubutama   Agua Prieta
Douglas

B A J A

Caborca   Magdalena
Puerto Lobos   Cucurpe   Bacoachí
Arizpe
Puerto Libertad
Desemboque   S O N O R A

Ángel de la
Guarda Is.   Río Yaqui
R. San Miguel
Rayón
Bahía de
los Ángeles   Tiburón   Hermosillo   R.
Island   Punta Chueca   Sonora   Mesa
Kino   Río   Tres Ríos
Bay   Sonora

S I E R R A

C H I H U A H U A

Guerrero
Negro   El Arco
Bahía   VOLCÁN DE LAS
Tortugas   Scammon's TRES VÍRGENES
Lagoon   San Ignacio   Santa
Rosalía   San Carlos
Bay

Natora
RASCÓN
RANCH
Maicoba
Yécora

Madera

Ciudad
Chihuahua

BASASEACHIC
FALLS
IKE'S
MINE

Sisoguíchi
Panaláchi

Nonoava

Mulegé

Guaymas

Navojoa
Álamos

M A D R E

PACIFIC

OCEAN

C A L I F O R N I A

G u l f   o f   C a l i f o r n i a

Río Fuerte

S I N A L O A

O C C I D E N T A L

La Paz

Culiacán
Altata

Mazatlán

Cabo San Lucas

0   300 Miles
0   500 Km

Oracle
Marana   SANTA CATALINA
MTNS   Redington
AVRA
Tucson   Cascabel   RUSSELL
RANCH
RYAN
FIELD
BABOQUIVARI   Benson
PEAK
Sonoita
U.S.A.
MEXICO
Nogales

Santa
Cruz
River

AVRA
VALLEY

San
Pedro
River

Desemboque
Cabo Tepopa
SIERRA SERI
Patos Is.
Tecomate
Infiernillo Channel
Punta
Bahía   Tormenta   Punta Chueca
Vaporeta
Tiburón Island   Kino   Río Sonora
Bay
San
Esteban
Island   GULF
OF
CALIFORNIA

1... THE GULF OF CALIFORNIA

*To Ike, the region surrounding the
Gulf of California was one of
the finest places in the world. The
Gulf had it all: desert, sea, exotic
islands, a rich array of wildlife.
It was wilderness, but it was also
home to people he liked and respected,
both Mexicans and Seri Indians. And
it was the place to visit his special
friends Ed and Becky Moser and their
daughter Cathy. The Gulf was where
many of his scientist friends needed
to go to pursue their research. And
it was a wonderful place for family
vacations. When Ike flew into Mexico,
the direction he headed most often
was toward the Gulf of California.*

1

Sinaloa Shootout

RICHARD STEPHEN FELGER

When we got back to Ryan Airfield Ike would say, "Made it again." It all seemed so matter of fact, spotting plants out the window, flying around mountains, landing just about anywhere. Going to see whales, meeting interesting people.

•••

Eelgrass grows in protected seas along temperate coasts around the world. It is well known in Sonora but factors affecting the southern limit and the situation in Sinaloa were still a mystery. A 1910 report mentions a specimen from Altata, due west from Culiacán in Sinaloa, and I want to go there. It is mid-March 1977, and at this time of year there should be detached eelgrass forming rafts at the sea surface. As usual Ike is eager to go—I just have to pay for gas. I ask Kim Cliffton, who works with me on sea turtles (they eat eelgrass), and Tom Backman, who did his graduate work in California on eelgrass, to come along. Four of us, a full plane.

We get to the Russell's early in the morning. Ike is rummaging through metal ammo boxes of nuts and bolts, spare parts, tools, and his medications. He spends a lot of time shuffling and packing. I don't question it; he is in charge of airplane matters. Sometimes he also spends a lot of time disguising things hard to get across the border to take to friends in Mexico. Finally, we all jam in his dull gray 1941 Ford pickup and drive out to Ryan Airfield in the Avra Valley west of Tucson, about 30 minutes from where Ike and Jean live.

Ike has a hankering for old pickups. Once on the way to Ryan, Ike made a U-turn on the Ajo Highway, opened the door, stuck out his long arm and scooped up a hubcap. "This is a good one." Like any old rancher he keeps a lot of parts. Once an attorney and I tried to run a rasty little ranch. An old Chevy pickup came with the ranch and I said the pickup is mine but the attorney would not give me the title. So I traded that rattletrap to Ike for a trip to Mexico and he took the truck to Mexico.

We're at Ryan and Tom probably thinks we are just going to climb into the plane and take off, and Kim has the patience of a turtle. More tinkering. Checking the engine and different parts of the plane. Ike gets into a deep conversation with Fred Grissom who takes care of the planes in this World

War II hangar—wide tongue-and-groove weathered 1940s wood outside walls, and cool and drafty inside like an opened cathedral. Fred wears overalls and fusses over the planes like a mother hen—Ike once said he was alive because of Fred. Airplane parts all over the place, his office boxed off inside the hangar, smelling of cigarettes and stale cups of coffee, and girlie calendars advertising tools and engines.

Fred teases Ike with intense concern about not bringing the airplane back again with a green propeller—it turned green the time we went through the tall amaranth at the mining claim. Fred once said, "Ike would fly in weather that would drown a duck." And there was the time Ike landed silently, got out and had his passengers help push the plane to the hangar. Fred said, "Cutting it a little close on gas, aren't you Ikey?"

Tinkering is a big deal for Ike. He loves to tinker the way I like field work and studying plants in the herbarium. Ike put a 1918 Dodge engine in the *Ofelia*—the ungainly little boat he had built in Guaymas modeled after a fisherman's *panga*—says it can cruise the whole Gulf of California on one tank of gas. It's loud, stinky, hot, and disgustingly slow but provides lots of tinker-time. He tinkers with his pickup. He tinkers with his airplane. I always carry a paperback book in my back pocket.

Finally when it's time to load gear into the plane he scrutinizes everything I bring. He picks up each item and dangles it up and down for weight. Everything is always too heavy. "Do you really need so many plant presses?" and, "Do you have to bring that thing?" There was the time Jean tried to put a sea-worn egg-shaped boulder in the plane—we picked up the rock on San Esteban Island and brought it to Kino Bay in the *Ofelia*. Then one day I saw that the egg rock had made it to Tucson and sat in a place of honor by the front door. Sometimes, especially in summer, I have terrible arguments with Ike about water. You can't win an argument with Ike for the simple maddening reason that he is always right—except about summertime drinking water. I won't give in on that one—you never forget close calls with water. I learn to bring twice as much water and twice the plant presses I really need so Ike can make me leave half. It's always half.

As I said, you never forget close calls with water. Once on Tiburón Island we flew around the east side of the big mountain—the Sierra Kunkaak—until we located the Sopc Hax waterhole, marked by bright green giant cane grass, tucked into a canyon recess at the toe of the mountain. We land at Palo Fierro and it seems like an easy few miles walk, but what's easy to spot from the air can be hard to find on the ground and we climb up the wrong canyon. Ike doesn't stop to collect plants and we get separated. I see smoke off in the distance. He's burned an old packrat nest for a smoke signal and next to it left a note stuck on a creosotebush stick: "I'll meet you at the big rock-fig that blocks the canyon." I take a short cut straight over the ridge to the next canyon and down to the big rock-fig blocking the canyon, but no Ike. He must be behind me, coming up the canyon bottom. I wait . . . and wait. Yikes, its late in the afternoon so I hightail it out of the canyon and head for the plane. I have very little water—we expected to fill canteens at the waterhole.

Night falls fast. Pitch dark and no flashlight since this is only a day trip. I keep bumping into impenetrable mangroves and try going around but too many cactus and spiny shrubs. I fall asleep on top of sharp rocks and scratchy cryptanthas and wake up with coyote breath in my face. I move and the coyote runs off but now it's cold and me with only a thin T-shirt. Dawn is way too slow. I am out of water. My tongue is huge and I can't swallow. I misjudged and have to go several more miles out of my way around the mangroves to get to the landing field. The sun is high, hot and swirling in a Van Gogh sky only it does not look pretty. The silver sea beckons but I keep forcing myself to realize it's not drinking water. I know the plane has to be way off to the left of the sea shine and keep forcing myself in that direction. I must be close but can't find the long low flat ridge with the landing strip. I pop a few bursera fruits in my mouth—the Seris say it helps make saliva run when you are out of water. The first time it almost helps. I climb up into a huge cardon cactus and don't see the plane. It has to be there . . . it has to . . . he wouldn't have left. I keep forcing the steps and just as I start to walk right through the plane without seeing it Ike hands me the last tiny bit of water in the half-gallon green glass bottle that's always in the plane. It's not enough but he is not much better off and has been saving this for me. We climb in and fly wordless across to Kino Bay, land at the edge of town and taxi up to Doña Gavina's little home-restaurant next to the beach. We walk in, pick up water pitchers sitting on the tables and drink, spilling water down us and all over the place. Don't get me wrong, it's not always like that. It's usually fun and easy.

• • •

So here we are at Ryan in this huge old hangar crammed full of airplanes. Fred has great talent for fitting the wing of one over the wing of the next one, and so forth. We move a few planes out of the way and roll out Ike's Cessna 185 which has a STOL kit (Short TakeOff and Landing) and other modifications. I take out my book and sit on an expensive airplane tire.

Finally we climb in the plane and take off, first for Nogales, Sonora. Always have to land in Mexico and get permits and clearance. I expect delay. If Ike would just give a standard little donation we would be on our way promptly, but he never does. Says if he does it once he would have to do it every time. More to the point Ike is just plain stingy, stubborn, and likes winning.

The officials know he brings "extra" stuff. They accuse him of flying into Mexico on business, being a commercial pilot paid to fly in Mexico. For such purposes one needs a commercial visa, which means lots of red tape and expense. He comes through too often, in and out, with too many different people. Nobody spends so much time and effort just for fun. The places we go cannot be for pleasure. He has to be up to something. Well, its not a truce, but there seems to be an understanding and somehow we always get through. In addition, this being Mexico, the airport *comandante* is responsible if anything happens to a plane that leaves under unsafe conditions. So there is real authority and concern.

The green propeller incident I mentioned a little while ago involves a trip to Ike's mining claim in the Sierra Madre Occidental in western Chihuahua. This time we are clearing Mexican customs in Hermosillo. Ike files the required flight plan from Nogales, Arizona. But before arriving in Hermosillo he makes an unannounced westward detour and lands way out in the desert. I nearly wreck my back helping him unload an unbelievably heavy wooden box we stash under an ironwood tree. I ask what's in it and he just says, "Dynamite for the mine." We arrive in Hermosillo flight-plan-late and things do not go smoothly. Ike won't pay an eight dollar special fee. The day wears on. I say I will pay it. This is not my idea of fun.

Ike goes to talk to El Comandante for the fourth or fifth time but El Comandante has "gone home for lunch." We get a taxi and go to his home. A woman answers the door and says El Comandante isn't in, although his car is in the carport. Back to the airport. Wait for El Comandante. Pretty soon it's too late in the day to leave. Taxi to a downtown hotel. Ike is a cheapskate unless it involves the airplane. He always picks cheap places. Mercifully this one is not absolutely the cheapest.

Ike worries that some cowboy might find his dynamite—about the only time I notice him being perturbed. This is costing more than eight dollars. Next morning after breakfast a taxi to the airport. Ike is having a long conversation with El Comandante without me present. We leave and pick up the box in the desert and head straight across the desert for the Sierra Madre.

We've been at the mining claim for two days and it's time to leave. But it's 4,000 feet elevation and over 100 degrees this afternoon so we have to wait until morning for cooler (denser) air to take off. Okay with me; I get more time to explore for plants, but Ike has a different plan. We chop amaranth and other weeds that have grown up at each end of the landing field with the summer rains. Ever chop fresh green amaranth as high as your head? Yellow pollen-rain mixes in sweat and runny nose and eyes. The landing field is not much more than several rows of corn Ike pays the owner not to plant. I don't like landing here. There are worse places but I only go to them once.

We leave soon after sunrise but it's still hot. The plane lifts off too slowly and the prop chops through amaranth just beyond the part we cleared. Barely clearing some scrubby boat-spine acacias and *mauto* trees we sort of sink into a vast canyon before the plane can lift up above the mountains.

I will never forget the way Fred shook his head when we got back to Tucson with a green propeller. I don't say anything to Jean and I doubt if Ike does. Ike and Bill Swan bought the mining claim from Bill's brother-in-law Pat Jenks who is notorious for treasure-hunting escapades in Sonora. I don't see how they expect to make money on the mining claim, but maybe that's not the issue.

Let me tell you about another dicey summertime event. We arrive in Nogales, Sonora, before midday. Plenty of time to get to Guaymas by early afternoon. It is clear and very hot in the middle of the monsoon season. Long conversations with El Comandante and a long delay. Billowing white cumulus clouds close in and turn to dark nimbus lightening, thunder, and torrential rain, and refreshingly cool. El Comandante declares it is unsafe to leave. We wait. I finish my book. The clouds clear and El Comandante almost lets us go but before another long conversation ends the clouds roll in again.

Finally a break in the clouds and Ike manages a breakthrough with El Comandante. Ike says, "Let's get out of here." I seldom see him move so quickly. Almost as soon as we are up in the sky the clouds close off the intended route. Ike says, "There's a hole over there, let's head for it." That route closes and we chase more holes in the clouds. Finally after chasing lots of sky holes, here we are again smack dab over the Nogales airport. Ike does not want to go back there again. The clouds are high enough so we fly under them. Ike follows the highway.

There is bright sunlight not too far off at the end of the valley. I look down at Emory oaks on overgrazed hills and when I look up the sunlight is gone, the ceiling sinks and it's dark and stormy. The plane tosses in wind and torrential rain. Ike says we have to land and manages a clear stretch of highway. Right away he gets the plane down off the blacktop onto a little dirt turnoff at a roadside ranchito. I hop out, open the flimsy wire and pole ranch gate, Ike drives the plane through. I close the gate and run up to the house for shelter but am already drenched. Ike stops the plane in front of the family gathered under the broad, low porch. They offer handshakes and "Mucho gusto en conocerle" (Very pleased to meet you). Homemade wooden chairs with crisscross leather strapping are placed at the table for us. Dark hot coffee and lots of sugar and pleasant conversation. The storm clears as fast as it came.

We are saying good-bye and thanking our hosts when The Head of Customs charges into the muddy yard in a chauffeured Thunderbird surrounded in a roar of police motorcycles. He announces, "We got you this time," and threatens to confiscate the plane. Ike and The Head of Customs are just beginning their conversation when two more motorcycle police roar up. They whisper something to The Head of Customs and without another word they all leave, sirens blasting down the highway.

We thank our hosts again, shake hands all around, promise to come back and see them, drive up to the highway, wait for the traffic to pass and take off. In just a few minutes we fly over a twin-engine Beechcraft and the Thunderbird next to the highway surrounded by the motorcycle swarm. Later we learn that they also made a forced landing and quickly paid a $2,500 fine.

• • •

Back to the Sinaloa eelgrass trip. This time we clear Nogales without incident. We head for the coast at Desemboque and hope to find Becky Moser at home. Ed Moser died suddenly last summer and Becky is carrying on her husband's work.

It is just a few years since Becky and I published our paper on Seri use of eelgrass—the first report of a grain from the sea as a human food resource. *Science* published it and put Helga Teiwes's haunting photograph of a Seri eelgrass doll on the cover. That paper made quite a splash. It was also a turning point for me. I had recently left a generous position at the Natural History Museum in Los Angeles. I had to be back in the desert, out of the smog and off the freeways, but the financial part of quitting was not realistic. The *Science* paper helped in getting sporadic grant support for the field work including airplane gas and launched me into the emerging halophyte-science crowd. Hazel Fontana made the first loaf of bread from the sea using eelgrass flour we bought from the Seris. It was bright green inside.

That *Science* article—as well as a few others—encouraged Becky and me to keep working on our Seri ethnobotany book. This book was still "almost finished" and I felt guilty not having it completed in time for Ed to see. It only took another eight years to finish. Without Ike and Jean Russell it would never have been finished, let alone started.

Ike Russell first brought me to Desemboque. We had been on Tiburón Island and I had a plastic bag full of plants that needed pressing. According to Becky, the first thing I said when I walked into their Shangri-La home was, "Where can I press my plants?" I was quite single-minded. Soon I discovered the Seris living in my study area and realized they knew more than I did about the plants. Those were wonderful times. I was finishing my Ph.D. Then some academic appointments. We were all so purposeful. Ike had to have a reason to go flying. My reason was that I had my work to do. It made a big difference to have Ike take me in his airplane. It was fun to go places with him, airplane or not. Everybody loved Ike, at least after the waiting. It was even more fun when Jean went along. We landed and camped just about anywhere. And John Dog often went with us.

The first time at Russells' for dinner, John Dog joined us at the table. Ike and Jean's son Luke had taught him to gingerly take food off a fork and eat politely from a plate—seemed like he had the best manners of anyone at the table. John's tail stuck out behind the chair. When John got too old to jump into the plane we lifted him up. He was a big Aussie weighing over 90 pounds. Then after John was gone Weni would go, especially if Jean went. Ike inspired Weni to growl, and Weni inspired Ike to growl, although Weni got along with everyone else. Then my dog would go along; her father was one of the Russells' big white dogs.

As I said, those were wonderful times. We could land just about anywhere. Ike seemed to know every rancher in Sonora, or knew someone who knew someone where we would go. We were always welcome and they were always welcome at the Russell's. I don't know how Jean did it—there was always room for another friend or friend of a friend. Their tree-shaded ranch along Cottonwood Lane was an international institution, like a grand hotel.

There was still no big drug trouble in Sonora. At least we didn't have to know about it or pay attention to it. Once in a while we would see a fast fancy plane on a dry lake bed and some city boys standing around waiting for someone. And only once were we clearly not welcome, when we landed at a forlorn ranch way out in the desert between Nogales and Desemboque.

• • •

Back to the Sinaloa eelgrass trip. We buzz the house, and Becky and some other gringos wave, and her daughter Cathy's lazy brown dog Slab is wagging his tail. Seri kids are running for the landing field and everyone is looking up. We land at the long, sandy smooth field near the shore north of Desemboque. Ike pays a Seri, José Astorga, to help keep it clear and had a sign made in Spanish and English that says anyone landing here should pay Astorga a certain nominal fee for his labors. Becky and her guests drive out to pick us up. The Seris press around us. They are not at all meek, always laughing and making fun of everyone, the women all at once trying to sell necklaces, baskets, and ironwood sculpture.

The Seris call Ike *Mericaana Cacösxaj* "Tall American." I am *Ctam Hehe Iyat Ctaamtim* "Guy Who Cuts Off the Tops of Plants." Ed Moser was *Moósni Ilit* "Turtle Head". We liked our names. Some people did not fare as well with their Seri-given names.

During those years when we sat down to eat in the cement floor dining room-kitchen-everything room in the Moser's beach-damp house, the Seris pressed around the windows staring at us, watching us eat. We were the best and only show in town. After the sun went down the kerosene Aladdin lamps were lit and it was the most peaceful place I have ever known. Sometimes Ed performed magic tricks. Becky and I worked on the ethnobotany manuscript. There were the day's notes to write up, plants for me to identify, revisions in the text, more questions to be answered. The action centered around the heavy wooden table in the kitchen.

The shower is behind the big silent gas refrigerator. Water is heated on the stove, poured into a bucket with a twist-turn sprinkler at the bottom and the bucket carried around behind the fridge and hoisted up on a pulley. You close the curtain and can keep on talking to the people in the kitchen. Ike all too often passes on the shower.

The next few days are occupied with field work along the Infiernillo Channel opposite Tiburón Island, botanizing and going places in the desert and along the coast with Seris, recording information on ethnobotany and sea turtles. After dinner, we spread out maps and look at the Sinaloa coast to Altata. The map shows some sandy barrier islands and huge complicated lagoons.

At bedtime we open up aluminum folding cots on the back porch. It is dark with only stars and the wet sound of the waves and dogs and sometimes donkeys and coyotes. Everyone else is asleep but just as I drift off another bunch of mangy Desemboque dogs starts barking and yowling from yet another direction . . . then silent torture waiting for it to start up again, over and over. When Cathy Moser was in college Ed sent her a double-sided tape of "Desemboque Sounds at Night." She thought the dogs and donkeys were wonderful.

Ike is in the little room off the kitchen—the dampness outside bothers him tonight. He is always coughing a bit. He has chronic health problems, which is why he ended up in Tucson in the first place, and self-medicates to keep going. With big parts of diseased lungs removed he has the choice of spending his time sitting in a chair or taking life-shortening drugs that enable him to live a heroic life. Like Franklin Roosevelt he is basically an invalid but nobody knows it. One day toward the long ending I walked into the house in Tucson and he calmly said, "I've got myeloma and I don't like that."

Sometimes I slept in that back room—unpainted cement floor and walls, plain thick wood shelves stocked with supplies and canned goods, bags of beans and potatoes, blankets, Seri crafts and artifacts on the walls, medications, paintings by John Houser and some by Cathy Moser. Flashlight always by the bed.

I am up well before sunrise and as always go for a long walk along the shore before breakfast. The beach drift is piled high with a fantasia of sea shells and marine life. Paper-thin bleached piddocks, sea urchin testa, and coralline algae, bubble shells, pectens, tiny perfect sand dollars, coffeebean cowries—the whole list is longer than this chapter. There is no way to avoid crunching them but their life is gone. (The beach in southern California where I grew up was also once like this.) At this time of year lots of eelgrass and winter seaweeds make up most of the beach drift, and I notice the first plastitrash.

I used to also go out for a long walk right after breakfast, when Ed would read from the New Testament. One day he informed me that I was the only visitor who did not stay for the Bible readings. So I put off my walks until after his reading. There was a clarity and calmness to his readings that I later learned were a mark of deep spirituality. Ike was truly interested and would engage Ed in Bible discussion, although he would admit to no organized religion.

Ed and Becky of course were passionate about the New Testament—their purpose for being at Desemboque was to translate the Bible into Seri. Along the way they published scholarly works on Seri culture—often but not always coauthored with specialists—made Seri a written language, taught Seris to read and write in their own language as well as Spanish. They were forever on call to take someone in need to the hospital in Hermosillo, fix the water pump, etc. There was never-ending action, and Ike constantly brought things people needed and flew them to Desemboque, especially medicines. Ike's friend Dr. Bob Thomas provided medical help, and long after the good doctor was dead mail-order discount medications bought on his name continued to go to the Seris in Ike's plane.

I don't know how Becky put up with all the commotion or got so much accomplished. Everyone going through stopped in on them, including of course us. The Mosers were the most tolerant people I ever knew. Over the years we maintained a close friendship although the Russells and I sharply disagreed with many of their political views. My life has been vastly enriched by Becky, Ed, Jean, and Ike. They influenced my whole career. Ike and Jean contributed so much to my work, and to just about everybody else I knew doing research in Sonora and even Baja California and sometimes Africa, South America, and Madagascar.

•••

Ike knows the desert. He knows the sea. He knows the Sierra Madre. He knows ranching. He has vast practical knowledge of the Sonoran Desert and people and places. He can fix anything. But you better be prepared for Ike Russell time and you better like plain Ry Krisp crackers because that's often all we have to eat.

But I learn to be wary of landing too late in the day, too close to darkness or even in the dark, and try to devise ways to avoid such events. There is the time we are coming into Kino Bay a bit late in the day. We are just going from Desemboque to Kino to deliver some guinea pigs Jean is sending to Doña Gavina. We are coming in for a landing in a strong wind when I spot utility poles and wires strung all over the place. They weren't here last time. Ike pulls up fast and we search for another landing place. The wind really picks up and dust nearly obliterates the view. Landing into the wind means landing into low-angle blinding sunlight albeit through murky dust. We can't be sure where the wires are and keep searching to no avail for a place to land in increasingly poor visibility as darkness descends. Now it's too dark so Ike keeps circling—a message to meet the plane. Finally someone savvy to the ways of small planes drives out to the paved highway and shines headlights in the right direction. We land and taxi in front of the headlights the half mile or so to Doña Gavina's little home and restaurant by the beach. As we get ready to leave in the morning a cop drives up and hassles Ike for improper landing behavior.

Another time we fly out of Kino Bay after a week-long trip to San Esteban Island in the *Ofelia*. It's the old story—it is a bit late but we can always stop in Desemboque or find somewhere to camp. Now it's getting dark so we land on a convenient dry lake bed. Oh well, a nice campfire and plenty of food. But the place is barren and not a scrap of firewood in a cold biting wind. We didn't think to tell each other, but I left what food I had with Doña Gavina, Jean did the same and so did Ike. To make matters worse our sleeping bags are way too thin. While we shiver Ike says, "This qualifies as an emergency." He finds a small Phillips screw driver in one of his metal ammo boxes and methodically starts taking apart the backs of the front seats. Tough little plastic lab bottles full of tequila are securely duct-taped end to end to the tubular framework.

• • •

It's time to leave Desemboque and head for Altata. Becky and her guests drive us out to the airfield over the sandy road. In the usual bright clear sky we finally take off for Altata. You might wonder why I use the word "finally" so many times. When you travel with Ike it is on his time. He is methodical. He is not like the rest of us. Nothing makes him hurry. You accept his pace or you better stay home, which is no fun compared to going on a trip with Ike.

We fly down the coast south of Guaymas. Hours and hours of wide green ribbons of mangroves clog long lagoons. I don't see the anticipated floating eelgrass rafts but in northern Sinaloa I see long rows of big beach houses on sandy shores. As in a Fellini movie, most of them are silently falling into ruin. Maybe it was a hurricane. The scene keeps repeating between more mangroves and then we land at Altata. It is near dusk as we set down on coastal salt flat dampened bare ground in a wide place in the road at the edge of town. We climb out and stretch. Coconut palms lean over dilapidated houses strung along the strand above a broad waveless beach on an inlet bay. There is no breeze and everything smells moist and tropical. Nobody greets us. Tom and I walk down to the beach and look for eelgrass in the drift but only find *Ruppia*, another kind of seagrass. A nice botanical record but not what we are looking for.

Ike stops at a few houses and asks about a place to stay and buy meals. Nobody offers information. That's strange—even in the smallest place in Sonora there is always an older woman, often a widow in black, who fixes meals and lets travelers use an extra room or the porch for a modest donation. It's getting dark.

I walk over to some fishermen hanging out next to beached *pangas* and ask about eelgrass—*zacate del mar*—describing it in detail. They act like they don't know what I am talking about. They're not like fishermen in Sonora. They don't laugh, not even at me. This place is creepy. Too late to go anywhere else. A bunch of gun-toting teenage soldiers announce they are guarding the airplane, which means we will have to pay them.

Finally a gringo I will call "Joe" materializes and offers us meals and a place to stay. He lives here with no visible means of support. Like the rest of the house, the unpainted wooden floor sags and the view is obscured by grime-clogged rusting screens. The old woman who serves us doesn't speak. I go out to the beach again and talk to fishermen still hanging around their *pangas*. We talk about sea turtles and again I ask about *zacate del mar*. They remain reserved and only slightly more friendly than before.

It has been a long day and I am thankful for a safe place to put a sleeping bag. The place is unbelievably dark and quiet. It seems like a different country from Sonora. In the first light I search the beach drift and skirt a mangrove lagoon but there is only *Ruppia*. While I was at the beach Kim and Ike have been talking to Joe. I don't want to stay here. There is no eelgrass and we would make better use of our time going back to Desemboque.

Joe didn't know jack about eelgrass last night, and now says he knows where it is and can take us there in his pickup. I think he is lying, but what for? I get out our maps and ask him to show me where the eelgrass is. He looks at the map of the Altata region for a long time. Maybe he doesn't know how to read maps. He's a strange duck but then I suppose we are too. Why would anyone come here looking for something called eelgrass? Joe shows us a place way back in an *estero* (lagoon) where he says eelgrass grows. I know eelgrass does not grow in stagnant backwater. The place he points to consists mostly of barren, dry salt flats we saw flying in yesterday. I ask how long it takes to get there. An hour or so. Well, I am sure that means at least two hours and there goes the whole day for nothing.

I tell Ike and Kim I don't want to waste the time and expense. Tom does not say much. Both Ike and Kim are on my case. "What makes you think you know so much? This guy lives here and knows the place. You don't know everything." Something has happened and I won't go. Since I am paying for this trip I insist we go back to Desemboque. Ike and Kim put up quite an argument for going and seeing what Joe has to show us. This is one time I won't give in. I know about eelgrass and it can't grow there. I prevail and we put our things together. Still rather early and time to get to Desemboque at a reasonable hour.

Joe is really trying to persuade us. What the hell does it matter to him if we find eelgrass or not? Why does he care about it now? Oh well, maybe he is just lonely for American company or wants to earn a bit of money. We pick up our gear and head for the plane. Just past a muddy little alley one of the fishermen I was talking to last night darts out from behind a house and says, "You guys better get out of here as fast as you can" and runs off before I can say anything. I catch up with Ike—he's taller and always walks faster.

I tell Ike and Kim says, "What for? Didn't you ask him why?" I repeat we should get going, but Ike won't rush.

Ike checks the oil and fiddles with things under the cowl. The plane sits on a wide place in the road, next to a school yard full of kids. The soldiers guarding the plane have evaporated. "Well, at least we don't have to pay them," says Ike. Tom, Kim, and I climb in. Kim has a pilot's license so he gets to sit in front with Ike. Out of nowhere a single-engine plane swoops down—pow . . . pow . . . pooff . . . pooff . . . pooff—the place is sprayed with bullets. I yell to Ike we need to get the hell out of here—that fisherman knew something for sure. Ike closes the cowl, climbs in and starts up the plane, sticks his head out and yells the usual "Clear!" He radios to the other plane making another pass at us. No answer. More strafing. Dirt blows up in little puffs at the same time we hear the "pooff . . . pooff . . . ."

The school yard is empty. Ike taxies out, keeps trying to radio, and we are off fast and short. Now I remember Ike and Joe talking about the plane last night.

Whew . . . we've left Altata none too soon. From my cramped seat I look down at endless coastal plain of thornscrub and mangroves fringing the sea and look up to see the other plane coming at us. There he is right next to us. I am almost fascinated as the window gradually opens upward and in dreamy slow motion a steel cylinder slips out and spits fire. Shit! I am looking into a gun barrel firing at my eyeballs. I yell, "He's shooting at us!"

"What makes you think he's shooting at us?" says Kim in his ex-heavyweight-boxer studied macho manner. Bullets whiz in front of the windshield and Kim is a believer.

Ike calmly says, "I don't know what I can do about his shooting at us but I know what I can do." He plunges the plane down red-lining the tach to just above the water, wheels almost in the sea and slowly outdistances our adversary.

We keep going north, stop for fuel in Guaymas, and head home. We find out Altata is the drug center for the whole west coast.

•••

Ten years later: Sandy Lanham, who has a flying service out of Tucson for environmental scientists, takes a Mexican biologist working on Black Brant—the little goose that feeds on eelgrass—to the Sinaloa coast near Altata, where he collects a big bunch of eelgrass. He has Sandy bring it to me to verify.

2

Fuel Is Where You Find It

PAUL DAYTON

During the 1950s it seemed to me, a naive and impressionable teenager, that Ike Russell mostly lived in airplanes. He went to wonderful places, usually in Mexico, and had wonderful adventures that epitomized what life was about. To be sure, he permanently parked a few planes, but nobody seemed very concerned. "The wings are the most important brakes a plane has," he casually explained often enough that I assumed that every pilot used his wings in that way. On occasion Ike took me on flights, usually short hops such as transferring his plane from Ryan Field, outside Tucson, to Tucson International Airport. On these flights I always brought along tin cans and ice cream containers that I would use when the spirits moved my stomach.

Ike was a very skilled pilot, and his takeoffs and landings were brilliant. In Mexico, he often landed on roads when he wanted to visit people or to look at something, so that too was part of the routine that we all took for granted. He also had a rather casual attitude toward fuel, and my mother used to talk about his use of gas stations along roads as planned refueling stops on some of his trips to Mexico. So I always assumed that this too was a normal part of flying with Ike.

The Seri Indians were one of Ike's special loves, and he was good friends with several families in the Seri village of Desemboque. Indeed, with Bob

Thomas, the family doctor, Ike helped the small community in many ways. From Desemboque, Ike would often take short excursions in his plane while the rest of us camped out in the village. Often he flew south along the coast to Kino Bay, which at the time was just a very small fishing village. He would sometimes go there to get fuel if he didn't want to go all the way into Hermosillo. There was a drum of gasoline in Kino, and Ike would land right behind town on the main street. He also had a buddy, Arnulfo Montiel, who ran a garage near Siete Cerros along the highway between Kino Bay and Hermosillo. Ike often stopped to visit with him, simply landing on the deserted road.

One summer day Ike invited me to make a quick trip from Tucson to Desemboque to deliver some medicine from Bob Thomas and perhaps visit his friend Arnulfo at Siete Cerros. We flew to Kino Bay, fueled up, chased the kids off the street, and took off on the short hop up the coast to Desemboque. At that time the airstrip at Desemboque was simply the beach, and landings had to be made at low tide. Ike was in a hurry to deliver the medicines and leave because the tide was coming in, and he did not want to spend the night. So I stayed in the plane and contemplated the tide lapping at the wheels. With a fair dollop of splashing we took off, flew down the coast, turned left at Kino and headed toward Hermosillo. Ike seemed nervous, but I was concentrating on my guts and did not realize that there was a problem until the engine coughed and sputtered, quit and restarted, and then quit completely.

By this time I had heard so many stories about Ike running out of gas that I considered it normal. Dying in Ike's plane was not possible; after all, there were always two good brakes. So to me it was nothing more than an inconvenience, since there was the highway below us anyway. Ike chased a car off the road, but a pickup truck thought he was playing chicken and did not give. Somehow Ike got the left wing over the truck and brought the plane in with one wheel on the road. We veered right as we slowed down and Ike parked on the shoulder, with the plane pointing down and the tail still almost on the road. He muttered about almost hitting the prop. I thought it was a planned parking job. In hindsight I think the right wheel, which was off the road, had hit a hole and thrown us into that slow-speed turn. But to me at the time, anything Ike did was part of the bigger plan, and I was never worried.

It turned out that the gas cap had come off and the fuel had siphoned out. There was some complaining about who had screwed up, but I could not remember who had done it. The first pickup truck down the highway stopped to investigate the plane parked with its tail almost on the road. Ike bummed some gas from the driver and even got him to help us get the plane back up on the road. Ike stuffed a rag really hard into the gas tank opening. He muttered and pounded on it, then we got back in the plane, took off, and flew to Hermosillo for fuel. The plane longed for a bit more octane, and I worried that the rag would come out. The rag stayed put, but I was sufficiently worried that I forgot about getting airsick until we approached Hermosillo. I would have made it too, but we had to go around once and we found some thermals, which got me. After we landed and taxied up to the fuel pumps, Ike had a hard time getting the rag out. As I stood there holding my ice cream container with my lunch in it, Ike threw the gas soaked rag to me, and the smell almost got me again. I dropped the rag into my lunch, and after searching in vain for a trash receptacle, I simply set the unholy mixture down behind the terminal.

It took Ike some time to find another gas cap, and it was pretty dark by the time we landed back in Kino. Considering all the dogs and kids that frequented the Kino Bay airport, the dark landing was probably more dangerous than playing chicken with the pickup. At the time it seemed as though these types of landings were so ordinary that nobody ever bothered to talk about them. It was only much later that I realized that playing chicken with a pickup truck on a dead-stick landing was not really all that routine even for Ike. And eventually, Ike and his son Luke welded little rods on the gas caps so that they could see that the caps were in place and make sure that Ike's fuel would not spew out over the countryside.

3

Landing in the Dark

BRUCE HAYWARD

Memories of times spent with Ike and Jean Russell come easily to me. But the moments I remember most vividly occurred during a trip in Ike's Cessna 180 from Tucson to Baja California, back over to Guaymas, and on north up the Sonoran coast to Desemboque in January 1964. There were four of us—Ike, Jean, Armando Maya, a good friend whom I have known seemingly forever, and me. Armando was studying fish-eating bats at the time, and he invited me to join them on this trip. They were going to look for landing places on islands in the Gulf of California so that Armando could return later and explore for caves and crevices with bats to expand his research. I was excited about this trip because I love adventure. It proved, however, to be more adventurous than I bargained for.

We took off from Ryan Field near Tucson and landed first at Nogales, Sonora, to clear Mexican customs. Ike then flew us across the vast empty spaces of northwestern Sonora. It was exciting to see this country from the air with its heavily dissected low mountain ranges and innumerable arroyos. Then we crossed the Gulf to Ángel de la Guarda Island. The island's rugged mountain ranges were far more barren than I had realized. I really enjoyed seeing this island that I had read about so often. Jagged peaks devoid of vegetation were cut by deep canyons, formed no doubt by flash floods. It was easy to see why no one lived, nor could live, on this chunk of rock. Ike continually scanned the shoreline for beaches where he might be able to put his plane down at a future date, and he also searched inland for potential landing sites. We flew great lazy circles over much of the southern end of the island, but as I recall he did not have much success finding places to land.

Next, we nipped over to Bahía de los Angeles on the peninsula, where we landed on a dirt strip among pigs, chickens, and screaming gulls. Ike taxied to a small adobe hut where he was able to buy fuel. He and the *señor* visited for maybe half an hour, and then we took off again. I didn't figure the chickens were much danger to us, but I was worried about the gulls flying into the propeller as we roared down that runway.

Once we were airborne Ike directed us over to San Esteban, a very rough, craggy island where Armando hoped some day to find colonies of bats. He commented that the island was extremely difficult and hazardous to get on to, even with a boat. The mountain slopes drop straight down into the water and there are almost no beaches. It was impossible by air.

We explored another island or two and Armando pointed out bat islands. Then we headed for Guaymas, arriving at the commercial airport just before sundown.

Armando owned a shell of a house out in a poor section of Guaymas, where there was a fine view of one of the many small, craggy harbors that surround the city. The house was completely minimal, the idea being that if there was nothing to steal, no one would break in. However, some of us stayed in that ancient, interesting hotel (now gone) on the city's main street. It was a classic old two-story hotel with a huge inner courtyard full of many kinds of flowers. The *señora* handed us large skeleton keys and we trudged upstairs to the balcony. The ceilings in the rooms were high, the beds sagged in the middle, and the showers came and went, seemingly on whim.

And so we had several excellent days in my favorite Mexican city. The day we were scheduled to start for home, Jean and Armando spent too much time fiddling around in town and we didn't get off the ground until late in the afternoon. Ike mused that we were awfully late, and he hoped we would not run out of daylight before we reached Desemboque, the first stop on our trip back. He had promised to visit several Seri Indian families there and stay overnight with his friends Ed and Becky Moser, who were translating the Bible into the Seri language. He thought we could probably make it, but it would be borderline.

The flight up the Sonoran coast has always been a thrill. I was riding in the copilot seat and had wonderful views of it all. The innumerable rocky coves, white sand pocket beaches, and the tall cardon cacti casting long shadows are permanent memories. How I love this country! I could probably spend weeks and weeks in these places completely content and happy. Ike chatted about "cabbages and kings" and we compared great moments from that weekend, while Jean and Armando chattered in the back seat.

Meanwhile, the cardon shadows grew longer and longer. Shadows of mountain peaks spread across wider and wider areas. The light was going fast. We left the rocky bays and approached the sand beaches of Kino Bay after the sun went down. The horizon glowed bright orange. I remember the twinkling lights of the village and the shimmering bright orange of the bay itself. We probably should have landed there, but Ike had promised to be in Desemboque that night. There was no way he could contact anyone there to say he wasn't coming.

"Ooooh," I thought, "This is not good. We still have 35 miles to go yet."

Ike said softly, "This is going to be tight." The late light on the desert below gradually faded. Instrument lights in the cockpit became necessary. Tiburón Island faded slowly into the blackness. Ike set a compass bearing and became intense. We were pretty quiet. The instrument lights were dimmed to maximize night vision. I looked around and saw nothing but blackness.

I suppose I am a fatalist in times like this. It's not that God is looking after me; I just have faith that things will work out well. I trust the pilot, driver, whomever, implicitly. There is no point in my getting excited. If it's time to go, I'll go without complaining. Ike was a damned good pilot—who better to trust at a time like this? But I really wondered how he was going to make this come off. Nobody in the plane said a word.

We droned on in the blackness. It was stony dark, no moon, no nothing. The instrument lights were now turned completely off. Ike mumbled, "I hope Ed will be out there with lanterns" (there was no electricity in Desemboque). After an eternity he said quietly, "There!" I looked off at 30 degrees and saw a tiny pin prick of light spinning in a circle. A closer look revealed two golden pin pricks of light set 40 or 50 feet apart with the swinging light in the middle. We had arrived.

But the problem now was getting down without crashing, a major feat that perhaps only Ike could pull off. Strangely, I was still not afraid; I felt no panic. All my senses were concentrated on that landing strip. "Ike can do it,"

I told myself. He flew past the swinging light and made a big turn. "How on earth does he know how much to turn?" I wondered. "How does he know how high we are? How can he find the runway?" I couldn't see a thing. He dropped the nose down some and flashed the landing lights for an instant— long enough to orient himself but not enough to ruin his night vision. We were too far to the right.

Ike made just the right correction, dropped down some more, and hit the runway with a pretty fierce jolt. The landing lights came on and we taxied up to the fellow with the lantern. We'd made it! I suppose there was a great sigh of relief throughout the cabin of the plane. But no one shouted, no one said a word. I suppose the others believed in Ike as much as I. He shut down the engine and we eased out of the cabin. We acted as though we did this sort of thing all the time. Ike and I stood up near the propeller, and I commented, "Wow! I didn't think we'd make it!"

He replied softly, "I didn't think so either." That was the time to be scared, I suppose.

Ike thanked Ed for his lights and chatted with him. We trundled off to the Mosers' adobe house where we ate a lovely supper, looked at some of their Seri ironwood carvings, and had a thoroughly entertaining time. We acted as though the landing had been nothing special, but was there an extra touch of hilarity during the evening?

I slept on a hard floor that night, but slept like an ironwood log. Next morning the sun shone brightly, as did our friends from the night before. The high peak of Cabo Tepopa sparkled beautifully just to the south. Ike wandered around the village visiting Seri families, asking how they were, and buying ironwood carvings. We feasted on a Mexican breakfast with the Mosers, said good-bye, then went out to the plane and made an uneventful takeoff. Ike flew us over the tiny boojum forest on the Sonoran coast north of Desemboque. Then we angled northeast over to Nogales, Arizona, for our entry back into the United States. It was a weekend I shall never ever forget.

4

A Greenhorn in the Gulf

JOY COOPER

In 1962, my new husband Fred and I set out for Tucson, Arizona, where we were taking our honeymoon before beginning our respective graduate programs at the University of Arizona. Fred had traveled a great deal during his life, for his father was in the U.S. Coast Guard. I, on the other hand, had lived a sheltered life, growing up in an ultraconservative family in the small farm village of Newfane, New York, near Buffalo. Until moving to Tucson, my greatest adventure had been defying my father and traveling a grand 300 miles from home to attend college in Albany.

Fred and I each had to get jobs to support ourselves as soon as we reached Arizona. I got a graduate research assistantship with Dr. William Heed in his "fruit fly lab". This was where Jean Russell worked, and she was the one to show me the ropes in the care and feeding of fruit flies. Since we were newcomers to town, Jean took Fred and me under her wing socially, introducing us to her husband Ike and their remarkable group of friends.

I think Ike was quietly amused by my naive Eastern ways. He was never critical but he gently showed us new worlds—both physical and intellectual ones—that were worthy of exploration. Among these worlds were some that he revealed to us with his airplane.

My first experience with Ike the pilot took place more than 35 years ago, but it was such a memorable time in my life that much of it is as clear as if it happened yesterday. It was early August 1964, and Fred was on a two-week trip in the Russells' boat *Ofelia*, exploring the Sonoran side of the Gulf of California with the Russells' son Bob. About a week into their trip Ike asked me if I wanted to join him on a flight down to Guaymas to meet the boat and see how they were doing. I was instructed to pack a daypack for overnight and to bring a sleeping bag. "Keep it light," Ike said, "the airplane will be full."

The Southwestern summer monsoon was in full spate, so Ike wanted to leave early to avoid the afternoon rains. The passenger list was made up of Cathy Moser, Richard "Dick" Felger, and me. We left Tucson early and landed at Nogales to clear Mexican customs in good time. However, we ran into a problem with the Mexican immigration officials. Ike had a firm policy of never paying bribes. He felt that bribery was corrupting the values of the Mexican people and government. He was also worried because he had some sort of contraband strapped under the pilot's seat, and the Mexican officials took a dim view of bringing illegal items into their country. In fact, they were downright nasty if they caught you. It took Ike nearly two hours to talk the officials out of searching the plane. Ike was jubilant, for he had gotten permission to fly on into Mexico and yet had avoided paying a bribe. Thanks to his fluent Spanish and quietly respectful demeanor, he had pulled it off.

As we took off from Nogales, we found ourselves looking into a circle of thunderclouds to the south where we were headed. Ike told us to hang on, because he was not going to fly back to the Nogales airport and the hassles that would await us there. So we hung on as Ike proceeded to descend for a landing. While we held our breath, he wove his way over and under some power lines to land us safely on the main highway south, somewhere between Nogales and the small village of Magdalena. As the plane rolled to a stop, children instantly flocked around us, chattering to Ike as we pushed the plane off onto the shoulder of the road. By now the rain started to come down in buckets. We were in front of an adobe house, and the kind owner invited us in out of the rain.

I do not know Spanish, but whatever Ike said was sufficient to prompt our host to strut about and proudly introduce his wife and children. We drank freshly roasted coffee in that tiny, two-room house, while politely excited children and chickens ran under foot. After the storm rained itself out, we pushed the plane back onto the road and quickly piled inside. We were just starting to taxi down the highway when we looked back and saw a jeep full of Mexican police coming down the road, waving their arms and signaling us to stop. Ike gunned the engine and we were out of there. The warm welcome Don Alejandro (Ike) had gotten from the locals and the thrill of being naughty remained with us as we soared out over the Sonoran Desert.

I seem to remember Ike saying that he later heard about this escapade from the Mexican officials.

We flew on toward our first destination, the Seri Indian village of Desemboque, on the shore of the Gulf. Dick Felger, who is a botanist, wanted to do an aerial survey of the condition of the desert flora as we flew toward the coast. The farmers had started to cut back the cactus forests in order to farm the valleys. The virgin forests of giant cacti were disappearing and being replaced by plowed fields with white rims around their edges, built up from salty irrigation water.

For me, this was not the best part of the trip. To accommodate Dick, Ike powered up the engine and set the flaps down for some low-and-slow flying. The plane rocked back and forth on its center of gravity, and I promptly got airsick. No problem, Ike quietly handed me a coffee can and made sure we had plenty of fresh air. Feeling a bit better, I became fascinated with the scene below as we flew low over the desert floor, with Dick pointing out the various types of vegetation. Ike noted that you could often see ancient Indian building outlines and fire rings while flying slowly just above the desert like this.

Ike mentioned, though, that this kind of flying made him uneasy. When he flew over remote stretches of desert he preferred being high enough to constantly keep sources of water in sight. Then, if he should experience engine trouble, he could glide down to as close to water as possible. Survival in the summer in this portion of the Sonoran desert would be difficult with the small amount of water we were able to carry with four people in a heavily loaded plane.

We approached Desemboque and landed on the dirt runway that had been cleared out of the desert by a Seri especially for Ike's use. Years earlier, Ike and a doctor friend had started bringing medicine to the Seri people. At that time, people were dying of diseases, and the Mexican government was doing little to help them. José Astorga, one of the tribe's most creative entrepreneurs, understood Ike's need for a runway if he were to regularly fly in to aid the Seris, so he took it upon himself to make the strip. Gradually the health of the tribe began to improve due in part to the medical efforts of these two men.

For Dick Felger, the main reason for coming on our trip was to continue his study of the indigenous use of desert plants by the Seris. Through José, he and Ike arranged a meeting with some of the tribal elders. Dick had brought a folder of pressed desert plants with him, and he wanted to quiz the Seri elders on the traditional uses of these plants as they remembered them.

While we were waiting for the elders to gather, Ike and José chatted. Ike had brought along a newspaper with pictures from the lunar explorer, *Ranger 7*, which had impacted the moon's surface a few days earlier. He figured that José would be interested in man getting ready to go to the moon. But José showed great disdain for the white man's bragging about going to the moon. He explained that he had traveled to the moon many times as a shaman. Ike asked him to describe the lunar surface, teasing about it being made of green cheese. With great dignity, José proceeded to explain that the moon was actually made up of gray rocks and dust, separated at intervals by ridged areas—an accurate description from a man who couldn't read. What had he seen? This incident taught me that there is much about existence and knowledge that science does not explain.

Finally, all the elders had gathered in the room. They were mostly elderly women who felt most comfortable seated in a circle on the floor. What beautiful faces; dark eyes, gray hair, wide smiles, and deep brown wrinkled skin gave grace to those experienced old faces. Speaking through an interpreter to the elders, Dick showed each of the local desert plants to the circle of elders. These plants brought forth not only information about each plant's use to the Seri people, but these old people were reminded of events in their past in this desert by the sea, when traditional culture dictated their lives. They told stories of their parents, friends long gone, and adventures they had had as young people. One woman related that as a child she had seen her father hanged by Mexican soldiers after an Indian rebellion. I sat fascinated for a couple of hours watching these elders softly speaking in the Seri tongue to the translator, who then repeated their stories and the information Dick sought in Spanish. Even though I didn't understand Seri or Spanish, I don't think much was lost in the translation.

After the session with the elders, Ike showed me around the village. Dick did not need a tour because he had been there many times, and Cathy, whose parents were linguists and missionaries, lived there. I watched women weaving intricate designs into baskets to be sold to tourists. Ike explained the designs woven into the baskets. He said that he was working through Astorga to get the women to do sea and desert animal designs that would appeal to tourists and bring the Seris a better price for their work. He helped me trade for one that we still treasure to this day. I watched beautiful, laughing, brown skinned children at play or sitting quietly by their mothers as they worked on their baskets.

A Seri man showed me a band of large cowry shells beaded together side by side. I asked Ike to find out if the man was willing to trade it to me. He was, and we concluded a deal that left us both happy. The cowry band was too small to go around my neck, so I wore it around my brow as a tiara. Suddenly there was great laughter among a gathering crowd of Seri men. Puzzled, I looked to Ike to explain what was going on. He started laughing so hard that he could barely tell me that cowry shells represented testicles, and the men were delighted to see a young woman so boldly wearing a wreath of testicles. It was a red-faced young woman who walked away before quietly removing that cowry headband. It now sits on a shelf among our Indian artifacts as a reminder of one of life's humorous, if embarrassing, moments.

Then the four of us got back in the airplane and flew to Tiburón Island, where we were going to spend the night. We landed on the beach and walked out to explore the island. Ike had explained that this island was sacred to the Seris. I fell behind as I looked around at this place that was special to the people I had just met. As I walked, I noted coiled circles marking the sand here and there. "Wow," I thought to myself, "are these sacred signs drawn in the sand by the Seris, much as petroglyphs are pecked into rock by other Indians?" I hurried to catch up with the others to ask about these figures. As I climbed over a ridge of sand, my foot was poised in midstep when I sighted a coiled sleeping rattler right where my foot was about to land. Luckily, the snake was sound asleep and I had enough balance to step back.

Panicked, I ran back shouting that I had almost stepped on a rattler. "Where?" asked Ike and Dick. I pointed to where the snake still lay sleeping. Dick got a stick, and he and Ike proceeded calmly to catch the sidewinder. Ike went back to the plane to get a burlap sack to put it in. The poor snake had just eaten and was rudely surprised at having been caught napping. Cathy and I had the privilege of having the bag with Mr. Snake in the plane just behind our heads for the rest of the trip. The snake was headed for the Wildlife group at the University of Arizona. My question about the circles in the sand had been answered. Sidewinders coil into the sand to warm up. Tiburón Island had its share of snakes.

As the sun set we pulled out our sleeping bags and spent a restful night on the beach within sound of the waves. We arose at sunrise and rolled up our sleeping bags. As I lifted my air mattress to deflate it, three small white scorpions scurried away from underneath. Again, I felt the adrenaline start pumping. Ike calmed me down by telling me that scorpion bites were highly overrated. Besides, only the white ones caused any real trouble for a healthy person. "But these *were* white!" I protested. I still don't know whether or not he was teasing me, but I have my suspicions.

We took off and flew out over the Gulf of California to begin looking for Fred and Bob in the boat. We passed over Patos Island, a small islet with an unusual flat area on one side of it. Ike informed us that long ago Patos had been mined for its bird guano, to be used as a nitrogen-rich fertilizer. The guano was gathered and bagged by prison labor, and the flat area was where they stored the guano for loading and shipping. We spotted a herd of sea lions lazing on the rocks off the island. Ike said that he had landed on this tiny island once before and that he thought he might like to go for a swim now.

Down we went. I was horrified when I saw basketball-sized rocks littering the small flat area where we were to land. Ike pitched the plane into the steep descent required for a short landing area. If he overshot the area, we would end up nose first in a rock wall. Once the plane hit the ground, Ike had to rock the craft's wheels up over the rocks so that we didn't come to an overly sudden stop and wind up trapped on this island with broken landing gear. Miraculously, we came to a safe stop. Dick, who had flown with Ike many times before, acted as if he did this kind of thing every day. Me? I think that I had run out of adrenaline. Ike remarked that the landing had been relatively easy; the short takeoff would be much harder.

We scrambled out of the plane, over the edge of the island's landing area, down to the water, and plunged in for our swim among the sea lions. Ike pointed out the huge bulls lounging up on the rocks, keeping wary eyes on the cows and pups swimming in the crystal-clear water. He cautioned us to not approach the females or pups or in any way alarm the bulls. As we swam, curious cows and pups frolicked around us, barking and skillfully diving to see these funny human creatures moving clumsily through the water. This was the stuff of dreams for an upstate New Yorker living in the West. Here I was, swimming in a warm blue sea surging against the rocks of a desert island, surrounded by wild sea lions smoothly gliding through the waters.

After our swim, we cleared away some of the rocks from the landing area and climbed aboard for takeoff. Ike revved up the engine for a full-throttle takeoff. The little plane shook against its brakes before he loosed her to race towards the waters of the Gulf. We careened across the flat area and dropped over the edge with a swoop until the wings lifted us up, just before we hit the water. My introduction to small plane flying certainly wasn't dull.

Later Ike told us about an unfortunate pilot who had seen his tire tracks on Patos Island. He had tried the same landing, but hit a rock and broke his landing gear. He got off the island with the help of some fishermen. When he went back to rescue his plane, he found that it had been stripped of its engine and other parts.

Flying south toward Guaymas, we saw Bob and Fred in the boat below us. We circled and they waved. We landed on the shore near a small village, and they beached the boat and came up to meet us. It was great to see them safe and hear of their adventures, for boating in the Gulf was still exciting in those days before it had been fished out and its shores built up with tourist developments.

With our mission accomplished we left Fred and Bob and flew back to Nogales—this time to the Arizona side of the border. Ike didn't like landing there, but that's where we had to go through U.S. customs. He told me that a tricky crosswind often blew up on the plateau where the airport was located and that he had once made an especially hard landing there, damaging his plane. A crosswind was blowing now, and as he powered down and slipped the airplane it looked to me as if we were going straight into the ground. But he pulled it out and we settled safely onto the runway. A quick hop to Tucson and our wonderful journey was over.

5

A Fine Day for Playing Hooky

CATHY MOSER MARLETT

Desemboque, the seaside Seri Indian fishing camp in Sonora where I grew up, seemed a place set apart from the time and events of the outside world. We didn't have electricity or running water, and our life centered on what was happening around us in this small isolated corner of the Gulf of California. We did keep in touch with world events, and news such as Kennedy's assassination was relayed to us through the radio that hung on our whitewashed kitchen wall. It was sometimes surreal to hear people sitting on our back porch discussing town events in the Seri language while we listened to the U.S. noon news, complete with traffic reports from the Los Angeles freeways!

Visitors were rare. Since there was no phone we usually had no advance notice, so the arrival of a truck in town was a matter of great interest, and we all watched the approaching trail of dust on the long winding desert road from the south. It could be Oscar Topete, the storekeeper next door, with a load of fresh groceries to sell and several weeks' worth of our mail from Hermosillo. Or perhaps it was a caravan of tourists coming to buy Seri artifacts. When friends came we were always ready to provide them with a place to sleep and a welcome bush shower in a discrete corner of our kitchen, or to open up a few more cans of food and have them join us for a meal. Most outsiders arrived by the road, but a few came in by airplane, landing on the airstrip west of town. And there was never any mistaking Ike Russell's arrival in Desemboque.

Since educational resources were limited there, I was home-schooled and spent my mornings at a card table desk facing the ocean. My usual school day would stretch long before me while my black cat Clara dozed on the windowsill. My mind would drift with the billowing curtains that were filled with tantalizing ocean smells bringing daydreams as full as the tide pools I planned to explore at low tide. Suddenly the *deafening* roar of a diving airplane would blast through the quiet village sounds—coming from about 20 feet over my head. Only one person ever announced his arrival like that. Gleefully, I would tear outside in my bare feet and run screaming along with a group of excited Seri kids appearing out of nowhere, "Mericaana Cacösxaj quih ti mxoa! Mericaana Cacösxaj quih ti mxoa!" (Tall American is coming!), sometimes throwing dirt into the air to help the celebrating. I'd hop onto the running board of our old green Chevy Carryall and hold on as my father drove the mile out to the sandy airstrip. School was suddenly over for the day, and I eagerly anticipated all the wonderful things Ike's visit might hold. The tiny red and white plane on the airstrip grew bigger as we approached, and I would try to be the first to see who was getting out of the plane. Through the desert haze I could pick out Ike by his shape—tall and thin. He always had someone with him—it could be a botanist in search of plants, geneticists looking for fruit flies on rotting columnar cacti, a man studying bats, university students, or best of all, Ike's wife Jean, with her Great Pyrenees dog in tow. It was exciting if they had unloaded lots of stuff, which could only mean they would be around a while. I waited in eager anticipation to see if somewhere there might be a present for me. One I still treasure is a gray locking metal deed box painted with, "To Cathy for shells and octopus legs," that held some small stainless steel tools which opened up a new world of biology to me. Another time it was a pillowcase containing two tiny black polydactyl kittens—and I could keep one! So I carefully counted and chose the one with the most toes—eight, seven, six, and five.

When Ike walked into our small adobe house, he had to stoop to get through the short doorways because he was so tall. The first thing he would do was sit down at our long pine kitchen table, take his small green enamel teapot out of his rucksack, and make some tea. I can still see him sitting sideways with his long legs crossed so that he could fit at the table. He always kept a little record book in his shirt pocket that reminded him of things to tell us, or in which he wrote down things he wanted to remember as we talked. I could hardly wait to regale him with my news ("I caught a *huge* octopus the other day!" or "Look at this really strange beetle I found!"), and he would always be interested. Life overflowed when Ike came to town.

Often the group would head out for some interesting place beyond Desemboque, and sometimes if there was room I would be invited to fly along on their adventure. One time Ike, Richard Felger, Joy Cooper, and I flew over to the west shore of Tiburón Island and camped out. It was in the awful heat of August, and I can still remember the smell of the hot interior of the plane as we took off. We climbed over Desemboque and I looked down in wonder at my favorite clamming spots and the best octopus hunting places and the sand spits where I gathered seashells with my friends. There were large manta rays swimming in the beautiful clear green water of the shallows, and an occasional hammerhead shark. We headed out over the deeper blue-green water off Cabo Tepopa and took a special detour to tiny Patos Island, where guano had been harvested early in the century. We landed there on a flattish spot strewn with rocks, near some white rock walls left from many years past. On the shore nearby, sea lions basked on rocky ledges, and the others thought it would be great fun to swim with them. I hesitated going in, but since everyone else was and my parents weren't around to think about sharks, I climbed down the rocks and started swimming too. After all, it was never complaining time when I was with Ike, and I did my best to go along with the group. That swim painted vivid pictures in my memory, of sea lions curiously watching us, and triggerfish swimming through deep rock crevices below me.

One never knew what interesting cargo might fly with Ike. On that trip we captured a rattlesnake that Richard stowed in a sack right behind our seats, and I kept thinking about the knot he used on the rope to close the sack. Another time on Tiburón we found chuckwallas that wedged themselves into cracks between boulders by puffing themselves up, and I carefully pried one out and took it home, where I fed it desert flowers.

On one of the last flights I ever took with Ike, he, Richard, and I hiked deep into Tiburón Island with Rosa Astorga, a Seri woman who guided us to the craggy hillside where she recalled seeing tepary bean plants growing many years before. Amazingly, we did find a solitary bean plant growing there! I was along as interpreter, and walking through the desert with a Seri so knowledge-able was a delight. It was like going back in time and hearing the desert tell its stories. We followed Rosa, an imposing figure, dressed in colorful clothes and using her large walking stick as she pointed out things of interest. She was a deep well of information and answered our questions with ease. I could imag-ine what it must have been like when Seris came to Tiburón, not in airplanes but in raft-like reed *balsas*, in search of food and water or to take refuge from their enemies in the high rugged mountains.

After reaching our goal that day we stopped for lunch and roasted a piece of meat over coals in a shady canyon surrounded by steep rocky walls. Prob-ably we were the only people on the whole island. But no matter how great the pleasure of being in such a remote world, it was always a comforting feel-ing to me to hike back in the right direction and finally touch reality again when we saw the plane anchored where we had left it. Arriving back tired and thirsty in the late afternoon, we all shared a drink of water, taking turns from the glass jug that Ike always carried with him from Tucson. Since I was used to our alkaline well water, the Tucson water tasted wonderful and civilized to me, even though it was very warm. After resting a bit, we climbed back on board, buckled ourselves in, and shut the doors on another adventure. As we rose and flew above Tiburón's vast landscape of old ironwoods, animal trails, and ancient Seri history, I knew that the solitude and uniqueness of that little-explored corner of the world had become a treasure I would always savor. Because of Ike, I was blessed with wings that let me briefly touch down there.

When I flew with Ike, I took it for granted that he knew what he was doing, and I never doubted that we would step out of his airplane onto solid ground again. One time after taking off from the hard-packed sandy strip at Kino Bay, I noticed some liquid streaming off the wing next to my back seat window. I watched for a while and either thought it not important enough to mention, or I was too embarrassed to, since I was only a kid. It was quite a while before I finally brought it up, realizing that if it were just water condensation it surely would have dried up by then. When I did tell Ike about it, he landed the plane and replaced the missing gas cap. He didn't seem troubled by all this, so it sure didn't trouble me. And I figured the less said, the better the chance that my parents would let me go along the next time. Later, we made an unplanned landing on a highway near Guaymas, and as I trusted Ike, it didn't seem too important to ask why. Leaving the plane business to the grownups, I wandered away to hunt for arrowheads, and found one. After all, new places always presented fresh opportunities!

Once in Desemboque I was a *little* troubled when my father was worried because Ike was overdue. As twilight turned into night, he was very relieved when we finally heard the plane, and he was ready at the end of the airstrip to guide Ike in with our car headlights on high beam. I think from then on I was highly impressed by the clear connection between flying and daylight.

It was always wonderful to get back home and share a meal with Ike and the others at our kitchen table, recounting the day's adventures, pressing plant specimens, looking at treasures found. The kerosene Aladdin lamps added a warm glow to the white kitchen walls, and the food tasted heavenly, with crab or abalone or fish accompanied by real lettuce and fresh tomatoes flown in from Tucson. Afterwards we would sit and talk, or invite Oscar Topete over to visit and sing for us, and he would sing the songs he had sung in the music halls of Buenos Aires many years before. The rest of Desemboque was asleep, with only the rhythm of the ocean waves and the barking of dogs to break the night stillness, and the million stars overhead covered us like a living blanket. But the lamps were on at our house, and we were having fun!

When the morning came for Ike and company to pack up and leave Desemboque, we would drive them out to the plane and watch while it was loaded. Then we would quickly drive down to the end of the airstrip and wait while the engine revved up and the plane headed rapidly toward us. It would rise above us and we would stand and wave as it climbed and circled back overhead, dipping a wing, while tiny pale people waved down at us. We would watch until the plane became a small speck and finally disappeared into the bright Sonoran desert sky. And I would know that another school day had begun.

6

Cebúfaloed in Guaymas

JAIME ARMANDO MAYA

On a balmy day late in May in the early 1960s, I followed a goat trail which led across a mountain and down to the old local fishermen's camp at Paraje Viejo, near Guaymas, Sonora. I had just left Jean and Ike, who had become interested in this first journey to look for the fish-eating bat (*Pizonyx vivesi*). They had helped me carry some of the equipment as far as the top of the mountain where they turned around and waved good-bye. From that day on, they would remain central figures in my research. Since *Pizonyx* is found mostly on the islands and surrounding shores of the Gulf of California, Ike offered to fly me to these locations whenever he went there. Most of these trips, drops and pickups, were freebies.

● ● ●

The Spanish nymphet in my clock has spoken: "Thon[1] las cuatro horas cero minutos" (It is four o'clock). I have been awakened from a vivid dream: I am standing at the end of the long dining room of a Mexican restaurant crowded with people. The room has double doors that open onto a patio with a lush garden. Ike is sitting at the last table in the room near the doors. Suddenly, the room is filled with music and a row of Tehuanas[2] can be seen coming down a cobblestone path in the garden. They are carrying large fruit-filled wooden trays on their heads. They start singing, "Todos me dicen El Negro, Llorona, negro pero cariñoso" (Everyone calls me El Negro, Llorona, dark but affection-ate).[3] I start singing and yell at Ike who is sitting with his legs crossed, busily writing in a small spiral notebook. "Hey Ike, come on, let's sing!" Ike answers, "In a minute, Myers,"[4] and keeps writing.

This particular trip had many purposes. Ike was going to work on his boat, *Ofelia*. I wanted to see how the construction of my boat was progressing.

---

1. *Thon* is the clock's pronunciation of *Son*.
2. Women from the Isthmus of Tehuantepec region of southern Mexico.
3. In Mexico, "Negro" (Dark One) and "Llorona" (Bright-eyed One) are both terms of endearment.
4. While living with the Ike and Jean, I once received a letter addressed to Jaime Myers.

And once and for all, we were going to acquire the title (we had been working on this for three years) to the lot we had bought and paid for in Guaymas—right near the water, on a hill near town. From Tucson, we had phoned El Ingeniero (The Engineer) in Guaymas, told him we were coming and that we were serious about taking possession of the title papers. We plotted and schemed against "El Inge" all the way to Guaymas. Dreamers? Of course, but we loved it!

• • •

I am flying a plane along the coast of Sonora. Ike had told me which rudder pedal to press for what and how to operate the yoke. He had pointed to a mountaintop and said, "Keep it steady that way."

I am petrified—a Chac Mool having mobility only from my ankles downward and from my wrists outward. There is little lateral movement in my eyes. If I force them to their extreme left, I see Ike. He is an elongated and pale-faced man—a person in an El Greco painting. Is he Count Orgaz or Saint Andrew? Ike has taken his metal-rimmed glasses off, folded them, and placed them in the left pocket of his khaki shirt. He buttons the pocket carefully, checks the button of the right pocket (where he keeps a spiral notebook and pencil), takes his green cap off, gives a raspy cough, twitches his nose, folds his arms and goes to sleep. Besides the khaki shirt, he wears his usual garb: Levis and Red Wing three-quarter lace-up boots. To the tops of these he has added wide leather strips that can be buckled with three straps. (The careful dusting of his feet, lacing, and buckling of boots every morning is a ceremony to be seen! I guess he would be Saint Andrew.) A strange caricature? No, he is carefully dressed and, other than the often gangling arms, extremely graceful. I manage to center the eyes of my frozen face and look at the scenery in this gradually warming day in June. "I'll take it from here, Jaime." I relax and breathe deeply. We talk and sing; he indicates many of the fascinating areas below. Ike opens one of his shirt pockets, takes out two orange pills and offers me one. "Will you have a pill with me, Jaime?"

I reply, "May I save it for supper?"

• • •

Before long we were flying over San Carlos Bay. Ike fiddled with the buttons of the pockets of his shirt, pulled the trouser legs up ever so slightly, coughed, looked around and settled the plane softly and cleanly onto the ground.

We got out. I carefully closed the door. (If you want to see Ike become fury incarnate, bang the door of his plane, or even worse, separate two fighting dogs.) The plane was tethered, and we went to pick up Ike's vehicle in Guaymas. I decided to defecate and went to the side of the road behind a pile of rocks and sand. Ike decided to join me and we squatted there and chatted. We finished, passed the paper, stood up, and noticed that on the road to our left a man on a horse was coming toward us. Following them was a dog. We continued straightening our clothes and watching this group. As they came even with us, a car came by, hit the dog, and drove on. The rider stopped his horse and stared back for a minute. Then he dismounted, walked back, kicked the dog, took out his gun, and shot it! We stood there and shook our heads. Ike said, "You know, that was the only thing to do."

I reminded him of the time we were near Hermosillo when a truck had just run over a bicyclist. "Remember how the trucker pulled the young man from underneath the truck and started hitting him on the butt? These acts are very much alike. It is the fury at the dictates of the unknown that always amazes me."

Ike nodded, "Displacement behavior." A truck stopped and gave us a ride to Guaymas.

We went to the Hotel Casa Grande and Ike signed in. I was going to sleep somewhere on the shore near San Carlos. We cleaned up a bit and went to eat at Paco's. We entered the restaurant and carefully gleaned the leftovers from the tables as we walked to an empty one. Ike took everything. I took *bolillos* (Mexican bread rolls). Paco came over and we talked to him; we were served and ate as we conversed. "Jaime," Ike asked, "how come you are so different from the other Mexicans from the States?"

I answered, "Who knows. I guess because I have lived so long in Mexico. Besides, most of the Mexicans you now deal with are from Mexico. Do you really know that many from the States?"

"No," he answered, "but let me ask you another question. If the United States and Mexico went to war, what would you do?"

I said, "I don't know."

Ike said, "That's a good answer."

"Ike," I said, thinking to the errand ahead, "what about El Ingeniero? I think he has us buffaloed."

Ike made an animal face and said, "Like this?"

And I said, "No, that is *cebúfalo*, not *búfalo*!"

And Ike answered, "Or as they would say in the States, *bufalo*!"[5] We got up laughing. Ike took out a roll of pesos and said, "Allow me to pay for this one, Mr. Myers."

---

5. There is a play on words here. *Cebúfalo* refers to Ike's capacity to imitate the face of a *cebú* or Brahma bull. Further, the omission of the accent in *búfalo* obviously changes its pronunciation.

El Ingeniero's home was just a few blocks away. He was the city engineer and as such he had the power to sell city properties and to give land titles. When we arrived, the secretary asked us to come in. It was a light green office/living room. We asked for the engineer, and the secretary said he would be in shortly. We sat down, crossed our arms and stared at the secretary as she typed. After five minutes, the engineer came in. His right arm was bandaged. While we were exchanging greetings, his wife came in and handed him a baby; he held the child with his left arm. The child obviously had a critical brain injury. The engineer excused himself, and said that hopefully he could meet us tomorrow when all the papers would be drawn up. We thanked him, wished him well and left. Out on the street Ike reached into his small bag, took out his teapot and said, "Jaime, what about a spot of tea?" We laughed all the way to Paco's. I think we both knew "El Inge" had beaten us again. It was a dandy end to our attempt to own land in Mexico and we never went back again. We lost the fabled lot on top of a hill in Guaymas, Sonora, Mexico.

We went back to the hotel. I grabbed my sleeping bag and research equipment and hiked to San Carlos.

•••

Two fishermen and I are hunting marine turtles late in the evening. Fernando and Poncho paddle the boat quietly; a brightly glowing gas lantern is on the bow. They speak softly, "¡Para allá! ¡Aquí, no, allí!" (Over there! Here, no, there!) At about 10 p.m., they harpoon a sea turtle. We continue our vigil of the bats as they fish. "¡Mira Armando, allí buscan algo!" (Look, Armando, they are looking for something over there!) We grab a shrimp the bats were pursuing. The men speak on the way back, "Nos fue bien, Armando." (We fared well, Armando.)

"Sí. Gracias a ustedes." (Yes. Thanks to you.) Indeed, it had been a great night. I go to sleep on the sandy shore. Fishermen murmur softly all through the night.

"Levántate y échate un taco, Armando." (Get up and have a taco, Armando.) After spending the night in the fishermen's camp, they dropped me on one of the islands where I spent half a day walking along the cliffs searching for bats. The fishermen picked me up from the island at noon. An ice truck gave me a ride to Guaymas.

Ike was working on the *Ofelia* at Ruiz's boat dock. "How did it go, Jaime?"

"Look at this, Ike." I showed him the shrimp. "First time I caught one! The bats were chasing it!"

Ike said, "That's wonderful!" Then he took me over to the boat they were building for me. "You know Jaime, this is really a beautiful boat. Look at all the work they have done—the mangrove wood on the back for the outboard, the wonderful matching and shaping of the mesquite ribs. Look at the cotton cloth sail! Do you know that they actually went to the mountains to hunt for a plant whose stalk can be curled to make the hoops for the sail?" He went on and on.

We drove to San Carlos that afternoon, got in the plane and headed for Tucson. I hadn't bathed in three days and stank like a free-tail bat. As such, I flew the plane more freely during Ike's snooze on the way back. "Hey Ike, wake up!" Ike awakened and I started to sing, "No sé qué tienen las flores, Llorona, las flores del camposanto. Que cuando las mueve el viento, Llorona, parecen que están llorando." (There is something wrong with the flowers, Llorona, the flowers of the graveyard. When the wind moves them, Llorona, they seem to be weeping).

"Jaime, I never heard that verse before! How does it go?"

We landed at Ryan Airfield. We unloaded and got into our respective vehicles.

"See you later, Jaime."

"Adiós, Alejandro."

7

Flying with Mexican Fruit Flies

BILL HEED

One day in 1960, when I was a new assistant professor busy with my fruit flies in my small crowded genetics laboratory at the University of Arizona, an attractive woman in skirt and blouse knocked on the door. She was accompanied by a tall angular man with close-cropped gray hair wearing army boots and blue jeans. Her name, she said, was Jean Russell, and the tall man was her husband. His name was Ike.

I was immediately struck by Ike's uncanny resemblance to "Vinegar Joe" Stilwell, the World War II army general who commanded American forces in the jungles of Burma. Ike had the bearing of a general, but he didn't say much, and I noticed he kept shifting a very weathered Stetson from one hand to the other. Was he a rancher, I wondered, concerned, perhaps, about a fence that needed repairing?

Jean brought my drifting thoughts back to reality. She said the reason she and Ike had stopped by was that she was looking for a part-time job, and someone in the Zoology Department office had told them I was looking for a laboratory assistant. So I explained to her that I needed someone who could maintain the Drosophila fruit flies we used for our studies and prepare slides of their chromosomes, often dozens at a time. I cautioned her that it was a meticulous undertaking, but she thought she could handle it. I thought so too, and Jean played a vital role in my lab for the next 20 years.

Very quickly after that first meeting, the Russells and the Heeds fell in together like old friends. Jean and my wife, Sarah, had mutual interests, especially in music and literature, which brought them together very naturally. Some of our budding friendship was through our children. I remember how surprised and pleased I was many years ago when Luke, Bob, and David Russell came over for dinner one night—how they competed to be No. 1 dishwasher and how much fun it was to see all that cheerful and activated maleness in a domestic setting. And then one day Jean brought over an Australian shepherd puppy for our oldest daughter Ellen. We enjoyed Greta so much that we have had Aussies ever since. When scientists came to visit the lab, we would often take them over to the Russells'. Jean and Ike loved the intellectual company and the visiting scientists invariably found the Russells to be fascinating people. My graduate students began visiting them also. For the Heeds, life after meeting the Russells took on an extra dimension that continues to this day.

With Jean working alongside a growing number of graduate students, everyone in the laboratory learned to collect and rear the different species of Drosophila flies that could be trapped within easy reach of Tucson. Jean never played up Ike's expertise as a pilot, but the group in the laboratory soon realized that her trips to Mexico with Ike could be very useful to our research. When she learned I was particularly interested in Drosophila that lived in decaying cacti, she began collecting pieces of soft-rot from a variety of species every time she and Ike flew to Desemboque, the Seri Indian village on the Gulf of California. She would bring them back to the lab and we'd raise the adult flies from the larvae they contained. In that way, Jean became an invaluable field worker as well as a laboratory partner.

Eventually, Ike began flying my graduate students and me to Mexico specifically for field work. Each stop in the desert was a window of opportunity to sample the immediate area. We would make the most of it by scurrying through the underbrush—machete in one hand, aspirator in the other—simultaneously trying to avoid the ever-present cactus spines. Ike's fluent command of Spanish and understanding of Mexican culture were extremely valuable, especially on our return trips. The Mexican border official would see all those wet chunks of fermented cactus wrapped in newspapers and ask, "What are *those*?" No doubt, they thought we were smuggling something, and it fell to Ike to get us cleared, since those were the days before permits were necessary to bring plant material in and out of Mexico. Just about every official on both sides of the border in the Nogales area knew Alejandro and they were unfailingly interested in seeing what he would bring next.

I flew with Ike about a dozen times. Several of those trips were quite memorable. Sometimes it would be just Ike, Jean, Sarah, and me, and we would fly to Mexico for a short vacation. One time in the 1970s, after a long day of sight-seeing in Baja California, which included eye-to-eye contact with the magnificent gray whales in Scammon's Lagoon, we decided to make a late afternoon stop at a small village on the Pacific slope of the peninsula. We hiked a long mile to town to seek out a family that would serve a meal to hungry *estranjeros*. Ike found a house where we might be accommodated. He rapped softly on the door. It slowly opened, revealing a weather-worn crone in a faded wash dress. When we inquired about a meal the old lady replied, "Lo siento, no hay mucho, solamente langosta" (I'm sorry, there isn't much, we only have lobster). We lamented with her that this sounded like a pretty hopeless situation, but we agreed to chance it anyway. It was a great meal!

One of my first flights with Ike, back around 1962, was a collecting trip with Larry Mettler, a colleague who was then at the University of North Carolina. We had been to San Felipe and other locations in northern Baja California and were heading north in the lee of the peninsular mountains. Suddenly we were in the midst of a very mean wind storm coming from the Pacific side and we were caught in its trough. The plane was tossing violently. White-faced Larry was sitting in the back seat surrounded by smelly insect traps trying desperately to keep his breakfast in place. I was seated next to Ike holding on with very sweaty hands to anything that was available. It seemed as though we were bouncing around the sky every which way but straight ahead. I was wondering what would happen if the wings were suddenly bent out of shape. I turned toward Ike looking for reassurance from our leader. I couldn't believe what I saw—there was Ike, casually leaning halfway out of the window enjoying the dust-driven scene below and taking pictures with both hands! Under the circumstances this struck me as a little *too* casual—another inch and he might have fallen out of the plane!

After what seemed like an eternity we landed at Chiriaco Summit in California. "That's it!" I said. "I'm taking the bus home. I'm not getting in that plane again!" We went into a cafe and had a long cup of coffee. Ike had his usual tea. By the time we finished Larry and I had calmed down, and the winds seemed to have subsided a little too. The rest of the flight home was unremarkable. But to this day, I don't know if Ike was hanging out the window because he really wanted those pictures or if he was just showing off. It may be that he was trying to allay our fears, but if he was, it had just the opposite effect. With nobody at the controls, I was seriously wondering just who was in charge there. As it turned out, Ike revealed later that he too had been "shaken up a bit." It was good to discover that Mr. Cool was human after all.

Around 1975, I had another unnerving trip with Ike. This time it was to Desemboque. It came about because we were looking for a new department head. One of our applicants was a geneticist, Francisco Ayala, who was then at the University of California, Davis. By that time Ayala was quite well known in his profession. He was a member of the National Academy of Sciences and had been awarded several other honors. He came out to Tucson for an interview, and when he gave his talk to the department, the auditorium was crowded with professors and students eager to learn about his latest research.

Two years before Ayala's interview, the distinguished geneticist, Theodosius Dobzhansky, also from UC Davis, visited my laboratory. Dobzhansky was strong on human genetics and evolution, and so Ike and Jean and I took him to Desemboque to visit the Seri Indians. Oddly, he didn't seem much interested in the Seris, but introducing him to our linguist friend Becky Moser, who lived in Desemboque, saved the day, and the two of them had a nice long chat. Ayala, of course, knew all about Dobzhansky's trip since their laboratories at Davis were next door to each other. So when Ayala came to Tucson for his interview, he too wanted to go to Desemboque. That was fine with me because at that time Desemboque was a popular area for our genetics research. The village is located on the edge of a large stand of *pitahaya agria* cactus, host plant for *Drosophila mojavensis*, a species of fruit fly that was becoming widely known from our work with it. I wanted to show Ayala the setting, so I asked Ike, "How about it?" and Ike agreed to take us there.

It turned out to be quite a planeload, because Ayala had brought his whole family to Tucson. We all piled in. Ike and I were in front. Ayala, his wife, and their two small boys somehow jammed themselves into the two rear seats. Looking a little like a flying sardine can, we took off for Desemboque.

Usually the weather is clear near the Gulf of California, even if it's not too good getting there. This time it was just the opposite. We had an easy flight down until we started heading out toward the Gulf. Low clouds were hanging over the entire region. The closer we got to the Gulf, the more the clouds and rain seemed to close in around us. The coastal hills lay ahead of us and we could see that their tops were completely socked in. Undaunted, Ike dropped below the clouds and began to maneuver his craft between the dimly illuminated hills. On we flew. Everyone was on Red Alert as we weaved our way up the blind valleys. Ike told us, "I'm not quite sure where I am but we're headed in the right direction." Maybe he said that intending to reassure us. We knew that once we got to the coast he could turn and follow the shoreline right to Desemboque. But we had to find the coast first. It was tense. Then Ike in his singular style began to tell stories about the Seris, how they hunted for sea turtles in their open *pangas*, how they used the plants of the desert for medicine, and so forth. We listened eagerly to those stories and began to relax. All of a sudden we saw the Gulf dead ahead. Ike turned to follow the shoreline, and before long, we were circling above the homemade landing strip at our destination. Once again I was mighty glad to be back on the ground, and so were the Ayalas.

The trip back to Tucson was much less nerve-wracking, and we made it without incident. Ayala did not become our department head but he probably did not forget that trip with Ike for quite some time.

•••

One of the delights of trips with Ike was that he had his own unique ways of doing things. Before he started his plane, he would always yell out the window, "Am I clear?" He performed this warning ritual whether or not there was anyone under foot and most of the time, when he was out in the desert, there was no one within miles. But the thing that pleased me most about Ike's question to hypothetical bystanders was the ease with which anyone could imitate it. Before long I found myself putting that same question out the window of the family Suburban whenever we were ready to set out for a long trip to the beach. I had the inflection down pat—especially the last syllable, which has to be emphasized with a long, drawn-out rising pitch. It delighted our three girls and it caught on like wildfire. The Heed family had a mantra. I do believe it protected us on our many camping trips to Sonora. In any event, it surely was a fun way to begin a trip.

Tea time with Ike was special. Wherever his Cessna took him in the desert, the ritual would begin the moment Ike's feet hit the ground. A tin cup and a small blue enamel kettle scorched black on the bottom would appear from the military gas mask bag he used as a satchel. A small fire soon followed, constructed of cactus skeletons or dead ironwood branches, whatever was available, and a handy grill from under the pilot's seat would be placed over the top to heat the water. Tea bags would emerge from his shirt pocket along with powdered milk, Ry Krisp crackers, and cheese from his satchel. Ike was now ready to relax with his passengers.

Ike was a thoughtful man with many interests, and he was a fine conversationalist. He also liked verbal sparring with anyone who took an interest, including my graduate students. Ike held extremely conservative views about certain things, but my students were mostly liberal by nature. They could hardly believe anyone could say some of the things he did. Often they'd end up arguing with him until late into the night. Ike loved these heated debates. I suspect he did not always speak entirely from conviction—sometimes he would bait them just to get a startled look on their faces.

•••

One of the things that was special about the Russells was their limitless hospitality. Their house on Cottonwood Lane was never locked, and, at times, it seemed like Grand Central Station. There were always interesting people under their roof, from celebrities, scientists, authors, and musicians to relatives, friends, and neighbors. Any excuse was cause for celebration, whether it was the visit of a distinguished personality or merely someone's birthday, and we were all invited.

Party time at the Russells' was an event. They were very organized affairs in a loose sort of way, and they usually began around three or four in the afternoon. You always knew the party had begun when the music—which might be anything from Mexican *ranchero* to Guatemalan or Greek music—originated simultaneously out near the pool and in the living room. The rhythm pervaded everywhere and people would soon be dancing. Mona Dayton's daughters would put on big red and blue Mexican skirts and really cut loose with their own interpretation of *la bamba*. Those who weren't dancing would be swimming, and the dare of the day was to dive into the pool after scaling the big mulberry tree overhead. Eventually, those in the know appeared in the kitchen, one by one, to receive a bit of refreshment. Jean made the best tequila drinks to be had anywhere. She started with a tall ice-cold glass filled with ice cubes, added water or soda, and layered the tequila on top (it had to be Sauza brand), then squeezed in two or three Mexican limes. But no stirring! On a hot day in Tucson, these drinks were life savers.

Amid the noise and mayhem of the music, the dancing, the swimming, and the tequila drinking, Ike would be holding forth trying to discuss the affairs of the day from his command post in the kitchen. Ike did not drink at all, and he pretended not to be a party person, but you could see that he was having a pretty good time anyway. However, I do believe he was happier when he was in his shed next to the pool tinkering with his machine parts and ancient tools, scrounged from dear knows where, preparing for his next flight.

Dinner was the high point of the party and it was served whenever Jean and her help could get it fixed. There was always a table inside or outside for everyone. Without exception, the menu was prepared to Ike's taste—homegrown beef, achingly garlicky salad, and fabulous home-cooked pinto beans that none of the rest of us could ever quite emulate. Those beans were the gold standard of Cottonwood Lane. And then came the dessert—vanilla ice cream on pound cake topped by whatever kind of berries from Oregon that Jean had in her freezer.

Finally, most parties were topped off with a slide show. Sometimes one of the guests would show slides, but usually we'd be looking at Ike's aerial views of landscapes. By then the tequila would be catching up with us and after an hour of slides in the darkened room, most people would be nodding off. By 9 or 10 o'clock the party would be over.

At first, our daughters were a little young to appreciate Ike's art form, no matter how intricately he described all those landscapes. So for them the slide show became the time to surreptitiously extract berry seeds from their teeth. The girls loved the liveliness of the Russell parties, but they had their own agendas. They spent their time searching for eggs in the hen house, counting the toes on the Russells' polydactyl cats, cuddling the guinea pigs, and cornering Sonie the rabbit in the shower for a love-in.

As the girls grew older, these gatherings became much more important events in their lives than just ordinary social occasions. Perhaps their perspective is best of all. As Sarah and I later learned, they eventually began to feel a little confined in Tucson, and came to look upon the Russells' parties as a refreshing window to the outside world. There were always interesting and cosmopolitan people there, and what's more, they were people who would talk with them as equals. A truly wonderful thing about the Russells' parties was that the generations mingled freely and everyone was made to feel valued as a person, no matter who they were. It's just the way it was done at Ike and Jean's house, and it is something our daughters remember and value to this day.

8

Mexico without a Permit

DAVID POLICANSKY

I met Ike Russell in 1969 in the best way I can imagine—through his wife Jean. While I was a graduate student at the University of Oregon, I had come to Bill Heed's laboratory at the University of Arizona. Jean worked there; we soon became friends and she invited me to their house, where I met Ike and so many other wonderful people. Some time later, Ike and Jean invited me to fly with them for a few days at San Carlos Bay, near Guaymas, on the main-land side of the Gulf of California. They had a boat there that needed a little work, after which we would go exploring.

I was thrilled at the chance to go on this expedition, but hesitant as well. I was then a South African citizen on a student visa, and Mexico had no diplomatic relations with South Africa's apartheid government. How would I get into Mexico, and—more importantly—how would I get back into the United States?

I asked Spencer Johnston, one of Heed's graduate students who knew Ike and Jean well, what I should do. "Go," he said, "it will be a wonderful adven-ture and you can't turn it down." Ike assured me that getting into Mexico would not be a problem, and the U.S. Immigration and Naturalization Service (INS) assured me that although I didn't have the right papers, they would let me back into the United States if I actually got into Mexico. And so I signed on.

Shortly before we departed, I was at Ike and Jean's house discussing how I would get into Mexico. Jean showed me two blind stamps that Ike some-times used to make largely undecipherable but official-looking documents that would cajole Mexican officials into issuing tourist cards and visas. One stamp was from the American Shoe Company. "We can make you the papers you need if it's necessary," Jean said, and I was reassured. "Midnight permits" was the term they used for these home-made documents. But Ike didn't think I'd need them.

The weather at departure was good, and Ike, Jean, and I climbed into his big Cessna 185. I loved flying in that plane with its huge 300-horsepower Con-tinental engine. As Ike used to say, having lots of power is a great confidence-builder in an airplane (not that Ike ever seemed to lack for confidence). The airplane climbed strongly over the rich and diverse Sonoran Desert landscape. Ike fidgeted with the controls, as always, but he was a smooth and skilled pilot.

"Calma, libre" (Calm winds, cleared to land), said the controller as we approached the airport in Hermosillo. We landed and headed for customs and immigration. I was nervous; Ike hadn't made any phony papers for me. Ike showed no trace of nervousness as he calmly and cheerfully walked up to an agent and said in Spanish, "Good day. Here's a gift for you," handing the man a dollar (Ike did not part with dollar bills lightly). "This is my friend," he said, indicating me. "He lost his tourist card; can you make one for him?"

The agent agreed to make me a card and asked me where I was from. "Stanford, California," I said, naming the place I knew well enough to answer geographic questions about. What questions might have been asked are beyond imagining at this remove, but for the purpose of obtaining a tourist card, one place was as good as another. I gave the address where I'd lived for three years as an undergraduate; the card was typed and we were on our way.

Ike later explained his method. "If you start a conversation with a gift—openly and without asking for anything—things always seem to go better. It's not a bribe because you've asked for nothing, and so there's nothing to hide." Ike had a way of distilling such issues to their kernels. He once told me that the one fatal flaw in a marriage is total recall, which is as succinct a distillation of that complex subject as I've heard. And so I've always remembered his approach, and it has worked well.

From Hermosillo, we flew west toward the coast and landed at the small airstrip at Kino Bay on the Gulf of California in time for lunch. We ate sea-turtle soup at Doña Gavina's restaurant—this was long before it became impossible to enjoy that delicious dish without feeling guilty about endangered species. Then we looked at Mexican ironwood carvings, imitations of those made by the Seri Indians living in villages farther up the coast. Ike and Jean lamented the quality of these mass-produced carvings, saying that those made individually by the Seris were more spirited and naturalistic. Although to my untutored eye they were delightful, Jean said I should wait until we got back to Tucson and she'd give me a quail that had been carved by the Seris. That quail remains a treasured souvenir of my trip and of the Russells.

After leaving Kino Bay, we headed southeast down the coast toward Guaymas. The flight down the Gulf was glorious. The stark desert scenery contrasted with the brilliant blue water. We saw a giant manta ray, birds, and other marine life as we flew, finally landing at San Carlos. (San Carlos, incidentally, is where much of the movie *Catch-22* was filmed after the cactuses had been cleared to make the scenery look less like the New World and more like the Old. A prominent feature there is a mountain named Tetas de Cabra [Goat Tits]. When I finally saw the movie it had been ruined for me; how could those lumbering old bombers make it to Italy in an afternoon from the Goat Tits in San Carlos, Mexico?)

Our stay in San Carlos was most enjoyable. Jean's cheerful enthusiasm and quick wit made a nice counterpoint to Ike's dry humor and occasional seriousness. We wandered the streets of Guaymas and San Carlos and we worked on Ike's boat. It turned out to need more than a little work, so the promised boat ride never materialized. Indeed, it seemed to be in such poor shape that, had we gone out in it, we probably would have been lucky not to sink! A young woman named Kit McCord swam to the boat one afternoon, her long hair flowing mermaid-like in the water while she held a pack of cigarettes above the waves in one hand. I don't remember where she came from but she was an enjoyable addition to the party. People moved easily into the Russells' circle of friends.

Our few days in Mexico passed quickly, and all too soon it was time to return home. Our departure time seemed to hinge on a number of factors mostly invisible to me, impatient as I always am to get into an airplane.

Again, the airplane's power, the striking scenery, Ike's seemingly infinite knowledge of this wonderfully exotic landscape and nation, and his flying skills made the trip back (like the trip out) seem like a wonderful dream. But once again I worried about the border crossing. Although the INS officials I'd spoken to before departure had assured me that there would be no problem returning to the United States, I had nothing in writing. However, back in Tucson, true to their word, they welcomed me back home.

Other expeditions to Mexico with the Russells followed. One of the later trips was to Madera, Chihuahua, in the Sierra Madre mountains. Ike was already unwell and I flew his Piper PA-14 much of the way down. And once when I took Ike in my plane (a tiny Cessna 120), he seemed delighted to be flying with someone else doing the planning and handling the controls. But the San Carlos expedition was my first long flight with Ike and my first trip to Mexico. It retains a special place in my memory.

9

In Search of the Wild Boojum

ROBERT R. HUMPHREY

The boojum tree (*Idria columnaris*), which grows primarily in central Baja California, is one of the most bizarre and truly unique members of the plant kingdom, and one with which I have had a long professional relationship. This relationship began back in the 1930s when I conducted a detailed study of the boojum's anatomy. Thirty years later I realized that in the intervening years no one had ever looked into the ecology of this peculiar tree. So, after retiring from the faculty of the University of Arizona, I decided that its ecology would be my initial research focus for as many years as were needed for the job.

Mother Nature had followed certain very definite rules in deciding exactly where the boojum should grow. In her original plan she apparently overlooked ease of access. Or perhaps she did this intentionally, which would explain why she placed it primarily in the heart of Baja California. In any event, only by chance did stands of our tree coincide with the location of readily passable roads. Even its presence or absence in some areas could only be determined from the air.

Twice I was able to arrange plane trips to the peninsula with Alexander Russell. I had met Ike, as he preferred to be called, through some of my fellow scientists at the University of Arizona, and we soon became good friends. Our first trip together, in September 1970[1], was the most far-ranging. Our goal was to determine the southern limit of the boojum's distribution in Baja California.

We took off from Tucson in a small Piper PA-14 and made our first stop just across the international border near Nogales, Sonora, where we cleared Mexican customs. From there we continued southwest over desert terrain across the state of Sonora. In the vicinity of Kino Bay we left the mainland, flying for 75 miles across the Gulf of California and landing 40-some miles inland at El Arco, Baja California.

Although originally a gold mining town of roughly a thousand inhabitants in the 1920s, El Arco had long since fallen upon hard times. At the time of our visit it might have had a total population of 100, the bulk of whom seemed to be children. It did boast of two places where gasoline might (or might not) be found. Gasoline was stored in 55-gallon drums, from which it was siphoned into five-gallon cans that were held shoulder high to permit siphoning into the occasional car. One never knew how much water or dirt might be included with the gasoline, so the experienced traveler made certain it was filtered through a piece of chamois skin or even an old felt hat. Both served equally well. The only available grade of gasoline was better than kerosene, but it had a lower octane rating than "regular" gasoline north of the border. Knowing this, Ike had not planned on filling up here but wanted to wait until we reached the Pacific coast town of Guerrero Negro, where he expected to be able to load up with high-test aviation fuel.

After landing at El Arco's makeshift strip, we taxied to the edge of town and tied the little plane down. By now, darkness was falling and we were hungry. A little inquiry led us to the only place in town where food was available, a private home where the *señora* served *frijoles refritos* (refried beans), *huevos* (eggs), and tortillas to those in need. To these were added the customary side dish of very hot chiles and some of the always available good Mexican beer. We feasted well.

That night we spread our bedrolls on the ground beneath the wings of the plane in a futile attempt to keep the heavy dew off. We were rewarded by a monotonous drip-drip-drip all night as the condensing moisture ran off the wings onto the ground and onto us.

The next morning we were up at first light and headed for our favorite restaurant and a hoped-for early breakfast. The door was open and again we dined well on *huevos con chiles*, *frijoles*, and tortillas, washed down this time with several cups of good black Mexican coffee. Mexican coffee is said to consist of a mixture of burnt coffee beans and charred sugar. These combine to

---

1. On page 37 of Humphrey's book *The Boojum and Its Home* (1974) the date of this flight is incorrectly given as 1971.

make a black, opaque brew. The usual initial gringo reaction is, "It looks strong enough to float a brick," and on tasting, "Well, it really doesn't taste much like coffee but since it's been boiled it should at least be sterile." Oddly enough, one soon acquires a taste for this south-of-the-border brew and many travelers make a point of asking for Mexican coffee when there is a restaurant choice.

After eating and packing our sleeping bags, we flew to Guerrero Negro to refill the plane's now almost empty fuel tanks.

Guerrero Negro was a bustling town of some 900 inhabitants that owed its existence to a thriving salt-processing and salt-shipping industry. The salt is obtained through evaporation of sea water in large shallow enclosures or salt pans several acres in size. This crude salt is then scooped up, trucked over a six-mile causeway to a deep-water port, and loaded onto ocean-going ships for export. Although the town had two small airports, everything—town, airports, and all facilities connected with them—was company owned. This put a slight crimp in our refueling plans. Ike was told, on inquiring, "Si, Señor, we have plenty of aviation gas but the rules permit using it only for company business." Most rules south of the border are flexible, but when it became evident that this one could not be bent, we had only two apparent choices: either fill up with low-octane regular gas, which could be purchased from a privately owned gas station, or settle in Guerrero Negro for the duration. Ike said he had used Mexican regular before and it had always worked pretty well and probably would again. So he climbed up on the wings with a funnel and a piece of chamois to empty in the five-gallon cans of gas that were handed to him.

Then, with a full load of what we hoped was at least 80-octane gas, Ike started the engine. It sounded to me just the same as it had before, and I was reassured by noting that Ike seemed to have no qualms as we taxied down the short runway for takeoff. We were quickly airborne, and our new fuel seemed to function as well as the U.S. aviation variety that had brought us in.

Although our watches and stomachs were now telling us that the noon lunch hour had already passed, we had seen nothing in the vicinity of the Guerrero Negro airport that tempted us. Ike said he knew of a small fishing village on the Pacific coast where lobsters made up a goodly portion of the catch. The idea of broiled lobsters just over the horizon appealed to both of us, so we headed in the general direction of Bahía Tortugas and, we hoped, either a lobster or turtle lunch.

At that time, one flew in Baja California strictly by the compass and by recognizable landmarks. At any rate, we did, taking a general southwesterly course above the rolling dunes. We hoped that we might hit Bahía Tortugas on the nose, but we knew that in time we would at least reach the Pacific coast. And sure enough, the land beneath us eventually gave way to open ocean. But there was no sign of any human habitation. We finally made out a little-used set of tracks winding among the coastal sand dunes which we hoped would lead to our destination. A brief discussion and we turned northwest up the coast as our first directional gamble. Luck was with us, for in no more than ten minutes we were flying over a small group of houses close to the water's edge. This had to be our town, so we buzzed it in the customary fashion by circling low overhead a couple of times. Then we flew to a landing field visible a couple of miles away, landed, and waited for transportation into town. After perhaps 15 minutes, here it came—a stake-body truck that served as the town's taxi.

When we made our dining wishes known, the driver said there would be no problem—two places in town could provide us with a lobster lunch. One place had lobsters and beer; the other, lobsters and girls. He was sure we would prefer the latter but we told him we could do without the girls, our main interest being lobsters. Although he seemed to understand this, apparently he did not, for we wound up at the lobster-and-girls establishment. We never did find out just what might have been available there on the a la carte menu. The *señora* who came out to greet us said she was sorry, but the lobsters for that day hadn't yet arrived.

By this time our driver, who now saw that we had a strong lobster bias, took us to another house for a second try. On inquiring here, the lady of the house said she had no lobsters on hand. But she did have some cold beer and it would take only a few minutes to get as many lobsters as we wanted. Her query as to how many we wanted took us back a bit, since neither of us had been thinking about more than one apiece. So we replied that a total of two would be plenty. She would have none of this, saying that we would need at least six. We were not in a position to argue, knowing nothing about the size of her lobsters, so we relaxed while she sent a *muchacho* (small boy) out to fetch our lunch.

After about 15 minutes the boy returned with a wet burlap bag slung over his shoulder. He up-ended the bag on the floor at our feet, dumping out six large, lively lobsters that immediately began crawling about in as many directions. But our *muchacho* was equal to the challenge. In his bare feet, he quickly stepped on the tail of each one, grabbed the head, and gave a twisting pull, separating heads from bodies. He tossed the heads, one after another, through the open door and into the yard. The *señora* picked up the tails and disappeared into the kitchen.

When she emerged a little later, we were served six of the most delectable broiled lobsters, *frijoles refritos*, tortillas, chiles, and cold Mexican beer I had ever tasted. I don't recall what she charged, but in those days a peso went a long way, and it was negligible for such a feast. And it turned out that we knew less about our lobster capacity than did our hostess; all six disappeared easily and in a surprisingly short time. When the time came to leave we bid our hostess "Adiós" and she replied with the customary "Vaya con Dios."

From Bahía Tortugas we flew a little south of east for roughly a hundred miles until we spotted Baja California's oasis supreme, San Ignacio, nestled among its thousands of date palms. We had both been there before—I by the slow, rough, and hot ground route, and Ike by air. The short landing strip lay about a half mile from town on a small, flat hilltop from which the native vegetation had been cleared. Ike said that despite the shortness of the runway, if we landed into the wind we should have no trouble stopping, and he was right. Our little Piper bounced to a stop just as we ran out of runway and the level ground dropped off into a rocky canyon.

Once again the day was ending and, as always seemed the case, we were hungry. This time we were not met by a "taxi," but we needed to stretch our legs and the short walk into town felt good.

My wife Roberta and I had our first view of San Ignacio about noon of a March day in 1961 after long hours of bumping over and dodging around rocks of every conceivable size and shape. That time, our first trip down the length of the peninsula, we were pioneering in a Volkswagen beetle. We had just about despaired of the rocks ever ending when a cool green forest of palms almost exploded upon us as we topped a rise and looked down upon the oasis below.

Several springs flowing from lava rocks combine here to form, unbelievably for Baja California, a small placid lake, lined with cattails and bulrushes, and adjoined by acres of date palms. When the area was first visited by the Jesuit Padre Francisco Piccolo in 1716, he found it inhabited by Indians who called it Cadacaaman. Twelve years later a mission, one of the first in Baja California, was established here. The old mission building, with its four-foot-thick walls of pale pink volcanic rock, faces the central plaza. It is one of only three in Baja California still in use and in good repair.

The original date palms were brought in by the Jesuits in the 1730s. Although dates are still the town's principal crop for domestic use and export, the oasis also supports fig trees and many vineyards from which a good local wine is made. Ike had heard of a family that not only made its own wine ("the best in town") but where the *señora* was an excellent cook and would serve meals to friendly, hungry wayfarers. We felt that we qualified on all counts, so we inquired in the plaza where the *señora* lived who made wine and served meals. A small boy offered to lead us there.

Our hostess was gracious and, although she spoke no English, we, with our survival Spanish, had no trouble making our needs known. Our main dish that night was a delectable *pollo con mole* (chicken with a chile-chocolate sauce), *frijoles refritos*, and tortillas. These were accompanied by as much of her good, light wine as we wanted. Was it all so tasty because we were hungry or would it have been as good with only so-so appetites? Even had we been inclined to be critical of the food, the wine would have taken care of that.

The moon was up by the time we left and made our way back up the hill to the airplane. We were fortunate to have this light, faint though it was, because it enabled us to make out and capture a rattlesnake that lay in our path. At that time, there was no prohibition against bringing rattlesnakes across the border, so I caught this one to turn over to Tucson's Arizona-Sonora Desert Museum.

Early the next morning we took to the air once again and flew toward the volcanic peaks that stood out high against the eastern sky. These were the three peaks of El Volcán de las Tres Vírgenes (The Three Virgins Volcano), about 25 miles northeast of San Ignacio. I hoped that we might find boojums on their upper slopes.

Although no longer active, the Tres Vírgenes were apparently newly quiet when the padres first set up housekeeping at Cadacaaman. These three isolated peaks are rugged and consist of a jumbled assortment of lava rocks that look as though they had cooled only yesterday. The peaks top out at an elevation of 6,500 feet, almost a mile higher than the rocky plain below. On later trips I climbed well toward the top of the mountain, but on this exploratory venture I was interested mostly in seeing where on the peaks the elusive boojum might have become established. As we circled the mountain, the boojums soon became visible not far beneath us. They occurred on all exposures, but only near the summit.

Mission accomplished at the volcanos, we scouted the terrain to the south. There we drew a blank, thus pretty well confirming earlier local reports that Tres Vírgenes represented the southernmost habitat of the boojums.

By now the sun was high. Our schedule, regretfully, called for a return to Tucson that night, so we swung off to the north and east. We took no time for either breakfast or lunch, nibbling instead as we flew on crackers, cheese, and raisins.

At the Nogales, Sonora airport we landed once again for customs inspection. The inspector must have climbed out on the wrong side of bed that morning or perhaps he had partaken of too much tequila the night before. In any event, he had an obvious chip on his shoulder and insisted brusquely that everything must come out of the plane and be opened for inspection. Ike's assurance that we had just personal items only seemed to make matters worse. Then our inspector reached the snake bag. He asked what was in it, and I said, "A rattlesnake." As I lifted the bag there was an ominous buzz.

The inspector jumped down, saying, "That's all, you may go now," and hastily retreated into the sanctuary of his office. We were glad to cooperate, so we repacked our belongings and took off for the Nogales, Arizona International Airport. Here we (including the talkative snake) cleared U.S. customs without incident and then flew home to Tucson.

All told, we had spent three days flying over some magnificent desert landscapes, and we had confirmed the southern limits of the boojum. It had been a productive and delightful trip.

10

Of Course There's Enough Gas

DEAN BROOKS

It began on a white-water rafting trip. My wife Ulista and I were joining our friends Bob and Pat Straub and two other couples for a five-day trip down the largely unexplored Owyhee River, a tributary of the Snake River in southeastern Oregon. One of the other couples was Bob's sister and her husband. Their names were Jean and Ike Russell.

Ike literally stood out in our group. Taller than the rest of us, he was a wiry man but without any hint of gangliness. He wore gold-rimmed glasses and a long-billed pilot's cap. And he wore leather boots. The rest of us wore sneakers—after all, this was a river trip—but there was Ike in his boots that covered the lower half of each calf.

And then there was the teapot. Ike was never without his teapot. Whenever the boats would land on shore for any reasonable period of time, Ike would break out his old, beat-up, much-stained teapot and have a brew. After his cup of tea, he would set off hiking in back of our landing area as far as time allowed. A curious sort he was—always looking, looking.

A happy outcome of that river trip was that a lasting friendship grew between the Russells and the Brookses, one that resulted in many wonderful and memorable occasions spent together. The one that clearly surpasses all the others was an airplane camping trip to Baja California.

One day in the early 1970s, we got a call from Jean inviting us to spend a week with them in Baja California during the winter calving season of the California gray whales. We would fly over the bays and calving lagoons on the west coast of the peninsula in Ike's plane for a close-up view of these gorgeous creatures and their babies. What an opportunity!

Ulista and I flew commercially from Oregon to Tucson and spent the night in the Russells' home. The next day we planned to leave the house at

9 a.m. for the half-hour drive to Ryan Field, where Ike kept his plane. Our means of transportation there was to be Ike's pickup truck. At least 25 years old, it was literally held together with bailing wire.

At the scheduled time the next morning, we had our things loaded in the truck and were ready to go. But as we were about to leave the house, we found that Ike was on the phone. He talked and he talked, and we waited and we waited. After an exasperating 35 minutes, we were finally under way to the airport.

From Tucson we flew first to Nogales, Sonora, where we cleared Mexican customs, and then on to Hermosillo, where we stopped for lunch and to gas up the plane. Then we took off and headed west, across the desert coastal plain and out over the Gulf of California. When we reached the peninsula of Baja California, Ike set the plane down on an empty beach where we made an overnight camp. Early the next day we breakfasted, packed up, and took off. We were now on our way to whale watch!

Ike flew us over several bays and inlets and we saw dozens of whales. Ike had a STOL conversion on his plane that enabled us to fly so slowly that we could practically hover over the mothers and their calves. We flew under a hundred feet—and it seemed as though we could almost reach down and touch these marvelous creatures. It was an absolutely unforgettable experience!

From the whale lagoons we flew southeast to the city of La Paz, where we gassed and stayed the night. That evening, after checking into the Hotel La Perla, we went out to a nearby restaurant and were looking forward to a delicious meal. By then I had come to realize that Ike was Ike no matter where he was. I knew that he was somewhat of a skinflint, but still I was not prepared to see him break out his teapot right there in the restaurant and ask to have it filled with hot water. Ike had brought his own tea bags with him.

The next morning we took off from La Paz and followed Baja California's east coast southward all the way to beautiful, breathtaking Cabo San Lucas. Then we flew northwest for a while up the Pacific coast. That night we landed and made our overnight camp on a hilltop. Then the next day we crossed over to Mulegé on the Gulf coast for our last night on the peninsula. By this time we again needed gas. But Ike balked at the price and would purchase just enough to get us back to the United States. I didn't quite understand his attitude, especially since I was paying for the gas.

At any rate, we left Mulegé and headed for the Seri Indian village of Desemboque, on the Sonoran coast, where we were to spend the final night of the trip with our friends Ed and Becky Moser. As we flew over the Gulf of California Ike spotted a finback whale below us. We were all excited to see another species of whale, so he descended and we circled it a couple of times.

We finally landed at the little airstrip at Desemboque, and we spent a wonderful evening with the Mosers. They told us there had been some excitement earlier that day, for the Federales had come through the village looking for some criminals. The speculation was that they were smugglers, maybe drug runners. They were in a small plane and had so far managed to elude the Mexican authorities.

The next morning we packed our belongings and loaded the plane, ready to head back to Tucson. After saying good-bye to the Mosers, we took off. Ulista, Jean, and I were expecting a fairly short and direct flight to the border at Nogales, Arizona. But Ike was not quite ready to head back. We didn't realize what he was up to until we heard him say, "There it is." We had not been flying toward Nogales—Ike had been silently searching for the smugglers' plane. We circled a couple of times while Ike radioed the authorities to give them the plane's exact location. Ike really knew this country, and so he had a pretty good idea of where to look for smugglers' landing places.

Now satisfied, Ike was ready to head for home. Turning toward Nogales, he asked me to keep the plane on course while he (and the two women) took a little snooze. I remarked to him with concern that the gas tanks were nearly empty, but he said not to worry—the gauge was not accurate. Trust him, we'd be okay.

At the controls as per instruction, I began to climb to 9,000 feet to clear the mountain range ahead. As we reached 7,600 feet the engine coughed. In an instant everyone was awake. Someone asked what was happening. I said, "Hell, we're out of gas."

Ike immediately took the controls, banked, and began looking for a place to put down in the desert. We glided for a few minutes and then he spotted an abandoned airstrip. We had no power, but Ike landed us safely.

We climbed out of the airplane into 100 degree heat. But Ike knew right where we were, and we were all happy to hike the mere two miles into the beautiful little town of Tubutama. When we reached the plaza the three of us passengers sat down in the shade while Ike left to see about getting gas. After a while Ike returned with the bad news. There was no gas of any kind to be had in Tubutama—he'd have to go to the next town 14 miles away, and all he'd be able to get there was ordinary car gas.

As Jean, Ulista, and I were sitting in the plaza I decided to ask a passerby where we could get a cold *cerveza*. He answered, "Buddy, if you want a beer, it's over there at the *cantina*." But he was curious about us, so he came over to inquire why we were there. We told him of our plight and of Ike's attempt to get car gas at the next town down the road. The man said we'd do no such thing—he would feel personally responsible if we should crash. He turned out to be an American mining entrepreneur and sometime pilot himself who happened to live in Tubutama. Moreover, he had 200 gallons of aviation fuel at his home! We found Ike and went with our new benefactor out to his house. Sure enough, there was the fuel, and we gratefully purchased enough to get us back to Tucson.

But our unplanned adventure wasn't quite over. The townspeople heard of our problem and they went into action. The woman mayor (*La Presidente*) organized a party to see that we not only had transportation back to our abandoned plane, but that we were properly fed before we left. So we wound up having a sumptuous meal in a family home. At least eight women prepared for us nachos, chimichangas, beans, and all the rest, a meal that was absolutely delectable.

When we could eat no more, the townspeople drove us to the airstrip. It seemed as though the entire community had come along. One vehicle, a flatbed truck, was loaded with men and boys singing the happiest of songs. We felt as though were being treated like royalty.

Soon the plane was filled with gas. We got in, taxied to the end of the runway, and took off to the cheers and waves of our new friends.

We landed at Nogales, Arizona, to clear U.S. customs and then flew on to Ryan Field. Back once again in Ike's old pickup, we were about halfway home when the engine sputtered and died—we were out of gas! But this time Ike had us fooled—before we left Tucson he had stashed an extra five-gallon can of the precious stuff in the back of his truck!

11

The Search for a Desert Bighorn Lamb

CHUCK HANSON

In 1973 the Arizona-Sonora Desert Museum undertook a major expansion of its facilities which was to include a large exhibit for desert bighorn sheep. As the construction for the exhibit progressed, the Museum initiated a search for animals to populate it. Inquiries of domestic zoos found many bighorn sheep, but none of these animals were true *desert* bighorns, which are a distinct subspecies. It became obvious that the Museum would either have to accept another subspecies or try to locate a desert bighorn somewhere in Mexico. Since it was well known that ranchers in Sonora would occasionally capture bighorn lambs and raise them in captivity, we decided to make a search of ranches in northern Sonora for such an animal. Botanist Richard Felger, who had done extensive field work in Sonora, suggested that the use of a small plane could greatly speed up the search. Moreover, he could recommend a bush pilot who lived in Tucson and had frequently flown him on research trips to Sonora. Thus did Ike Russell enter my life!

So I contacted Ike, and he and I made arrangements for the search trip. In accordance with our plan, he flew his Cessna 185 to the Seri Indian village of Desemboque, on the coast of the Gulf of California, while I drove down and met him there. Ike had friends in Desemboque which made it a convenient place to stay during the course of our search. From Desemboque, we began flying sorties throughout western Sonora, landing at ranches and inquiring if the rancher knew of anyone in the area who was keeping a bighorn in captivity. What was not part of the plan was that right away Ike began to teach me informally how to fly. Once we were in the air he would turn the airplane's controls over to me. I found out later that he loved to teach others to fly. At first, it was white-knuckle student piloting, but under Ike's calm encouragement, I soon found it to be great fun.

After several days of unproductive flights we heard that someone up the coast in Puerto Lobos had a small bighorn, so we flew up there to find out. It turned out to be a false alarm, so we got back in the plane and took off for Desemboque. That's when things took an alarming turn. We were hardly off the ground when Ike turned to me and said he was starting to feel sick. He asked me to fly while he rested. By now I had put in several hours at the controls, so flying back down the coast to Desemboque was easy. But I was concerned about Ike's condition. The idea of my having to land that plane at Desemboque had no appeal whatsoever! The little dirt landing strip was very short and it had a five-foot drop-off at both ends.

As we neared Desemboque I roused Ike and told him we were there, and that he would have to take the controls. He mumbled that he couldn't, that I would have to land the plane. My worst fears were confirmed! This is the sort of predicament one reads about but certainly never expects to have happen to them. I was scared spitless!

But there seemed to be no choice, so I turned the plane into the wind and began the approach. Ike occasionally mumbled directions and encouragement, but that five-foot embankment at the foot of the runway looked 100 feet tall. Ike would tell me to give it more throttle or less throttle, or that I was too high or too low, but he seemed unable to take over. That landing took ten years off my life! As we rolled to a stop Ike sat up, opened the door, congratulated me on the landing, and climbed out of the plane, apparently fully recovered. The rascal had feigned illness in order to force me to make the landing. It was obvious that he'd been closely watching the situation and would have taken over instantly if necessary. I wasn't sure whether to be flattered or angered, but I must admit that after that experience I felt entirely confident flying with Ike. This was a man who was so thoroughly in command of his airplane that he could even talk a neophyte into landing it successfully on a short strip!

Several days after my one and only experience landing an airplane, we were told that a rancher who owned a farm near Caborca was keeping a small bighorn lamb. We got directions to the farm and flew up there. Most farms and ranches in Sonora have cleared landing strips, but this one did not. Ike spotted a road that cut diagonally across the field by the farm house and decided it was good enough to land on. As we crossed the fence and set the airplane down Ike let out a grunt, saying he had miscalculated the length of the road. Although it was long enough for a landing, it wasn't long enough for a takeoff.

We got out of the plane to look for the rancher, but he wasn't there, so Ike began to work out the problem of takeoff. There were roads of sufficient length that ran along both edges of the field, but they didn't look promising because they were right next to fences, and some of the fence posts were higher than the wing. Nevertheless, Ike inspected the fence posts and figured out how we could do it. So we got back in the plane and Ike fired up the engine. As we began our takeoff roll down the road, Ike asked me to yell out each time we were within ten feet or so of a fence post that was taller than the wing. Each time I yelled Ike lifted the right wing just enough to clear the fence post. Thank God that little tail-dragger didn't require a long takeoff run. We made it off the ground without touching one fence post. A lesser pilot wouldn't even have tried.

Later Ike and I returned to Caborca, went to the rancher's home in town, and found the bighorn lamb living as a house pet in the rancher's living room! But by then the time I had available for the search had run out, so Mervin Larson of the Desert Museum staff took over the task of persuading the rancher to give the lamb up. It took much persuasion and several days of thought on the part of the rancher, but in the end he donated "Chivito" to the Museum. Ike, Merv, and Jean Russell flew down to Caborca to pick up the lamb, and bringing Chivito back to Tucson is Jean's story.

12

Bringing the Desert
Bighorn Lamb Home

JEAN RUSSELL

Chuck Hanson and my husband Ike flew to Sonora to try to locate a desert bighorn lamb for the Arizona-Sonora Desert Museum, and they found one living in a rancher's house in Caborca. Unfortunately, Chuck didn't have time to follow up on their discovery, so it fell to Merv Larson to take over the delicate task of persuading the rancher to donate the lamb to the Museum. This took a lot of time and effort, but Merv finally convinced the rancher that he really couldn't keep the lamb when it grew up, and it truly would be better to let the Museum have him.

When the rancher finally agreed to part with his pet, Merv had to figure out a way to get the lamb up to Tucson without traumatizing it. It seemed like the gentlest way to do this was to fly him in Ike's airplane to Ryan Field, which is very close to the Desert Museum. But there are no U.S. Customs facilities at Ryan, and nobody wanted to subject the lamb to an extra landing at Tucson International Airport. Besides, there was always a possibility of delays and perhaps even having to hold the lamb there if they ran into unexpected red tape. So Merv also did a lot of negotiating with Customs officials and finally got clearance to bring the lamb straight to Ryan. All we had to do now was go pick it up.

So one morning in 1973 Ike, Merv, and I took off in Ike's plane for Caborca. Merv had let the rancher know when we were coming, and he was waiting for us at the airstrip when we landed. After we were all introduced, we climbed into the rancher's pickup and drove to his house in town.

It was such a strange experience to walk into the rancher's house and see the bighorn lamb right there in the living room, sitting quietly on the top of an overstuffed chair where he had a view of the whole room. He was so young—practically a baby—and he was a true pet to the rancher. He was completely tame, and our arrival at the house didn't seem to bother him a bit.

We didn't stay at the house very long, just an hour or so to exchange pleasantries with the rancher's family and get instructions on how they had been handling the lamb. Merv gave them all kinds of thanks and assured them again that donating the lamb to the Museum really was the only thing to do, because the family just wouldn't be able to handle the animal when it grew up. I think he also gave the rancher a life membership in the Museum.

The rancher and his family were genuinely sad to see the lamb go—they really did love him. When the time came, we took the lamb outside. Ike asked, "Now how are we going to load him into the pickup?"

The rancher said, "Oh there's no problem—he goes with me everywhere in my truck." He was too little to climb in on his own, so we lifted him in. He sat down in the front seat beside the rancher, just like a dog that's completely used to going places in a car. The rest of us got in, and off we drove.

When we got back to the airstrip, Merv lifted the lamb from the truck and put him in the back seat of the airplane. I climbed in back next to him, and then Merv got in the front passenger seat next to Ike. Ike started the engine and we prepared to take off. We didn't know how the lamb would take to flying, so Merv was on the alert. He was turned around in his seat, facing the lamb and ready to grapple with him if he started trying to leap out of the airplane. But that darling creature sat there quietly in the back seat with his feet tucked in like a Buddha, just looking around and gazing out the window. He was so tame and so used to being taken everywhere by the rancher that he didn't move during the entire trip.

It was a wonderful flight back with the little lamb. We flew straight to Ryan Field, and when we landed there was a car from the Desert Museum waiting for us. We lifted the lamb out of the airplane and into the car, and the Museum people drove him off to his new home.

The Museum staff named the lamb "Chivito" (Little Goat) and he lived at the Desert Museum for several years. The animals there all have large enclosures that are part of the natural desert, and Chivito's space had the same kind of rocky ledges and cliffs that would have been his natural habitat in the wild. But sadly, Chivito didn't take kindly to other desert bighorns. A while later a female was introduced into his enclosure, and one day she was found dead at the bottom of the cliff. He may have pushed her off, or perhaps she jumped off to get away from him. At any rate, the idea of producing more Chivitos didn't work out too well, and Chivito ended up being the Museum's only desert bighorn for quite a while. He had been so wonderfully tame with people that flying him back to Tucson had been an absolutely joyous experience for Ike and Merv and me. But having been taken by humans at such an early age, apparently he never had a chance to learn how to get along with others of his own species.

13

The One Percent Flight

THOMAS BOWEN

There is a saying among pilots that flying is 99 percent boredom and 1 percent stark terror. On January 24, 1976, Richard White and I managed to get in on Ike Russell's one percent.

It all started because Richard and I wanted to explore the archaeology of Tiburón Island, the traditional homeland of the Seri Indians. Richard was spending the year in Sonora working for the Instituto Nacional de Antropología e Historia (INAH), and I had nearly a month off between teaching semesters. Beatriz "Tita" Braniff, codirector of the Hermosillo office of INAH and Richard's boss, arranged for us to join forces for a couple of weeks of field work around Tecomate, the famous Seri camp on the northern end of the island. Not only was this area archaeologically important, but there was a good boat landing, a small shelter house where we could stay, water, and a graded airstrip. We would also have neighbors, for a squad of Mexican marines was stationed there to guard the island against unauthorized visitors, especially the drug runners who had become an increasing problem in the 1970s.

The first week in January, Tita handed Richard and me an INAH permit for our archaeological work and waved "Adiós" as we drove off toward the Sonoran coast. Our staging area was to be the mainland Seri village of Desemboque, about 25 miles north of Tiburón Island. Desemboque was the home of Ed and Becky Moser, my linguist friends and Richard's uncle and aunt. It was also the place we got our first inkling of the confused jurisdictional status of Tiburón Island.

In Mexico, all archaeological field work is authorized by INAH, so we had assumed that our INAH permit was all the authorization we needed. The Seris, however, didn't agree. The Mexican government, after years of restricting Seri access to Tiburón, had just returned the island to the tribe and decreed it legally Seri territory. The Seris have always considered Tiburón Island rightfully theirs, so it is no wonder they were feeling a bit proprietary toward it just then.

When Tribal Governor Roberto Herrera heard of our plans, he promptly informed us that we couldn't go to Tiburón without a permit from the tribe. Roberto and I already knew each other, but his official demeanor was anything but encouraging. A permit, he said, would require a meeting of the tribal council, and at the moment all the council members happened to be 40 miles away in the other Seri village of Punta Chueca.

"We've had it," I thought gloomily. I imagined precious days passing before the council's next meeting, and more days slipping by as the members deliberated our fate.

"We'll go in your car," Roberto said, pointing at my yellow VW squareback.

"Go? What do you mean—where are we going?" I asked him, feeling thoroughly confused.

"We're going to Punta Chueca."

"You mean right now?"

"Yes. Now."

I wasn't quite sure what Roberto had in mind, but he was insistent, so we climbed in my car and set off on the bone-jarring drive over the recently "improved" washboard road to Punta Chueca. When we arrived, Roberto disappeared inside several houses in quick succession and then vanished altogether. Fifteen minutes later he reappeared at the car.

"The council says you can go to Tiburón," he said, grinning, as he thrust a hand-written permit toward me.

Thank you, Roberto! Infinitely relieved and grateful for Roberto's good will and political clout, I started the car and we rattled our way back to Desemboque.

Bright and early the next morning, with two permits now in hand, Richard and I loaded our gear in a Seri fishing *panga*. The fisherman cranked up the outboard motor, and off we headed for Tiburón Island. As we neared shore we could see the Mexican marines trotting down toward us, toting their automatic rifles and hastily putting on various parts of their uniforms. It was clear that they were going to make their own determination of whether we would be allowed ashore. The squadron commander gravely inspected both our permits, declaring finally that we seemed to be properly authorized. The Mexican Marine Corps would allow us to stay on Tiburón Island.

With the national security now insured, the atmosphere lightened considerably. The marines were clearly delighted to have company at this lonely outpost, and they helped make short work of shuttling our gear up to the shelter house. The house itself had just two small unfinished rooms, one of which was completely taken up by pieces of an airplane that had crash-landed on the beach a few years earlier. The fuselage, we eventually discovered, still lay half-buried in the sand. So we settled into the other room with high hopes for two tranquil weeks of field work.

We soon found out, however, that we were still not free of the long arm of Mexican bureaucracy. Word of our arrival must have been gotten out quickly, for the next morning we had a visit from some officials of the Programa Forestal y de la Fauna Silvestre, the Mexican forest service, who were stationed on the east side of Tiburón at Punta Tormenta. A few years earlier Tiburón had been declared a wildlife preserve, so naturally the Forestal people claimed jurisdiction over the island and wanted to know what we were doing there. They were not overly impressed by our INAH permit and they just laughed at the one from the Seris. We admitted that we did not have Forestal authorization to be on Tiburón, but to our relief they didn't press the issue. After some discussion among themselves they reluctantly told us we could stay.

For a remote island, Tiburón turned out to be a busy place. Mexican and Seri fishermen, of course, came and went. What amazed us was the number of small airplanes flying overhead. Richard and I began to appreciate the importance of light aircraft in making the Sonoran wilderness accessible. And it wasn't long before we were hitching rides with two of the region's finest bush pilots.

A few days after we arrived, Albuquerque pilot H. H. "Pat" Patterson flew in to Tecomate with Roberto Herrera. Pat had been visiting Ed and Becky in Desemboque and had promised Roberto a tour of Tiburón Island from the air. When he learned that Richard and I were there, he just dropped by to see if we wanted to ride along. So we climbed in and the four of us took off on a spectacular flight around the island.

Pat wanted especially to show Roberto the infamous stone "corral" on the east side of Tiburón, where it is said that many Seris were incarcerated and killed by Mexican troops in the late nineteenth century. It is a small structure set against the side of a cliff, so when we were directly overhead, Pat stood the airplane on its wing and turned in a series of tight circles so we could look straight down on the corral. Richard was feeling a bit green after this maneuver, and when we landed he stumbled out and hung on to the fuselage for a few moments to regain his composure. Roberto, who was obviously feeling none too well himself, swaggered over to Richard and asked with a phony taunt, "What's the matter, boy, you sick?" We could hardly believe our ears! Naturally, Roberto spoke Seri and Spanish, but this was the first time any of us realized that he had somehow picked up some English!

It turned out that Richard had been worrying about some unfinished business in Hermosillo, so he decided to ask Pat if he could return in a couple of days and fly us over to the mainland. Pat is a man who loves flying, so when he appeared two days later he treated us to another spectacular aerial tour of the island before ferrying us to Desemboque.

From Desemboque, I drove Richard to Hermosillo and the next morning returned to the coast alone. That afternoon, Pat flew me back to Tecomate. As we headed out over the water I noticed that we were fairly high up and still climbing steadily. It was such a short trip to the island that I asked Pat why we were gaining so much altitude. "Well," he said, "the middle of the Gulf isn't the best place to set an airplane down if the engine quits. I always like to be high enough to glide to solid ground." There was obvious wisdom in this view, but it certainly contrasted with my one previous flight over the Gulf. I told Pat about the almost magical trip I had taken ten years earlier with Ike Russell, when he dropped us right down on the deck near San Esteban Island to watch a school of giant manta rays leaping out of the water. Pat and Ike were friends, of course, for the fraternity of pilots who fly the Sonoran backcountry is a small one. Pat smiled as I told my story. Then he said simply, "You know, Ike's a very fine pilot, but different pilots have different styles of flying." At the time I didn't fully appreciate how true this was.

Pat dropped me off at Tecomate, and I had the next four days to myself, more or less. Late the third day I returned from surveying to find signs that the Forestal people had been prowling around inside the house. They came again the next day, and this time they waited for me. They had the marines in tow, looking very uncomfortable, apparently as a show of force. "Uh-oh," I thought, "this doesn't look good."

"Buenas tardes," I said uncertainly.

There was no beating around the bush this time. "You are here illegally," their spokesman said bluntly. "Tiburón Island is a wildlife preserve that belongs to Programa Forestal, and you do not have a permit from our agency. You and your friend must stop what you are doing and leave immediately."

"But can we stay if we get a Forestal permit," I asked, "and can I get one at your station over at Punta Tormenta?"

"You can stay if you get a permit, but we are not authorized to issue them at Punta Tormenta. You must go to the regional office in Hermosillo. Until you get a permit you must leave the island. We expect you to be gone tomorrow."

"This is totally nuts," I thought. First INAH, then the Seris, then the marines, and now Forestal. Who's going to be next to claim this godforsaken chunk of desert?

The next morning Pat flew Richard over from Desemboque, and I immediately filled Richard in on the permit situation. We decided that the Forestal action was more likely harassment than official policy. Anyway, if they were serious we knew they'd be back. We never saw them again.

The evening before we planned to leave the island, Ike Russell flew in just before dark and spent the night with us. He and Jean had flown to Desemboque to visit Ed and Becky, and they had told him that we were just finishing our stint on Tiburón. So Ike, with characteristic good will, figured that he could fly us out and save us the hassle of a *panga* trip. Besides, he thought we might like a side trip over to Bahía Vaporeta on the west side of the island. It was one of his favorite places and he knew some interesting archaeological features in the area. Better yet, he knew a place to land. His idea was to drop us off, and while we surveyed the area, he would ferry our gear over to the mainland. Then he would pick us up late that afternoon and fly us back to

Desemboque. For Richard and me it was a windfall opportunity, and it would be a wonderful finale to a pretty chaotic field trip.

Late the next morning we were on our way to Bahía Vaporeta. Ike flew low and slow over the landscape and we were able to pick out several man-made features, including some sinuous lines of rocks and a heavily occupied cave we could hike to after we landed. Unlike Tecomate, there is no airstrip at Vaporeta. Years earlier, during one of his many exploratory flights around the island, Ike had spotted a level patch of ground that was pretty much free of brush and large rocks. It seemed long enough to land on and, more impor-tantly, to take off from. He had performed his usual touch-and-go test, which was to fly in slowly, briefly touch down with the wheels, and then take right off again without really landing. Then he had circled back around and, flying slowly just off the ground, inspected his tire prints to see if they looked solid enough. Everything seemed okay, so he came around again and landed. After a little shovel work to remove plants and rocks, he had made himself a nice landing spot in one of the most inaccessible reaches of Tiburón Island.

Ike told us all this during the short flight there. One nice thing about this place, he said, was that his wheel tracks healed themselves pretty quickly, so the location wasn't obvious to other pilots flying over it. As far as he knew, no one else had ever landed there or even knew about the spot. He seemed to take great pleasure in being able to set his airplane down in wild places that only he knew.

So Ike pointed the nose of the plane downward and aimed for a patch of desert that looked to me pretty much like every other patch of desert. As the wheels touched down we were thrown forward in our seat belts in a sudden deceleration. A moment later we stopped.

We got out and Ike immediately inspected the landing gear and our tracks. The ground was a lot softer than he had anticipated. The main wheels were buried in the spongy soil up to the metal hubs, which explained why we had come to such a grinding halt. Thankfully, there was no damage to the undercarriage. We had landed roughly but safely at Ike's secret spot at Bahía Vaporeta.

While Richard and I unloaded our survey packs, Ike began striding rather purposefully away from the plane. A hundred yards out he bent down, picked up a tin can under a rock, and walked back to the airplane with it.

"What's that, Ike?"

"Oh, it's just a notebook. I like to keep a record of the landings I make here."

I didn't get a very good look at it, but the notebook seemed to have at least a dozen entries. Ike penned the date of our landing and then sauntered off to put the notebook back under its rock. I've often wondered if it's still there.

By now it was nearly noon. As I launched hungrily into a squashed sandwich, Ike gathered a few dry twigs and built a tiny fire under the wing. Then he got out the teapot he always carried with him and he and Richard brewed up a pot of tea. "How utterly civilized," I thought, as I munched away on my peanut butter sandwich. Here we are in the most remote part of a remote island in a remote corner of Mexico, and Ike and Richard are sitting in the shade of the wing drinking tea!

When tea time was over, Ike draped the spent tea bag over a convenient bush, climbed back into the airplane and fired up the engine. He turned the plane around and slowly taxied to the edge of an arroyo that defined the northern end of the landing area, giving himself the maximum amount of runway. At the lip of the arroyo he turned the plane again and revved the engine to full throttle. The plane lurched forward, accelerating slowly and kicking up big plumes of dust as the wheels bulldozed through the powdery soil. Ike was clearly having a tough time picking up speed, and I think Richard and I both breathed a sigh of relief when he finally lifted off. "If the plane was having this much trouble getting airborne with only Ike in it," I thought uneasily, "what will the takeoff be like late this afternoon with an added 300 pounds of human cargo?" I wondered if Richard was also having unsettled thoughts. If he was, he wasn't saying anything. Anyway, this was something we could worry about later. Right now, we were standing in the midst of some of Tiburón's most interesting archaeology, and it was time to refocus our attention and get to work.

And what a spectacular afternoon it was. The sun was warm, the air was calm, and Bahía Vaporeta was loaded with sites. There was so much to look at that we hoped Ike wouldn't reappear until late. And indeed, the shadows were growing long when we heard the faint drone of the engine and saw the red and white Cessna cruising low over the mountains. A few minutes later Ike touched down and ground to another abrupt halt.

Considering the difficulty Ike had had getting off the ground earlier, I expected him to fly Richard and me out one at a time to keep the extra weight to a minimum. So I was pretty surprised when said, "Hallo boys, go ahead and put your packs in the back and climb on in." Of course, I knew Ike was a superb pilot with a lot of experience in places like this. He knew what his airplane could do and he had already taken off once today from this same spot, so I had great confidence in his ability to get us out of there. Still. . . .

We flung our packs in the baggage compartment and in we climbed. I crawled in the back seat and Richard buckled himself in next to Ike. The light was fading rapidly and we did not tarry. This time Ike was going to take off to the north, toward the arroyo. We taxied to the very end of the landing area and turned around. Ike gunned the engine to a fierce roar and let up on the brake pedals. The plane shook as the wheels began to lumber through the spongy soil. Ike was hunched way forward in his seat, his head close to the windshield, as if to get a better view of the runway. I recognized the body language, because it's the same thing I do in my car on a really bad road when I'm worried about ripping out the underside on a rock. I also knew it doesn't help.

On we rumbled, wheels plowing through the soft soil. I couldn't see directly in front because the nose was in the way, but I had a good view diagonally ahead out the side window. And what I saw was getting really scary. The arroyo that unequivocally ended the runway was dead ahead and we were not gaining speed very fast. I couldn't see Richard's expression but Ike's face was set in a look of intense concentration. Nobody spoke. Suddenly it occurred to me how surreal this whole scene must look—three frail humans encased in a howling metal container trying to bully their way out of this ancient and serene landscape in the light of a pastel sunset.

Maybe this was the sensation of stepping outside oneself that helps preserve calm in the face of terror. If it was, it didn't work. An instant later I was jolted back to reality by the sickening realization that the arroyo was now almost upon us, we were totally committed, and we were *not* going to get off the ground in time. A split second later the arroyo flashed underneath us and the plane sank downward and shuddered. A nanosecond after that we were airborne.

"Say, that was a little rough, wasn't it?" Ike said nonchalantly. Richard and I seemed to have lost our voices. "Could be we picked up a branch or two back there, so maybe we'd better just go over to Tormenta and have a look before we go on."

A few minutes later Ike set the plane down on Punta Tormenta's graded airstrip and we tumbled out to see what had happened. Ike cleaned the brush out of the tail wheel, but there didn't seem to be any damage. Still feeling a bit shaky, Richard and I climbed back in and we took off for the mainland.

The flight was short but twilight doesn't linger this far south, and it was nearly dark when we landed for the last time that day in Desemboque. Ike buzzed Ed and Becky's house to let them know we were there and then set the airplane down on the graded strip. Our "one percent" at Bahía Vaporeta had lasted only a few seconds, but as we unwound that evening in the blissful security of the Mosers' house, I think we all felt that it had been a very full day.

14

Marooned on a Desert Island

SUSAN RANDOLPH

The summer of 1977 lingers indelibly in my memory. It was a hot August day, and I was passing the afternoon with Jean over at Jean and Ike's house. Ike came in and sat down with us. He looked up at me with his characteristic sideways glance, peering obliquely through his glasses. "Hey Susan," he said, "do you want to go to Mexico?" It was more of a challenge than an invitation.

"Sure," I replied, "I'd love to. Where are we going?"

"Oh, just down to Ángel de la Guarda. I have to pick up Kris."

I was vaguely aware that Ike had come back the day before from an island in the Gulf of California where he had dropped off Charlie Sylber, a herpetologist who was doing research on chuckwallas. Ike liked to include others on his trips, so he had taken along a 12-year-old boy named Kris in the extra seat. Kris was the child of friends who were in a crisis, and he was one of many children and adults to whom Ike and Jean had offered temporary refuge over the years. Kris, it seemed, was still on the island.

Ike wanted to leave right away. "We'll be camping overnight," he said. "It'll be hot so maybe you'll want to bring just a couple of sheets to sleep on."

I quickly rounded up a few overnight things and a couple of books and magazines just in case, and off we went to Ryan Field.

My first hint that something was not quite right came when Ike guided me toward his Piper PA-14 Family Cruiser rather than the Cessna 185 he usually flew. Gradually, the full story behind our trip began to emerge. The place where Charlie wanted to put his camp—dubbed Black Rock—was a difficult place to land, even for Ike. To reduce weight, Ike had planned to drop off Kris and most of Charlie's water at a slightly easier landing place on the north end of the island and then fly Charlie and his water over to Black Rock in two trips. Then he would pick up Kris and head home to Tucson.

But when Ike landed with Charlie at Black Rock he touched down just short of the runway and snagged the tail wheel on a rock. He was afraid that if he tried to land with the damaged wheel back where Kris was he might not be able to take off again. Rather than risk being stranded there, he decided it was safest to fly straight to Tucson to get the wheel fixed and return the next day to retrieve Kris. He was pretty upset about abandoning the boy, but at least Kris had most of Charlie's water, so Ike knew he would be okay.

When he got back to Tucson, Ike tried every alternative he could think of to get the parts to fix the tail wheel, but there were none available. Fortunately, as a backup plane there was the Piper, which Ike and his son David had bought in Mexico and rebuilt together. David, who is also my husband, was not home that afternoon, so I was the one Ike invited to fly with him, and I thought it was a grand opportunity. Both David and I were low-hour pilots, and we knew well Ike's reputation for taking scientists, collectors, ranchers, and adventurers to remote and nearly inaccessible parts of the world. So the prospect of watching Ike Russell ply his legendary skill on a difficult landing spot (even the place where he left Kris was not a real airstrip) on a Mexican island was compelling. "Sure I'd like to come along!"

After flying south for two hours, Ángel de la Guarda loomed into sight. It lay like a giant sleeping lizard, pink and gray, stretching to the south farther than we could see. It lay astride the southward extension of the infamous San Andreas fault, and though it was riding on the ever-shifting plates, it seemed implacable and unbounded by time. Little did I know that Ángel de la Guarda would be my unbidden home for the next few days.

The north end of the island where we were going to land is its crown jewel. A picture-perfect bay with a curving white sand beach came into view as Ike set up his approach. As we neared the shore, we could see a small boy flailing his arms. Kris had expected to see Ike return in a couple of hours. Instead, he had been abandoned for a night and most of a day. He had been alone on an uninhabited island, where the daytime temperatures hovered around the 110 degree mark. This is the stuff fiction is spun from, but as with so many things in Ike's life, rescuing a small boy stranded on a desert island was part of his reality.

Ike reduced the power and the featherweight Piper wafted downward. Then we were buffeted by the winds born of the meeting of the land and the sea. As I looked ahead I realized with a twinge of panic that I was looking for the first time at an "Ikey airstrip." I glanced at Ike to see if there was some mistake. The strip was a narrow and barely discernible swath of ground a mere 800 feet long. On the approach end were the shoreline bluffs, and at the far end was a 200-foot-high cone-shaped mountain. Even with my limited piloting I knew this was a "no-go-around" strip—one where you'd better get it right the first time because there was no second chance. I wondered what Ike was thinking and feeling at a critical time like this. Was there any hidden emotion? His eyes under that khaki cap were gazing intensely ahead and his jaw and upper lip were protruding in almost a pout, framed by the collar of his tan work shirt. Before I could say anything he slipped the plane, dropping her sideways, her right wing tipped into the crosswind. The wheels touched lightly and we were down. It was a perfect landing.

Between Kris' tears and many questions, Ike in his calm way told him what had happened, explaining that he had not been able to pick him up in the Cessna because he couldn't land with the damaged tail wheel. What he needed to do now, he told us, was to fly some of Charlie's water over to him at Black Rock. He'd be back in an hour or two to spend the night with us. In the morning he would take the last of Charlie's water over and then he and Kris and I would leave for home.

Kris and I watched as Ike wedged his gaunt, lanky, and slightly hunched frame into the airplane and taxied to the top of the makeshift strip. We waved as he took off. The red and white Piper rose jubilantly with the power of her 150 horsepower engine and no weight save for Ike and the water.

The arrangement suited me fine. I looked forward to settling in for a bit of island life—having a swim and reading until Ike returned. Ángel de la Guarda seemed like a paradise with its crystal-clear bay and small jutting islets. There was nothing to the north of us except water, and one look down the rugged coast to the south confirmed that no one would ever appear on foot from that direction. Kris and I were essentially alone on this long, narrow, uninhabited island. I spent the remainder of the afternoon enjoying the magic of the summer sun and the cool water of my remote queendom. But as the afternoon faded into evening, I realized with a slightly sinking feeling that Ike would not be returning that day. I was more perplexed than worried. Perhaps he had gotten held up with Charlie. Kris and I had plenty of water and some tortillas and cheese. But it would be his second night on the island. He had many questions I could not answer.

Finally I lay down on the cotton sheets to sleep. I was grateful to have Kris' little heartbeat next to me, and I was comforted by the smell of Tide detergent in the sheets. I thought of Jean at home on Cottonwood Lane and wondered what she was thinking right now. Of course, she knew we were planning to spend the night on the island. I felt a small pang of guilt because I had left David only a brief note saying that I had gone to Mexico with Ike. He would have come home to an empty house, found my note, and then had to ask Jean for the details. I tried not to think about rattlesnakes and chuckwallas. Soon I drifted off into a light restless sleep, reminding myself that "Ángel de la Guarda" means Guardian Angel.

Morning came and went, and Ike's red and white plane did not appear. I knew now that something had gone wrong, but I still had faith that Ike would return to get us.

One-hundred-ten-degree-plus days are long when you have no shade and nothing to do. I read a little; Kris mostly just stuck pretty close. Neither of us felt much like eating. I found myself ruminating on how Ike had become such a good bush pilot. Apparently, when he first started flying, the hand-eye coordination of balancing the rudder, aileron, and throttle were so difficult for him that he spent countless hours of practice to make up for his lack of natural talent. Walt Douglas, the instructor who taught David and me to fly, used to say that farm boys made the best pilots because they have a natural feel for the machinery. Ike didn't grow up on a farm and he didn't have that intuitive feel, but he had risen above it and mastered the elements of the air with intellect and determination.

The romance of the island faded as the sun made its long relentless arc across the sky. Nothing moved, and the hot tedium made me wonder if anyone really knew just where we were. I felt sure that Jean knew something about the island, but did she know where Charlie's camp was or where Kris had been dropped? The day lengthened and my imagination played recklessly. The sun moved downward, the air cooled imperceptibly. Another day had passed. Nothing.

Morning came again. I wondered what David was thinking. David tends to be pretty independent and does not hesitate to act when he feels there is cause to do so. But would he realize that something was wrong and come rescue me? Or would he just assume that I was on an ordinary foray with Ike? And where was Ike? Kris and I were now into our third day on the island, and we needed someone to find us. If not David, maybe a fishing boat? Kris and I built a signal fire on the beach and were ready to light it if anyone came by.

Late that afternoon, as the light was once again fading, we trudged up from the beach to our pitiful camp site. Suddenly I heard something and my heart almost jumped into my mouth. Whirling around, I was certain I was hearing the familiar drone of an aircraft. Kris and I ran like children greeting a long-absent parent, ripped off our shirts, and waved them wildly in the air. The little twin-engine plane approaching us conjured up an image of Mighty Mouse coming to the rescue—so neat and tidy and fast and powerful did it appear. It circled as though preparing to land, and then it disappeared toward the west as suddenly as it had appeared. Why hadn't it landed? It must not have been David. I looked back at Ike's strip and gradually realized that only a fool or Ike would try to land there. The twin would never have made it.

Kris and I walked back to our camp with our heads drooped to our chests in disappointment. As I kicked at imaginary clumps of sod, I thought of having to spend another night here. The nighttime silence and starry splendor were rapidly losing their charm. Where was Ike? Where was David?

Wait! There was that engine sound again. I craned my neck looking upward, then wheeled around and ran toward the beach. This time the buzz-hum was coming from the water, not the air. It was a 25-foot fishermen's outboard *panga* instead of an airplane. Help was here! Our rescuers were Mexican fishermen.

The three fishermen just sat in their boat looking at us, patiently waiting for us to tell our story. I explained our plight. Kris described Black Rock as best he could, and the fishermen agreed to take us the 20 miles to Charlie's camp.

It was almost completely dark when we arrived at Black Rock an hour later. Ike hobbled down to meet the boat. He was hurting badly from cracked ribs and a damaged spleen, but as always he was cool, calm, and collected. I asked him if he could reward our saviors since I hadn't brought any money. He gave them the half-gallon Gallo wine bottle he used to keep water in his plane. He valued it because the cap didn't leak and the green glass kept the water from going bad. I thought it was an odd thing to give as a gift, but it was so like Ike to reward someone with an original and functional item rather than with ordinary money. I never could decide if Ike was simply parsimonious or just totally original in everything he did.

One look landward told me in a flash what had happened. The Piper sat pitched forward with her nose ground into a shallow gully. Her tail was raised in the air in an undignified salute. The gully lay at the end of another "Ikey strip," an 800-foot stretch of ground amongst volcanic rocks. Ike was not used to the Piper, which was much lighter than his Cessna 185. It floated like a feather and was hard to get down on the ground. The high temperatures and the wind had made him miss a perfect landing by about 20 feet. Ike had made a valiant attempt, but this time, even his luck had run out.

I stifled a sob for beautiful, reliable XB CUS (Ike and David had never removed the Piper's Mexican identification letters). Ike explained that the twin-engine plane had been David and Johnny Anderson who had come looking for us. Hearing the emergency signal that is emitted when a plane crashes, they had found Ike, communicated with him by radio, and found out where Kris and I were. After they located us they flew over to the Baja California port of Bahía de los Angeles, where they were going to hire a boat to come and pick us up. It would probably be out to fetch us in the morning.

Poor XB CUS. There was no way to get her flying from here. She was stranded in the middle of nowhere, and I was beginning to think that she would have to spend the rest of her days on this desolate island. Little did I know that Ike was already hatching a plan to spirit her away from the Guardian Angel, or that I would be returning to this desert island so soon.

•••

What a joyous sight! As we headed out from Bahía de los Angeles at daybreak, dozens of dolphins leapt and cavorted alongside our two *pangas*. I had never seen such a magical sight, and it only heightened my excitement about our expedition back to Ángel de la Guarda Island to rescue the little Piper. In

Bahía de los Angeles we had hired a small crew for the job. Heading the group was Ed Bernasconi, a talented American engineer who had married a local woman and was now living in Bahía de los Angeles. We had also hired three local fishermen to help with the airplane and run the two boats. Miguel was middle-aged, bronze, and quiet. Kiko and his friend Nacho were in their twenties. Kiko had a huge shock of black hair and kept us laughing with his jokes and teasing. Nacho, though small in stature, astonished us by single-handedly lifting a 55-gallon drum of gasoline into the boat. We knew we were in good hands.

Ike was back in Tucson, still laid up from the injuries he sustained in the crash. Although he was in no shape to come back down to the Gulf, he had been instrumental in planning our expedition. None of David's adventurous friends seemed interested in helping, so we decided by default that I would go back to the island with David. The plan was to drive down in David's ¾-ton Ford pickup. Ike insisted that we take a cattle rack that fit into the bed of the truck and that we bolt two 2 x 4s across the top to which we could fasten the parts of the plane. It was a good thing because otherwise we never would have gotten the plane back. From Tucson our route was to Guaymas, Sonora, across the Gulf by car ferry to Santa Rosalía, and from there northward up the peninsula to Bahía de los Angeles.

It was a long ride in the *pangas* to Black Rock and XB CUS. We needed to take the airplane apart, haul the pieces to the beach, and somehow get them lashed to the boats. Ed assumed leadership of the project, gave us each a tool from the great arsenal he had brought with him, and told us what to do.

We worked until midday, and then took a long break from the scorching heat, trying hard to keep cool under scant shade. We had food but it was so hot nobody could eat anything except canned fruit cocktail. We resumed work, and by day's end we had the wings off and the engine out of the fuselage. We would haul the parts to shore and load the boats in the cool of the morning, and then head back to the village.

That night we settled into our sheets for a nice restful sleep on the beach. David and I drifted off with the satisfaction that the dismantling process had been completed. But our slumber didn't last long, for we were quickly discovered by *jejenes*, the ruthless no-see-ums whose vicious bites can drive a sane person mad. During that long sleepless night we saw the fishermen take a *panga* out onto the water so they could sleep undisturbed by these hateful insects.

Getting licensed to fly doesn't include instruction on how to carry large airplane parts to the beach and load them on two small open boats. Kiko and Nacho solved the problem for the engine by finding two tree branches to use as poles, which they roped together in a sort of sling. With one of them on each end of the two poles, and assisted by my encouraging cheers, they somehow managed to carry the engine to the beach. Among the six of us, we were able to pick up and carry the wings and fuselage to the boats. After much discussion, we put the fuselage and engine together in one *panga* and the wings in the other. The wings were lashed to the gunwales, one on top of the other, which left just enough room in the stern for someone to operate the outboard motor.

We were finally ready to leave with the late afternoon sun. We decided that two people should go with the wings and the other four with the engine and fuselage. I staked out a spot next to the engine. We were just barely away from shore when we noticed the wind picking up. Soon the sea began turning rough. Within an hour it was obvious that we were not going to get to the village that evening. The fishermen pulled into a pretty little cove, well protected from the wind, where we would spend the night.

David and I were looking forward to a good night's sleep after our awful episode the night before with the *jejenes*. If there were any of those infernal creatures around this beach, we figured the wind would keep them away from us. It did, but as the night progressed, the wind blew with ever-increasing fury. Flying sand stung our faces, and soon we had to roll up completely in our sheets like the stuffing in a burrito. Between the wind, the sand, and worry about the *pangas* with the airplane parts, we passed another long miserable night punctuated by short bouts of restless sleep.

By early morning the wind had subsided, and we again set off in our little boats. Near the southeast tip of the island we stopped for a couple of hours at a tiny islet called Estanque. Here we watched the fishermen at their finest. They stripped down, dove for oysters, and made a fire to roast them. It was a pleasant feast with much laughter, and it took our minds off the long night and the transport job that still needed to be completed.

Rested and well fed, we set out again into a calm sea. And once again the calm was short lived. We watched anxiously as the clouds gathered, the sky darkened, and the waves grew. Before long we were in the full face of the storm. The waves were huge and ragged, and spray was flying everywhere. I crawled under the fuselage for shelter. Occasionally, I would look up at Kiko and Nacho, and the sight of these two fishermen plying their craft inspired a lot of confidence. One man worked the outboard motor while the other manned the bow, giving directions on the character of the waves. Working as a team, they would steer into each wave at exactly the right angle and speed, timed perfectly to ride over the crest instead of getting knocked sideways, flipping, or swamping the boat. I was afraid, but I also felt like giving in to whatever was happening at the moment and riding it out. As we crested each wave, I was thankful to be just that much closer to land.

After what seemed like hours at sea, we finally arrived in Bahía de los Angeles. By now it was completely dark, but we were welcomed by the lights of the little village and throngs of villagers who were worried about us out in the storm. It was then that we learned that we had returned from the island through the edge of a hurricane.

Dozens of men came down to the beach to help bring the *pangas* ashore. Without a word they lifted the boats, looking like some primordial beasts with their airplane parts tied on, and carried them about 75 feet into shore. Tired, relieved, and emotionally drained from the trauma of a storm at sea, I just watched these heroic fishermen silently carrying the boats. Suddenly it dawned on me why Ike was so attracted to Mexicans in general and the people of the Gulf in particular. It was the heroism that these people displayed in their everyday lives. It was a quality Ike understood, for it was a quality he himself exhibited every day of his life as he continually forced himself to overcome his own disabilities.

The next morning we loaded the engine and fuselage into the bed of David's pickup and laid the wings on top of the cattle rack, with mattresses sandwiched in between for padding. We must have made an odd and fantastic sight as we slowly pulled out of Bahía de los Angeles—a blue truck with pieces of a red and white airplane on board. But we had accomplished our mission. We had rescued XB CUS from the desolation of Ángel de la Guarda Island, and we were ready to begin the long slow journey home.

II... THE SIERRA MADRE OCCIDENTAL

If there was any place Ike loved as much as the Gulf of California it was the Sierra Madre Occidental—the incredibly rugged mountain range that straddles the border between Sonora and Chihuahua. Many of the villages and ranches in that country were only accessible by horseback or by airplane, and the mountain airstrips that served some of these communities were among the most difficult in Northwestern Mexico. Ike loved the country, the people, the isolation of it all, and the challenge of flying there. For many years he and his friend Bill Swan shared ownership in a gold mine over on the Chihuahua side, which probably served more as an excuse to fly into the Sierra than as a serious business venture. The Sierra was one of the first places Ike explored when he began flying in Mexico, and he continued to fly there until a few months before his death.

15

Bones, Boundaries, and the Tarahumara

BERNARD L. FONTANA

My first involvement with Ike Russell as a pilot was not as a researcher, but as expediter for three scientists. Early in 1963, archaeologist Robert F. Heizer, who had once been my teacher and employer, called to say that he, archaeologist Theodore McCown, and geologist Howel Williams needed to fly to Arizpe, Sonora. As representatives of the University of California at Berkeley, they had been invited to be present that February when Arizpe residents were to replace the old wooden floor in their eighteenth-century church, where it was known Juan Bautista de Anza, the younger, had been laid to rest in 1788. People in San Francisco, California, who viewed Anza as their city's founder, had agreed to pay the cost of installing a tile floor with the proviso that experts would be on hand to identify Anza's remains when they were uncovered.

I thought of Ike right away, and he agreed to pilot the trio of professors to their Río Sonora destination. They didn't take part in the excavations but stood by as observers while laborers ripped out the wooden floor and began exposing burials. McCown later remarked, "It was a regular charnel house. Bones were flying everywhere. But those we identified as Anza's were the only ones in a coffin, and he was dressed in a Spanish officer's uniform. The Mexicans were more interested in their new floor than in finding Anza, and it was impossible to be more systematic."

Ike took a few pictures of human bones resting on church pews, but he and geologist Williams decided their time could be better spent discussing the area's geology from a hill overlooking the town—not surprising given Ike's interest in mining. As it later turned out, a church burial register indicated that the costumed skeleton of the soldier in the coffin was not Anza's, but belonged to a fellow Spanish officer, possibly Manuel de Echeagaray.

It wasn't until the end of May 1975 that I first went aloft with the man who was then known as the region's best bush pilot. Along with botanist Richard Felger, I had been invited by Beatriz "Tita" Braniff Cornejo, archaeologist and codirector of the Centro Regional del Noroeste of the Instituto Nacional de Antropología e Historia (INAH), to fly along on an aerial reconnaissance of the Río San Miguel in northern Sonora. Tita, who was stationed in Hermosillo, was interested in the archaeological boundaries between the historic Pima (Northern O'odham) and Opata Indians whose territories merged in this region. She wanted to acquaint herself with the topography, ecological boundaries, and archaeological potential of the San Miguel drainageway. Richard was well acquainted with the various life zones in Sonora, and I knew something about Piman archaeology—ceramics in particular—and ethnohistory. INAH was footing the bill for our expenses and gas for Ike's Cessna 185. Later, Tita carried out archaeological investigations in this and adjoining regions that resulted in her doctoral dissertation. At least a few of her other publications were also based on her work in this part of Sonora.

Our flight began at Ryan Field, west of Tucson. Richard Felger and I arrived about 3:30 p.m. at "Fred's Hangar" where Ike kept his trusty aircraft. Fred Grissom told us, "He said he'd be here at three. We put his plane out there. Don't worry. He'll be here. He's always late."

Ike's clock ran on what locally is known as "Indian time," and "I'll be there this afternoon sharp" was usually about as close as it got. Sure enough, Ike showed up; I took a picture of him and a bearded Felger standing next to the plane. We took off on the short hop to the Nogales, Sonora airport to clear Mexican customs. Then we flew the 60 miles south to Magdalena de Kino where we were to rendezvous with Tita for the next day's flight.

The Magdalena "airport" is a landing strip about midway between Magdalena and the more northerly town of San Ignacio. At that time it was simply a flat strip of land, a couple of small hangars, and a wind sock. We spotted a yellow Volkswagen "bug" by one of the hangars, but concluded Tita wasn't there. So Ike buzzed the Kino Motel in Magdalena three or four times, hoping either to see Tita or to alert some taxi driver that we'd need a ride from the landing strip to the town, some two or three miles away. With Ike's plane making noisy circles overhead, everyone in Magdalena knew we were there.

We landed on the Magdalena-San Ignacio strip and, much to our surprise, Tita had been waiting in the yellow Volkswagen. The three of us somehow crowded into the tiny vehicle and Tita drove us to Magdalena where rooms had been reserved for us in the motel. Ike, Richard, and I walked to a store to buy cheese, *bolillos* (Mexican bread rolls), and pineapple juice for the next day's breakfast. We split the cost, each of us contributing 50 cents.

After relaxing over a few drinks in the motel bar, we were joined for dinner at the Tecolote Restaurant on Magdalena's plaza by Arturo Oliveros, the other codirector of the Centro Regional. Arturo picked up the tab, which included my four beef enchiladas, beans, coffee, and beer. Back at the motel we pored over maps and photographs until a little after 10 p.m. Agreeing to get started early, I volunteered to knock on everyone's doors at 4:30 in the morning. I woke up a little before four, took a cold shower (the only kind available), dressed, and awakened the others at the appointed time. We got a cup of coffee in a tiny cafe, and by 5:40, Tita, Richard, Ike, and I were in the air for our tour of the Río San Miguel.

Ike headed the plane southwest 27 miles to the town of Cucurpe, situated near the headwaters of the San Miguel. Cucurpe had marked the northern limit of Opata occupation in Spanish times; Pimans were in villages just to the north. We headed south, following the river to Rayón. Ike put the plane down next to town on a dirt landing strip, part of a local road. We got out and walked around for about 45 minutes looking for archaeological sites. During Spanish times, beginning about 1638, the settlement was known as Nacameri, but in 1825 the name was changed to honor General Ignacio L. Rayón. It had been an Opata village in pre-Spanish times, but in the 1740s, Spaniards settled a large number of Seri Indians there. It was a place with interesting archaeological possibilities.

From Rayón we flew south. Near the juncture of the San Miguel and Río Zanjón we doubled back to Rayón. Then we left the San Miguel, detouring northeast to Bacoachi near the headwaters of the Río Sonora. This side trip had nothing to do with archaeological reconnaissance, but everything to do with the fact that Bacoachi was known far and wide as a place where some of its inhabitants distilled a superior brand of *bacanora*, a regional variant of mescal, from the hearts of local agaves. *Bacanora*, also occasionally referred as *lechuguilla*, is a Sonoran version of moonshine. The makers of this potent spirit market it for local consumption without bothering with such aggravations as government approval, taxes, tax stamps, and those kinds of things. The Bacoachi product is famed for being especially smooth, gentle on the palate, and warm to the stomach.

Ike put the Cessna down on the dirt road next to the village cemetery, remarking that many landing strips in Mexico were conveniently near cemeteries. From there it was a short walk into town where we inquired about the availability of *bacanora*. No one professed to have any, but we were told by someone that a man who lived about four miles to the north had a barrel filled with some that was 15 years old. The barrel, though, had started to leak, so he had decanted the contents into gallon jars. Our informant thought the man might sell us a jar or two, but a four-mile walk each way on an uncertain mission seemed like a bad bet. Reluctantly, we abandoned our search, got back in the plane, and headed again to Cucurpe.

Earlier in the morning we had simply flown over Cucurpe, but now Tita elected to land there. Ike brought the plane down on a mesa that stands at the north edge of the town on the east side of the Río San Miguel. We landed in the vacant plaza in front of an arched church begun by Franciscan missionaries in the early nineteenth century but never completed. Very quickly a large contingent of townspeople walked up the road to the mesa and gathered around our plane, the *presidente municipal,* or mayor, included. Tita explained the nature of our business, and after considerable polite discussion in which it was made clear we were welcome to be there, the *presidente* mentioned to Ike, almost apologetically, that Cucurpe's landing strip was on the opposite side of the river. No one, it seems, had ever landed a plane on this mesa before.

Soon afterward I saw Ike walking in a straight line toward the far edge of the mesa, staring at the ground as he moved along. I thought he was looking for pottery sherds or other artifacts until I came up behind him and heard him counting out loud, ". . . a hundred six, a hundred seven, a hundred eight . . ." and so on with each step. He was pacing off the distance to the edge of the mesa! When we got there and he had made his count, he asked me, "How much do you weigh?"

As it turned out, he was wondering if we would be able to take off with such a short runway. He calculated the distance, our total weight, the temperature, and the altitude of Cucurpe above sea level and concluded that we could probably make it. The alternative would have been the inconvenient one of flying the plane solo to the real landing strip and retrieving his three passengers there, delaying us as much as an hour. Not wanting to wait and trusting completely in Ike's judgement, we got into the plane. I took up my usual position in the front passenger seat and tried to relax as we went roaring toward the end of the mesa. As the plane came off the edge it made a slight dip and I instinctively lifted my legs and drew a deep breath as if to make myself lighter. There was a house perched just beneath the mesa. It seemed to me that the wheels of our landing gear missed its chimney by fewer than ten feet. But miss it they did, and we were safely up and away.

By 11:30 a.m. we were back on the Magdalena-San Ignacio landing strip where the yellow Volkswagen was parked. We drove to Magdalena for lunch and said good-bye to Tita. It had been a wonderful morning and I had two rolls of black-and-white film to show for it, pictures taken from the air that someday might be useful for comparative purposes.

We landed at the Nogales, Sonora airport early that afternoon to clear Mexican customs. The airport's *comandante,* who was a friend of Ike's, and another official wanted to go to Hermosillo. Ever mindful of Mexican tradition and the reciprocal nature of doing favors, Ike obliged them while Richard and I sat in the airport eating our supply of *bolillos* and the white cheese that is the region's specialty. While we waited, Richard regaled me with information about Sonoran vegetation zones.

Soon after 5 p.m. Ike returned from Hermosillo, gassed up the plane, and took us on an uneventful flight to Tucson International Airport where we stopped to clear U.S. customs. That done, it was back to nearby Ryan Field where we landed at 6:30 p.m. under clear skies. The trip had been a fine one.

•••

It would be a year and a half before I would fly with Ike again on what turned out to be our last excursion together. It marked my introduction to the Tarahumara Indians of Chihuahua. Eventually, it would lead to more visits with a different pilot, Larry Bornhurst, and four publications relating to the Tarahumara, including a book, *Tarahumara: Where Night Is the Day of the Moon.*

Ike and his wife Jean had been to Tarahumara country before, but when we took off from Ryan Field in the morning on January 5, 1977, it was my first foray into that magnificent region of great mountains and deep canyons. Helga Teiwes, photographer for the Arizona State Museum, rode with Jean in the back seat of the plane. A mutual acquaintance of ours, Canadian trader Edmond J. B. "Ted" Faubert, had told the Russells there would be a splendid Tarahumara celebration of Epiphany in the new church at Panaláchi, and that it would be possible for us to attend it and for Helga to photograph it. I was the ethnologist at the Arizona State Museum, and Ted had been anxious to have me visit the Tarahumaras, people among whom he had been trading for a few years and whose language he had learned to speak. The Russells had contributed to the Jesuits' Tarahumara mission program, one that included much-needed medical, educational, and social services. They seized on the opportunity to pay a visit, and Helga and I were invited along as guests.

It was cloudy and cool, about 50° F, when we cleared Mexican customs at the Nogales airport shortly before noon. It was a windy day, and Helga, unused to flying in small planes, was fighting off air sickness in the back seat. The plane rose ever higher to clear the crest of the western Sierra Madre, and I noticed that Ike was breathing oxygen through a tube in his mouth, an early indication of the disease that eventually was to kill him. About 2:15 p.m., we dropped down to attempt a landing at the settlement of Panaláchi where we were to meet Faubert and attend Mass with the Tarahumaras.

The landing strip at Panaláchi was more than 7,000 feet above sea level on a mesa overlooking the settlement. It turned out to consist of a few adjoining bulldozer swaths through a stand of pine trees, narrow and utterly without pavement or serious compaction. As we approached the strip, fierce cross winds jostled us every which way, but Ike determinedly kept the plane on a downward path toward the clearing between the trees. It was only at the last possible second, with the plane yawing fiercely from side to side, that he gunned the engine and we soared aloft out of harm's way. He circled around and flew to nearby Sisoguíchi, a place a little lower in elevation and where the landing strip, one that boasted a wind sock, was in an open valley. There was also less wind and the landing was a smooth one.

Ike and I walked up to the Jesuit mission and hospital in Sisoguíchi to see about getting someone to drive us to Panaláchi. As we walked slowly to the mission, with Ike breathing heavily and pausing often, he volunteered matter-of-factly, "I could have landed at Panaláchi, but with the wind blowing that hard, sometimes you bounce on the runway and your wings fall off."

Later, Jean asked me, "Weren't you afraid he was going to land at Panaláchi?"

"Not at all," I said. "I don't know anything about flying. I figured Ike knew what he was doing."

"Well," said Jean, who had flown many thousands of miles with her husband, "I was afraid!"

I daresay that Helga, who by then was quite ill from air sickness, had been afraid too.

We got a ride to Panaláchi with Father David Brambila, the Jesuit priest and 40-year veteran missionary among the Tarahumara who was to officiate at the Mass. We also rendezvoused with Faubert in Panaláchi, where later that night we attended the spectacular service in the new and modern-appearing Catholic church. Observances began well after dark when two dozen Tarahumara *matachín* dancers, accompanied by violin players, emerged from the church. They made a counterclockwise circuit around the plaza and edifice before going back inside and escaping the freezing cold night air. The Mass at which Father Brambila officiated included music provided by nine Tarahumaras playing their homemade violins, music whose strains reverberated throughout the building in a joyful celebration of God's presence. After Mass, music and dancing continued until about one in the morning. Besides the Tarahumara dancers and musicians, Faubert had brought four friends with him to Panaláchi, a Mexican, two Guarijío Indians, and a Mayo Indian. Faubert and the Mexican wrapped their legs with strings of cocoon rattles (*teneboim*) and performed *pascola* dances while one of the Guarijíos played a harp and the other two Indians played violins. It was a musical, visual, and spiritual experience never to be forgotten.

We spent the early morning hours sleeping on the floor of a storeroom owned by one of the Mexican residents of Panaláchi. We awoke to discover that the *matachines* were dancing beneath a nearby red bluff just as the moon was setting and the sun was coming up. Helga and I took pictures of the group while Faubert traded for Tarahumara pottery and woven blankets. Later in the morning, the Guarijío harpist provided a solo concert for all who cared to listen. Father Brambila had said he'd come by in the early afternoon to drive us back to Sisoguíchi and our plane, and true to his word, he dropped us at the landing strip by midafternoon.

The flight home was through clear skies and smooth air, to Helga's great relief. It was cozy and warm in the cabin, a warmth abetted by a couple of swigs shared by Jean and me of her good Korbel brandy. Our in-flight meal was a continental lunch of cheese, sausage, crackers, and tangerines. We cleared Mexican customs at the Nogales, Sonora airport and U.S. customs at the Nogales, Arizona airport, getting back to Ryan Field a little after 6 p.m. on January 6. It had been an Epiphany to remember and a perfect ending for my flights with Ike.

16

Letter from the Rascón Ranch

JEAN RUSSELL

Tuesday Nov 10 [1976]

Dear Luke & Marjorie,

Last weekend I flew with Ike to the Rascón ranch in the center of the deepest part of the Sierra Madre, in Chihuahua. All weekend I kept thinking so much about you, I guess because the memories aren't lately evoked of [the] old days—old beloved memories of sights, smells, experiences we shared—and here they were all there as fresh as yesterday and as strong.

I had expressed an interest in seeing Leo's still where he is making sotol (mescal, or bacanora). So after Arnold & I had ridden horseback up 1,000 ft. from the ranch below to the airstrip & cowboy's house at the top, Arnold asked the old (62!!) cowboy to take me to see the still, while he stretched himself out & sipped sotol from a small saucepan. I was behind, and we were winding along down a trail along the bottom of an oak-filled canyon when the cowboy lighted a cigarette. The smoke drifted back & almost unseated me it was so delicious. Oaks they call cusi grow there which have <u>soft</u> light green leaves, not deciduous, & these occur side by side with encinos—the more typical large live oak. Both oaks are real trees—not scrub.

The still was very simple—consisting of 2 holes lined with rocks where they roast the mescal [agave plants] 2 days & 1 nite. Then [there were] wooden troughs & boxes and underneath chambers whose function remains as much a mystery now to me as before it was carefully explained in Spanish. I kept looking at the setting & loving the trees & the cigarette smoke & the man, who came from Agua Prieta.

Ike had a flat tire on his airplane that had to be fixed before we could take off, so the wing was manually lifted by 8 men (where did they all come from?) & the spindle set on a rock. Ike mended the tube, but the tire pump he carries in the plane had gotten busted just the day before by a passenger whose weight over it in the back seat was too much for it. So after they tried unsuccessfully inflating the tire with a foot pumper for an air mattress & a propane torch affair, Arnold sent two cowboys on horseback 4 hours ride away to the nearest place possible to find a pump. This was Nátora, down on the river, also unreachable by road, only horseback. The reason they would have a pump is that they are on the river & have a rubber life raft. The guys got back at 1 a.m. with the pump—moonlight helped light the way.

None of these places has roads in, only trails. Nátora, by the way, is where Gavina was born, & Ike flew her and Nacho there so she could visit her ancient mother. Ike's funniest story—about the privy being a board across an abandoned well & the old mother falling in & having to be pulled out—was about Nátora.

Mornings, the men get up early & get a small bonfire going in front of the cowboys' shack, which looks like the mesquite-beamed barn Jesús Sánchez had at our ranch. They sit on their heels & stand around it, drink coffee, smoke cigarettes, talk. There were two children, 5 & 3, who took their place as if they were little men—no one excluded them from the grownup world. The 3-year-old drank his coffee (no cigarettes tho) as if he weren't 3.

The ranch house is in the bottom of a bowl with high red cliffs all around, the moonlight by nite & the sun breaking in the morning changing the colors constantly. The moon rose behind a single pine growing in the saddle. Ramón is Mexican, his wife & wife's kin are Pima. The 5-year-old looks pure Pima, the 3-year-old pure Mexican. The wife's brother rides 2 days into Madera for supplies for all of them & 2 days back. We ate venison (they shot a deer when we first got there), flour tortillas, butter & cheese (they milk all the cows when they calve), coffee from beans they roast themselves. Sotol from the same beat-up enamel cups they drink their coffee from.

Arnold & Leo Rascón are the perfect hosts, always looking out for you, gentle, kind, considerate. They are 2 of 11 children all born right here, raised all together on the food provided by the ranch, with a lot of hard work. Just imagine—on a ranch 2 days by horseback away from the nearest town with transportation—a man & his wife raise all the food & the necessities for themselves and eleven children. This is what went on in the covered wagon days but I guess it is my first personal encounter. They raised beans & corn in the fields, shot deer, fished from the big river that goes thru the ranch, & raised cattle—which gave meat, milk & cheese. They had a kitchen garden that raised onions, tomatoes, chilis. It's Arnold's, Herman's, Hector's, Arturo's, Leo's idea of Heaven to go back for a weekend, a week, even a day, and now that I've been there I can really see why. Leo said, "My father really made us all work hard in the fields, even the girls." The huge corral is made of a massive stone wall 5 ft. across at the base, 3 ft. at the top, 160 ft. from one side of the corral to the other. This wall, 6 ft. tall, [was] built all together by the father & the children. [It was] made of stones carried to the corral in home-made baskets astride burros—not mortared, but just stacked.

So Luke & Marjorie—do remember that we have shared trips like this in the past, and that there is nothing else in the whole world that I have ever known to equal the thrill, except violin music, perhaps.

Love from
Jean

17

Chasing Birds in the Sierra Madre

H. RONALD PULLIAM

I first heard about Ike from Dick Felger. Dick and I were neighbors and lived in stone cottages near the mouth of Esperero Canyon outside Tucson at the foot of the Santa Catalina Mountains. We were talking about my research plans, and I told Dick that I was looking for a bush pilot. For several years I had been measuring seed production and counting sparrows that spent the winter in the grasslands of southeastern Arizona. I had found that there were 10 to 100 times more sparrows in the winters following wet summers, with heavy grass seed production than in winters following dry summers. I wanted to know where all of those sparrows were going when they couldn't find enough food in the Arizona grasslands. I suspected they migrated farther south after dry summers and spent the winter in the mid-elevation grasslands and woodlands of the Sierra Madre Occidental.

Dick told me that I needed to meet Ike Russell, a retired rancher who liked any excuse to fly into Mexico. I called Ike and told him that I wanted to visit a number of sites in the Sierra, ranging from 4,000 to 6,000 feet in elevation. The sites were in Chihuahua, Sonora, and Durango. Ike was enthusiastic and agreed to a four-day trip. He would pilot the plane if I would pay the cost of gas. What a deal!

I first laid eyes on Ike early one morning in February 1974. The man standing by a hanger at Ryan Field fit my image of a rancher—tall, fit, and lanky. We exchanged hellos, and I introduced him to my field assistants, Ted Parker and Nick Waser; he introduced me to his plane, a single-engine Cessna. Ike didn't say much at first. He just told us where to put our gear and where to sit in the plane. The first real conversation was about two hours later. We were near a little mountain village in eastern Sonora when Ike tilted the plane way to one side and excitedly asked, "See that? Right there. The glint of metal." I was sitting up front next to Ike and admitted to seeing a glimmering of light from rocky ground several hundred feet below us. "That's ol' Dave Coughanour. Crashed there in '65—had a heart attack in midair and went down with two passengers. Best damn bush pilot I ever knew. Taught me everything I know about flying in these mountains. That's the way I want to go someday." Ike pulled the plane back up to a steep ascent. I felt a little woozy and wondered what I had gotten myself into.

We spent the first night near the small village of Mesa Tres Ríos in the mountains of eastern Sonora. First, we circled around the village a few times, and I scanned the landscape in search of good bird survey sites. After a while, Ike said, "We'll land over there."

I didn't see a landing strip and asked, "Over where?"

"In that big cornfield," he replied. The landing seemed very rough to me, but in retrospect it was one of the better ones.

A small crowd of children had gathered near the field. We saw them whispering and pointing at us from a distance, and before the propeller stopped turning, a group of the bigger boys came up to the plane. Ike hopped right out and started speaking with them in Spanish. I caught a few words of what they were saying, enough to know they were talking about mothers and food and where to spend the night. Soon a couple of the boys pointed at one of the others. Ike said something more to the boy everyone was pointing at, and after nodding agreement several times and both of them pointing back toward the village, the boy ran off.

"What is going on?" I asked Ike.

He explained. "I asked them whose mom is the best cook, and when they decided, I gave the boy a few dollars and sent him to ask his mom if she'll fix a meal for four strangers."

An hour later, we were sitting in a small, tidy house, taking tortillas directly from a wood-burning stove, and eating some of the best *chile verde* I ever had. We spent the night in a pine grove near the plane, and I thought to myself, "This isn't so bad after all."

After a morning of bird surveys, we flew southeast across the mountains into southern Chihuahua. We were looking for a good grassland site on the eastern Sierra slopes. We weren't having a lot of luck finding good sites, and late in the afternoon Ike said he had heard there was a landing strip at Nonoava, a small town nearby, but that he had never landed there. From the air the town looked more like a medieval Middle Eastern village than a Mexican town. There were rows of small, whitewashed stucco houses, surrounded by stone-walled pastures. The landing strip was dirt but well maintained. As soon as we landed, a jeep drove up and parked about 100 feet away from the runway. Two armed military-looking men got out of the jeep and waited. Ike said to the rest of us, "You better wait here." They talked for quite a while, and when Ike came back, he just said, "There is a landing fee." A short while later, Ike had negotiated not only the landing fee but dinner and lodging for us at one of those small stucco houses. We had a great meal and spent the night in our sleeping bags on the floor of the house.

The next morning I decided to look for some local sites to survey birds. Nick, Ted, and I rode in the back of an old pickup out to the countryside. Ike seemed uneasy and said he was going to stay in town. We got back in the late morning, and I was eager to leave and find some survey sites farther north in Chihuahua. We found Ike at the landing strip, and he didn't look too happy. He said the plane had been "commandeered." We looked across the landing strip, and next to the plane were the same two uniformed soldiers who had greeted us when we first landed. They were standing guard by the plane with guns. Big guns. We walked with Ike back toward town and before long came to what looked like a warehouse. Ike seemed to have been there before. We were escorted into the building by a guard and taken to a small office where an officer sat at a desk. The officer seemed friendly, shaking hands and smiling. He asked a lot of questions, and Ike translated. Yes, we were scientists and yes, we were studying birds. No, the plane belonged to Ike. He was our pilot. After a while, Ike said we should go outside and wait. When we were finally back in the air, Ike told us how much it had cost to get his plane back. It was a whole lot more than the gas money we were paying, but Ike said he'd take care of it.

We flew north along the eastern edge of the mountains in Chihuahua. The weather was good and the skies were clear. Ike asked if I wanted to fly the plane. "Sure," I said, and Ike told me what to do. It seemed easy. Late in the afternoon we found a beautiful place to land, in a pasture atop a mesa high above a river. Ike had been there before and spoke fondly of the two brothers who owned the land. They had a business in Ciudad Chihuahua, 50 miles away, and took turns on the ranch, apparently a two-day horseback ride from the nearest road. Ike said they had a small *casa* an hour's walk from where we had landed. He told us that the house had no plumbing or electricity, but that it was full of literary novels the two brothers had carried in on horseback.

We camped in the pasture by the edge of a cliff. The river was at least a couple of thousand feet straight below us, in a steep-sided canyon. Late the next morning, after our surveys, we found Ike standing in the middle of the pasture near the plane. He licked his index finger and held it up in the wind. I knew that look, and once again he didn't look too happy. "Can't take off in this wind," he said. The pasture was short, and Ike was very worried about getting up enough speed to lift the plane off the ground before we reached the edge of the cliff. That sounded pretty serious to me, so we spent the next few hours clearing rocks and limbs out of the pasture. Every now and then, Ike stopped, licked his finger again, and stuck it in the air, always with the same result—he shook his head and said, "I don't know." In the early afternoon, Ike announced, "We'll have to wait until tomorrow."

The next morning, Ike repeated his ritual of licking a finger and sticking it up to feel the wind. Then he said, "The wind is still not what I'd like, but if we're going to leave, we'd better do it now." We climbed in the plane and buckled up. As we raced down the grass field towards the cliff, it was obvious we had not found all of the rocks and sticks. It was a bumpy start, but the plane gradually gained some speed. Just as we seemed about to lift off, we reached the edge of the cliff. The plane went into a nose dive and headed directly for the river below.

I had never before experienced such a sensation of weightlessness and disorientation. Gasps of fear came from the back seat. Ike looked intense but never seemed out of control. We came within inches of giant boulders in the river before the plane leveled out. Ike steered a path between the two canyon walls, which seemed closer together than the span of the plane's wings. Gradually, we gained height, and the canyon walls grew wider apart. No one said a word for five minutes or more. Nick, Ted, and I were too sick to talk, and Ike just stared straight ahead. Finally he said, "I didn't think we were going to make it."

When I finally regained enough composure to notice, we were flying almost due east, away from the mountains. I asked Ike why, and he pointed at a gauge. As best I could understand, that gauge had something to do with the plane's electrical system, and we were headed to Ciudad Chihuahua to find a new alternator. As we got close to the airport, Ike radioed ahead, but already the signal was weak and he spoke very loudly in Spanish. We spent several hours at the airport, while Ike disappeared looking for the replacement part.

Finally in midafternoon he came back, but he didn't look too happy. By this time, I knew that meant trouble. "Can't find the part. We'll just have to go without it," he said.

"Will it be safe?" I quickly asked.

"Yeah, it'll be safe enough, but you'll have to turn the propeller for me." I soon learned what he meant. Ted and Nick climbed in the back and Ike got in the pilot's seat, while I stood on the runway, both hands on the propeller. Each time Ike yelled, I pulled down with all of my might. The first couple of times, the engine just sputtered like my lawn mower does. The third time, the engine started, and I ran around and climbed into the copilot's seat.

The journey back seemed anticlimactic. The bird surveys had gone well. We had documented, for the first time, facultative migration in sparrows, which Ted and I would report in a 1979 paper in *Fortschritte der Zoologie*. We had all enjoyed the adventure, but it was about to come to an end. Although the sun was starting to set, the sky was bright blue except for a few clouds that looked like cotton puffballs. The mountains were bathed in warm light on their western slopes, and their shadows extended across the lowlands to the east. Ike asked if I would steer the plane. I happily agreed, anxious for my second flying lesson. While I steered the plane, Ike put on his headset and picked up the radio handset. He didn't look too happy. He told us that the radio was dead and that he wouldn't be able to make ground contact before we landed. "Is that a problem?" I asked.

"Yeah," he said. "We don't have a radio and we don't have any lights. We'll be crossing the international border after dark, and when we land at Nogales to clear U.S. Customs they'll think we're drug dealers."

"Oh," I said.

Sure enough, we landed in total darkness and, before we even touched the ground, I could see the lights of a couple of vehicles racing down the runway towards us. Once again, we were facing armed men on an airport runway, but Ike didn't seem worried. He brought the plane to a stop and turned around to Nick in the back seat. Nick was wearing a heavy down jacket, and Ike said, "Here, put this bag under your jacket." Nick looked confused but he obliged.

Ike opened the cockpit door, and I heard someone say loudly, "Oh, Ike. It's just you." We got out of the plane and I heard Ike start explaining. There were a lot of questions, but Ike always seemed to have a good answer, and I noticed everyone was smiling and seemed amused. Everyone except Nick, who stood a little off to the side and gave a funny little cough every now and then.

After the plane had been inspected and Ike had signed a couple of forms, we made the short flight back to Ryan Field. As we were walking to our cars, Ike asked Nick for the bag. Inside was a live Harlequin Quail chick. Ike said, "I've always wanted one, and the boys at Tres Ríos gave it to me." Nick explained that his coughs had been to cover the noise of the chick scratching in the bag. I was glad to know that we were not drug smugglers.

AUTHOR'S NOTE

I took two trips with Ike into the Sierra Madre Occidental. This story combines events from those two trips as if they occurred on a single trip. I have done this, in part, because I can no longer recall which events occurred on which trip. Ted Parker and I went on both trips, but Nick Waser went on only one. Steve Speich, another graduate student at the University of Arizona, accompanied us on the other. A sad and ironic footnote to this story is that Ted Parker, one of the truly great neo-tropical bird experts of our time, died in 1993 in a plane crash in Ecuador while conducting biological surveys. To learn more about Ted's adventures, see *A Parrot without a Name: The Search for the Last Unknown Birds on Earth*, by Don Stap (1990).

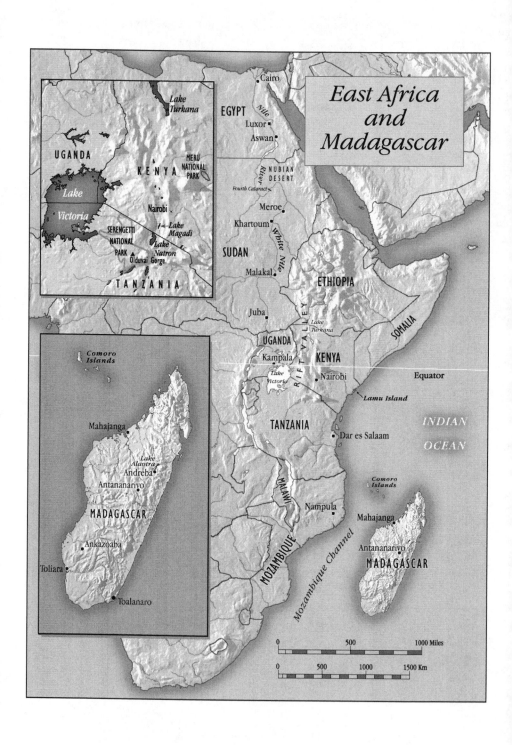

East Africa
and
Madagascar

Lake
Turkana

UGANDA
KENYA
MERU
NATIONAL
PARK

Lake
Victoria

Nairobi

SERENGETI
NATIONAL
PARK
Lake
Magadi
Lake
Natron
Olduvai Gorge

T A N Z A N I A

Cairo

EGYPT

Nile

Luxor
Aswan

NUBIAN
DESERT

River

Fourth Cataract

Meroe

Khartoum

White Nile

SUDAN

Malakal

ETHIOPIA

Juba

RIFT VALLEY

Lake
Turkana

SOMALIA

UGANDA

Kampala

KENYA

Lake
Victoria

Nairobi

Equator

Lamu Island

INDIAN

TANZANIA

Dar es Salaam

OCEAN

Comoro
Islands

Mahajanga

Lake
Alaotra
Andreba

Antananarivo

MADAGASCAR

Ankazoaba

Toliara

Toalanaro

MALAWI

Nampula

Comoro
Islands

Mahajanga

Antananarivo

MADAGASCAR

MOZAMBIQUE

Mozambique Channel

0   500   1000 Miles

0   500   1000   1500 Km

III... AFRICA AND MADAGASCAR

*By the mid-1960s Ike and Jean found
themselves at loose ends. Their three sons
were either away at college or had graduated
and begun to establish lives of their own.
Jean was working half-time in Bill Heed's
genetics lab at the University of Arizona.
But she and Ike needed a major challenge
to give their lives more direction. After much
discussion they applied to and were accepted
into the Peace Corps.*

*Ike and Jean had originally asked to be sent
to Kenya, but the agency decided that this
would not be a good choice because of the
country's generally high elevation and Ike's
severely reduced lung capacity. So instead they
were assigned to Chiloé Island, off the coast
of Chile. They were beginning to make final
preparations to leave when paleoecologist Paul
Martin approached them with a proposal for
an extended research trip through east Africa
in Ike's airplane. Ike and Jean had never flown
farther afield than Mexico and the Caribbean,
and Paul's idea greatly appealed to them. In the
end they dropped their Peace Corps plans and
in August 1965 embarked on a nine-month
odyssey to Africa and Madagascar.*

18

Corners of the Earth: Africa

PAUL S. MARTIN

I met Ike and Jean Russell through Marvin Karlin, a math teacher at Pueblo High School in Tucson. Marv had taught some of the Russell boys. He knew that Ike was a bush pilot who flew field biologists into the backcountry of northern Mexico. He also knew that I had started working on fossil pollen at the University of Arizona's Desert Laboratory and that I wanted to search south of the border for caves with fossils. So Marv got Ike and Jean and me together. We soon became close friends.

Beginning in May 1960, Ike and I flew on numerous trips into Mexico. The longest was more than a thousand miles, across the Mexican Plateau to the cloud forest just south of the Tropic of Cancer near Tampico, in southern Tamaulipas. Then in the spring of 1965, Ike and Jean and I began planning a much longer jaunt, one that would take us to East Africa and Madagascar. It would be the longest trip that Ike and Jean ever made in a small plane.

That fall I was eligible for a sabbatical leave from the university. To help in editing a new book on Pleistocene extinctions I wanted to visit Africa and Madagascar to learn more about their large animals, living and extinct. Above all I wanted to understand a peculiar and vital difference between Africa, Madagascar, and the Americas. In the New World, large animals vanished suddenly and massively at the end of the last ice age, around 13,000 years ago. Starting 2,000 years ago the same thing happened in Madagascar. Africa, on the other hand, somehow managed to escape severe megafaunal extinctions throughout the Pleistocene, despite the climatic hammer-blows of the ice ages that were experienced in all corners of the globe. How could all this be explained? What was going on?

I read what I could find on Africa, which only increased my appetite for the surprises, the freshness, and the novelty to be anticipated by field experience. What were Louis Leakey and other paleontologists discovering, I wondered? And then, what about Madagascar, an island almost as big as Texas, lying 260 miles east of the African coast? What were archaeologists finding there? Africa and Madagascar constituted a natural experiment in comparative biogeography. All I knew about Madagascar was what I'd read in David Attenborough's book, *Zoo Quest to Madagascar*.

It didn't take much talk about the glories of seeing Africa to catch the interest of Ike and Jean. Jean's mother had been a childhood neighbor of Osa

Johnson who, with her husband Martin, was among the first Americans to photograph African game from the air with a movie camera. Osa's book, *I Married Adventure*, which we had all read, aptly described her marriage to Martin, and Jean had done much the same when she married Ike. We'd also read *Serengeti Shall Not Die* by Bernhard and Michael Grzimek. What we learned in that book was more sobering, that young Michael had died in a plane crash in the African bush.

Of course, Ike had also had his share of mishaps. I learned about one of them on my first trip with Ike, a flight into the mountains of eastern Sonora. We landed at Yécora, a country town of perhaps 500 people. On our walk into town in search of a restaurant, I noticed pieces of an airplane decorating various backyards. I asked Ike whose airplane that had been. "Mine," was the laconic reply. I wondered what I'd gotten myself into.

But after several more trips and some flight instruction of my own (I got as far as soloing) I realized just how good a pilot Ike was. I was happy to leave the flying to him, especially in places like Africa.

In due time my sabbatical application was approved, and the Guggenheim Foundation came through with a fellowship. I wrote Louis Leakey and he agreed to let me accompany him on visits to Olduvai Gorge. I was ready to go to Africa.

•••

The trip began in August 1965, when Ike and Jean flew their Cessna 180 from Tucson to New York. There they had the wings removed and the airplane shipped by freighter to England. In early October, after it was reassembled, they flew to Spain to visit their oldest son, Luke, and his wife Marjorie, who were there teaching English. Then on October 17, joined by their old friend and one-time University of Arizona classmate, Bill Swan, Ike and Jean took off from Madrid and crossed the western Mediterranean to Algiers. From there, they intended to fly across all of North Africa and meet me two days later in Cairo.

Meanwhile, on the night of October 18, I found myself on a BOAC night flight from London's Heathrow Airport to Egypt. By midmorning as our jet circled the Cairo airport, the pilot announced a slight delay due to local traffic. Somewhere in Cairo I would find Ike, Jean, and Bill for the start of our flight south into East Africa and eventually to Madagascar. I hoped they hadn't run into trouble somewhere over the barren deserts of North Africa.

Finally we landed. Immersed in a queue of travel-weary passengers descending a flight of steps to the tarmac, I heard a familiar voice. Jean, Ike, and Bill had spotted me. They had just arrived themselves! They were the traffic that delayed our landing. Ike had indeed had his share of problems, having been required by Libyan air control to fly over the Mediterranean, out of sight of land, to avoid Libyan air space. Some days they don't, but on that day in Cairo the gods smiled; our rendezvous could not have been easier.

After two days of touring the Museum of Antiquities and the zoo, along with the inevitable rendezvous with the pyramids and the Sphinx, we were ready to start for Nairobi. Ike estimated that we could arrive in less than a week, with time for stops along the way. Bill Swan would leave us there and fly home with the Military Air Transport Service (MATS). A retired OSS major from World War II, Bill was entitled to fly MATS gratis when space was available.

On October 22 we filled the baggage compartment of the Cessna. Holding extra baggage on our laps, we started south. Ike said we were cleared to fly the commercial air corridor, the direct route over the desert for Aswan. But he thought it would be much more interesting to fly on a visual path of our own, winding our way up the Nile to Luxor and the Valley of the Kings. So that's what we did.

Landing at Luxor late in the day, we unloaded and tied down. Then, hoping not to attract undue attention, we proceeded to set up camp, boiling hot water for tea under the wing of the Cessna in the corner of the field, as was our custom in Mexico. But this was no remote, seldom-used dirt strip at the edge of a Chihuahuan corn field with only a family or two in residence. Luxor sported a modern paved airfield. There were jet fighters parked nearby. The tense Arab-Israeli standoff would soon erupt in war. Duly noting our failure to leave the airfield, guards in a jeep drove up to see why not.

We must have made a strange tableau. Dressed as usual in khaki, Ike wore a tan cap and sported World War II "Eisenhower" field boots. Above the shoe was a leather cuff with buckles, with room to tuck in one's pant leg, military style. Bill Swan dressed casually, but he had a military air about him. Like Ike, I was wearing khakis. Without Jean I suspect that we would have been detained as foreign agents or spies, up to no good. We exchanged pleasantries with the guards.

"There are fine tourist hotels in town," the officer suggested.

"We intend to fly out at dawn. We simply want to camp here," Ike replied.

The security guards stared at us in disbelief. After considerable discussion among themselves and after making sure they understood our intentions, the officer in charge proposed a solution. We could camp in our sleeping bags at the base of the tower under mercury vapor lights next to a military barracks, which reluctantly we did. The barracks were full of soldiers warming up for a riotous all-night binge, it was too hot to sleep inside a sleeping bag, and the mosquitoes were very bad. So was the idea of camping out at Luxor's airport.

The next day, after crossing the Nile to visit the archaeological wonders of Karnak, we flew on to Aswan. In the process, Ike discovered he had burned out his left wheel brake. We searched without success for a mechanic who might help with repairs. Ike thought we could get it fixed in Khartoum or Nairobi. That night we all agreed to sleep in a hotel. We found one which featured four-poster brass beds beneath inviting canopies of mosquito netting, sparing ourselves another night of misery.

On October 24 we cleared Egyptian customs and left for the Sudan. Depending on winds aloft, Ike wasn't sure we could reach Khartoum from Aswan. Since there was no aviation fuel at Aswan, Ike filled a five gallon can with car gas and loaded it into the baggage compartment. We abandoned the Nile where it makes a big bend in the northern Sudan and followed the commercial airline corridor straight for Khartoum. Our cruising speed of 130 miles per hour at an elevation of 3,500 feet was low and slow enough to inspect the surface of the Nubian Desert. We found an empty wilderness. Black hills (*jebels*) alternated between orange sand sheets, supporting no visible ground cover, no trees, no shrubs, and as far as we could see, no desert grasses. Apart from the barren floor of desert playas, we had seen nothing as lifeless as Nubia, not even in the most arid parts of North America, including Death Valley. This was desert with a vengeance.

Back over the Nile, below the Fourth Cataract, Ike spotted the town of Meroe. No one could be seen around the airstrip outside town. This was not a port of entry and we were not authorized to land. We landed nevertheless, taxiing back downwind to be ready for a speedy departure. Ike dumped the contents of the gas can into a wing tank. A dust cloud marked the progress of a large truck of armed soldiers bearing down on us. Ike thought it might be better not to trouble them with explanations so we took off, double quick. That night in Khartoum, dining on the roof of our hotel, we toasted our escape while watching the course of Comet Kohoutek.

At the university in Khartoum I found the Egyptian botanist Professor Kassass, who kindly took me out on my first African field trip. We found local species of *Acacia* trees, some more thorny than any I had seen in Arizona or northern Mexico. One acacia in particular attracted camels. They sought the bean pods, which looked similar to those on our mesquites that attract livestock. In early evening before dark, we watched as herders drove strings of goats or camels toward the city, raising clouds of dust which hung low to the ground, held there by cold air drainage. We had seen the same effect in American deserts when cars raise dust from unpaved roads, and the cold air of nightfall holds the dust cloud low to the ground.

In a few days we resumed our journey. The next stop was Malakal, on the White Nile in southern Sudan. Here we found ourselves at the edge of a war zone. Black Africans, some of them Christians, were fighting Arab Moslems (they still are, 35 years later). After refueling we saw no need to remain longer.

Ike taxied to the end of the paved runway, revved up, and at full throttle roared into our takeoff.

Suddenly, two men who had been out of sight cutting tall grass in a ditch next to the runway stood up and revealed themselves. Fearing that he might hit them, Ike cut power and jammed on the brakes. He forgot that only one brake worked.

We spun around in a ground loop, dragging and damaging the left wing tip and tail tip and collapsing the left wheel and strut. We were shaken up, but luckily nobody was hurt. A sizable group of people appeared from various quarters of the airport to help drag the plane off the field to an abandoned hangar.

This was a major setback for our trip to Nairobi. Ike and a few new friends with mechanical skills from the Malakal airport were soon at work disassembling the damaged strut and wheel. Jean, Bill Swan, and Ike decided to take the next scheduled Air Sudan flight back to Khartoum to search for a new wheel. I booked the next flight to Nairobi to catch Louis Leakey in time for our long-planned trip to Olduvai Gorge. Later I learned that the pilot of Ike and Jean's Air Sudan flight, after hearing of our accident, invited Ike into the cockpit of the turboprop Fokker to fly part of the route to Khartoum.

• • •

Louis Leakey was not happy to discover that I would be his only passenger to Olduvai. He had been expecting help from Ike on designing cattle tanks for the Masai tribesmen. The many goats and cattle of these herdsmen were seeking water sources in the bottom of Olduvai Gorge and were trampling Leakey's fossil outcrops, and Leakey had promised to provide a water source for the Masai at a safe distance away. From Ike's experience ranching in the San Pedro Valley of Arizona, which is about as arid as Olduvai, Ike would have been able to advise Leakey on how to design serviceable cattle tanks. Leakey rightly suspected that I was a useless academic, barely bright enough to pick his brains, with no practical experience in designing or building cattle tanks.

Despite my academic handicap, I gloried in four days of uninterrupted brain picking. We inspected fossil sites in Olduvai Gorge and localities important to the modern ecology of the region. Leakey would answer anything I asked him about ecology, fauna, paleontology, prehistory, and politics of the region. Back in Nairobi, though, Leakey was virtually unavailable. Although I appeared regularly in his office to pick up our mail, his tigress of a secretary protected him from distractions, for he was in the early stage of initiating the Leakey Foundation in the United States. Soon he left Nairobi to consult with his backers in California.

Meanwhile, in Malakal, Ike and Jean had managed to repair the Cessna enough to get it into the air. Despite vibrations from the bent wing and tail tip, they were able to nurse it from Malakal to Juba, where British mechanics jovially hammered the bent tail back into place. Juba was a dangerous place, though, with the Sudanese civil war raging all around. As they were coming in to land, Ike was instructed to maintain his altitude until he was right over the city, then descend fast to the airport in tight circles to avoid getting shot at by the Anyana rebels. Even the Air Sudan flights had to land this way. In town, Ike and Jean saw prisoners tied by their wrists in a guarded compound.

When Ike and Jean finally landed the damaged Cessna in Nairobi, it went back into the shop for proper repairs, and it remained there for three months waiting for a shipment of parts. In the meantime we decided to try a few pollen projects. Would the dung of living animals help reveal their diet, an approach that had yielded good results with fossil ground sloth dung? In Europe, archaeologists had discovered hyena coprolites in ice age caves. Maybe the coprolites harbored fossil pollen from the guts of the animals the hyenas preyed upon. The hyena was extinct by the end of the Pleistocene in Europe, but the same species, *Crocuta crocuta*, still thrived in Africa.

In a Volkswagen "bug" from Habib's Safari Rentals we set out for Serengeti National Park in northern Tanzania to look for Hans Kruuk, who was studying hyena life history. Halfway there we heard loud grinding noises from the rear end of the VW. Ike diagnosed the trouble as shattered wheel bearings, and inspection in a small roadside garage proved that he was right. Although some were in pieces, there were enough good bearings left to keep us on the road.

Near the headquarters of Serengeti Park, we found Hans Kruuk and his wife, accepted their invitation for lunch, and were told about their free-ranging pet hyena, Samson, who enjoyed soaking in their tub. That afternoon we left to explore a nearby *kopje* (isolated hillock) for possible hyrax middens, a potential source of fossil pollen. We noticed a hyena was approaching and began to get uneasy as it closed in on us, showing no sign of fear. It turned out to be Samson.

At the botany laboratory of the University College, Nairobi, we met algologists Edwin and Frances Isaac, parents of the soon-to-be renowned paleoanthropologist Glyn Isaac. They had left South Africa to escape apartheid. They offered us a hood and centrifuge for extracting fossil and modern pollen. Our attempts to trace hyena diet through pollen in hyena dung led to no breakthroughs, at least not in my hands, so I decided to try another tack.

Lake Magadi, southwest of Nairobi in the Rift Valley, was being mined for salt. The director of the Kenya Geological Survey, Brian Baker, told us of deposits of lake clays from some earlier high stand of the lake (possibly early

Holocene) yielding layers of fish bones. The chemistry of the lake had changed at some point, poisoning the fish. Except for the layers full of fish bones, the silty clays looked like the sort of playa lake sediments found in arid parts of North America that have proved rich in fossil pollen and revealed features of ice age climatic change. Jean helped me extract the clays, but our best concentrations yielded no more than a few microfossils, too few to provide a reliable paleoclimatic record of the region.

Then as now, Kenya attracted a variety of natural scientists involved in interesting studies. In Nairobi we met Jane Goodall and the Israeli paleontologist Etian Tchernov. North of Nairobi, in Meru National Park, we spent New Years Day with Joy Adamson, who was in a tizzy because her pet leopard was hiding out, jealously punishing her for keeping a pet cheetah in camp. Her husband George lived in a field camp of his own, inside a large cage. The idea was to bring visitors like us into the cage where we could observe in safety the young lions that were to be used in a movie based on the Adamsons' book, *Born Free*.

In Nairobi we met Larry Robbins, a graduate student in anthropology from the University of California, Berkeley. Larry offered to show us the Mesolithic sites in rock shelters and caves he was excavating on the west shore of Lake Turkana. I hitched a ride to a nearby town with the local District Officer, where I met Ike and Jean, who had flown in from Nairobi in a rented Cessna. Then the three of us flew south along the lake shore to Larry's camp. There was no airstrip but Larry said that at least in places the surface was flat enough to land, with no gullies or plants larger than low shrubs to cause trouble. Ike managed a bumpy landing on a gentle slope. The country looked (and felt) as dry and hot as summertime in the Sonoran Desert. It was the driest country we had seen since leaving the Sudan.

When we returned to Nairobi, we found that our Cessna had finally been repaired and was ready to go. We could now leave for Madagascar.

During a visit to Kampala, Uganda, we had encountered an affable young British zoologist, Alan Walker, who was a lecturer in anatomy at Makerere University College. Alan studied locomotion of lemurs, especially the anatomy of their grasping hands and feet. Since Bill Swan had returned to the U.S., we had room for one more passenger in the airplane.

"Come with us to Madagascar," Jean begged.

I could see Alan was sorely tempted. I hoped he hadn't heard about that ground loop at Malakal. Could he get a release from his teaching duties on such short notice? He'd need a visa for the Malagasy Republic, as Madagascar was then called. His wife was not thrilled to be left behind in Uganda for a month with their son Simon, a two-year-old. But Alan knew it was a unique opportunity to see the Great Red Island, up to then seldom visited by Anglo or American scientists. Because of its variety of living and extinct lemurs, Madagascar would be especially interesting to him. Alan finally gave in to our persuasions. Somehow it all worked out.

On the way we stopped in Dar es Salaam, giving us an opportunity to visit Tanzania's National Museum and to inspect the famous 1.75 million-year-old skull of *Zinjanthropus*, alias *Australopithecus boisei*, that Leakey had excavated from Bed 1 at Olduvai Gorge. Zinj was housed in a locked vault. In response to a heartfelt plea from Alan, the curator reluctantly opened the vault for us and let us examine the specimen.

On the next leg we flew south to Nampula in Mozambique, the logical jumping-off point for Madagascar. Mozambique was still under Portuguese control and known as Portuguese East Africa. Guerrilla wars raged in the hinterland. We lacked visas for travel there, and there were no "in transit" facilities at the airport. When an immigration official finally appeared after a long siesta, he announced that we would be detained. Ike insisted that we were merely passengers in transit and that we would start for Madagascar in the morning. Besides, we were harmless. None of this satisfied officialdom. We were delivered to the police station and obliged to cool our heels outside the chief's office. Eventually we were ushered in, to be told that we would spend the night in jail. We could see a cell through a rear door. Jean assured Alan that Ike would talk us out of this. I wondered if he could. While Ike never seemed to worry about a problem until he could not avoid it, he had one now. The chief gave Ike a tongue lashing in Portuguese, which is close enough to Spanish to pick up a few words. The unfriendly tone was plain enough. Ike persisted, ever respectful of bureaucrats (whatever he thought of them), his demeanor calm. Eventually we were allowed to go to town for the night, leaving our Cessna tied down at the airport.

In the morning the weather looked bad. The weather service reported and we soon saw for ourselves that eastern Mozambique and the Mozambique Channel were under heavy overcast. Fortunately, our destination in Madagascar, the coastal city of Mahajanga, expected clearing. Ike decided it would be okay. He explained to Alan that, ideally, for a long over-water crossing in a light plane, there would be boats stationed at fixed intervals along the route. The aircraft would have radio contact with the boats as well as with the airfield ahead. But Ike's radio wasn't working and any boats along our flight path would be fortuitous. Alan thought that Ike's explanation might have been intended to give him an opportunity to bail out and stay behind if he had any qualms. After all, it was Alan's first experience with madcap Americans exploring new country by Cessna.

Alan had already discovered some of Ike's idiosyncrasies, such as his aversion to the stall warning in the cockpit. The screech warns the pilot that his airspeed is marginal for safety. Ike wedged a matchstick into the air intake to silence it. He had an aversion to loud noises, and he didn't care to be screeched at just to be told what he already knew about safe airspeed.

As soon as we could, we left Nampula. We flew for two hours through solid overcast across the Mozambique Channel. Locked in on instruments, with no radio contact and no visibility, I had a sickening feeling that the compass lied and that we were flying in circles.

I felt a tap on my shoulder. Breaking the tension, Jean passed me her emergency tequila bottle. I took a sip, then another, and another, until I didn't feel any worries. Finally the clouds parted. Far below we could see the ocean. To my amazement it was not some shade of blue or green but brick red! The muddy flood waters of the swollen rivers were washing far out to sea. Soon the coast appeared, and at Mahajanga we made our acquaintance with French customs officials. Although it was a newly independent nation, the infrastructure of the Republique was still largely French. From Mahajanga we flew on to the Madagascan capital of Antananarivo.

We spent a month in Madagascar, traveling throughout the country by plane, car, and jeep to visit fossil localities and museum collections. But I will leave it to Alan to tell that part of the story. In March, I left Madagascar on a commercial airliner to begin the long journey to Tucson. Meanwhile, Ike, Jean, and Alan flew the Cessna back to Africa by way of the Comoro Islands. They left the plane to be sold in Nairobi and returned to the U.S. via commercial airlines.

• • •

The African and Madagascar experiences strengthened unconventional ideas I held about the relationship between the first arrival of humans and the extinction of megafaunal species in localities around the world. Research in Madagascar since our trip has lent further support for the causal role of humans in megafaunal extinction. It is now known that almost half of Madagascar's prehistoric fauna of 40 species of lemurs are extinct. All the extinct species were large, more than 20 pounds adult weight, and in one case as massive as a gorilla. Thus the species that disappeared were those with the most meat. The time of these extinctions has also been recently verified as quite late, around 2,000 years ago. This puts it much later than in Africa or the Americas. But in Madagascar, as elsewhere, the extinctions correspond roughly with the arrival of the first humans.

The trip helped me considerably in editing my book, which was entitled *Pleistocene Extinctions*. I was especially pleased that our new-found friend, Alan Walker, contributed a chapter on Madagascar.

19

Looking for Lemurs on the Great Red Island

ALAN WALKER

I have never kept a diary. All my life I've thought how useful it would be to have done this and I've envied those who had the discipline to keep one. So here I am, 35 years after the fact, trawling deep in the past for memories that never got away—memories of Ike Russell and the trip I made with him, Jean Russell, and Paul Martin to Madagascar in 1966. The trip affected me forever in a peculiar way, for apart from a short ride around southern England in a World War II bomber, as a Royal Air Force conscript, this was my first flight in a small aircraft. Thus, Ike's flying style is the one I came to think of as normal. This belief has served me well during the hundreds of hours I have spent since then in small aircraft going to and from homemade bush strips at fossil sites in East Africa.

I joined the Madagascar trip in an odd way. I was teaching medical students at Makerere University in Kampala, Uganda, and trying to finish my Ph.D. thesis on the locomotion of the extinct subfossil lemurs of Madagascar. I had worked on fossils in the British Museum and studied reports of the sites from which they came. I also had made comparative studies of the bones and muscles of extant lemurs as well as watched their locomotion in zoos and on old cine film. But, because worldwide air travel was still under development and very expensive in the early 1960s, I never had the chance to go to Madagascar to see the lemurs in the wild. Even when I took up the appointment at Makerere, my family and I had traveled from London to East Africa by boat, not plane. Then one evening I went to hear a lecture at the Uganda Museum. The speaker was Paul Martin, from the University of Arizona, and his topic was extinction. He gave an excellent presentation of his "prehistoric overkill" hypothesis, linking the sudden arrival of humans to the extinction of large and relatively defenseless animals throughout much of the world. He explained that he was on a worldwide trip to collect data about extinctions from as many places as possible. Among the places he was going to visit was Madagascar. I introduced myself to him after the talk and told him what I knew about the extinction of the subfossil lemurs there. I added that I myself thought that, directly and indirectly, human actions were responsible for the demise of many lemur species. My research had shown that the extinct forms were so recently extinct that they really had to be considered part of the modern fauna. Further, looking at their characteristics in light of an extinction hypothesis, I noticed that all the extinct lemurs were big, slow-moving, ground-living, and diurnal. In contrast, the surviving lemurs were small, fast, arboreal, and mostly nocturnal. This looked to me like a case of hunting overkill.

Paul wondered if I could possibly go along with him to Madagascar, because I knew the literature concerning the Madagascan lemurs and the fossil sites. I told him at once that I was teaching and that it was impossible for me to go with him. The next day he left for Nairobi, where he was to study the East African evidence. When I got a chance to tell my head of department at the medical school about this offer, he insisted that I should go. He even arranged for my teaching to be covered. (In point of fact, this was very early in my career. I wonder now if I had been such a lousy teacher of anatomy that the department head was delighted to get me out of his hair for a few weeks!)

And so I got in touch with Paul at the National Museum in Nairobi, borrowed money, bought what 8mm movie film and 35mm slide film I could afford, and got a flight to Kenya, where I joined Paul, Ike, and Jean. What Ike and Jean thought about this I don't know, and Ike's rather laconic manner didn't make it easy for me to find out, but there I was. All I had to offer was a lot of enthusiasm for Madagascan lemurs, fossil and living, and schoolboy French. In return I got the trip of a lifetime and enough data on the locomotion of lemurs and the fossil sites to make my thesis a much better contribution to the scientific literature than it would otherwise have been.

●●●

We were sitting on a bench at police headquarters in Nampula, a town in what was then Portuguese East Africa (now Mozambique). We had been sitting there all afternoon, our bags in a pile and our passports confiscated. We had flown down from Tanzania and had made our approach to Nampula airport about noon. Ike hadn't been able to raise anyone at the tower—we found out later that it was siesta time. We landed anyway. There were long rows of military planes parked next to the concrete runway. But we didn't yet realize that the Portuguese who ran the airport, and the country, were feeling distinctly wary of strangers on account of the fierce, ongoing war for Mozambican independence (which continued until 1975). As far as we could see, there was no sign of any war, and nothing much at all going on at the airport, so we didn't anticipate the problem that shortly arose. After landing, we hung about in the airport's dusty cafe trying to buy soft drinks from the woman at the counter, speaking to her in American Spanish which she dutifully and incomprehensibly answered in African-accented Portuguese. Eventually, a sleepy soldier came into the room and casually asked where we were from. At the mention of Tanzania, he leapt to activity. Mozambican rebels had bases in Tanzania, and the government there was actively supporting their activity. We had unwittingly breached Mozambique's security. Within minutes we were being hustled off to town in a military vehicle under armed escort.

Hours passed and it was getting to be quite late in the evening. Ike was doing his best in Spanish to negotiate our release with the minor officials we were permitted to see. Our concerns grew, especially as the language barrier between ourselves and the Portuguese officials had been by now amply demonstrated. Suddenly the door to the police chief's office opened and out he strode. It was the first we had seen of him. In perfect English he announced, "When in Lisbon I speak Portuguese, when in Paris, French, and in London, English. But this is Portugal." Then he left. Apparently, he had been perfectly willing to let us twist in the wind.

Shortly afterwards an aide gave us back our passports and gave orders to some people to carry our bags to a hotel across the street. He sternly told us to be in the air and out of Nampula early the next morning, and we agreed. We thought that the police chief had decided to get rid of us before we became even more of a diplomatic problem.

So the next morning we took off, fully fueled, for the trip to the coast and out across the Mozambique Channel, flying 475 miles to Mahajanga on the northwest coast of Madagascar. There were only three life vests for the four of us, but as I thought our chances of survival if we had to ditch were hopeless anyway, I was not much bothered. Ike took the plane up to altitude and set the pitch and mixture for the long leg over water. We were at least a hundred miles away from the island when we saw the sea change color from blue to red. The lateritic soils of Madagascar were bleeding out to sea. We made the crossing without incident. It was the monsoon season in Mahajanga, and that afternoon we watched the rain pouring down on the rickshaws in the street. Flying on to Antananarivo, the capital, we crossed over the central plateau and were amazed at the fantastic landscape of rounded grass-covered hills with their *lavakas*—enormous erosion gullies caused by centuries of overgrazing and burning.

We made several trips from Antananarivo to fossil sites on the central plateau and in the south of the country. Sometimes we were accompanied on these journeys by researchers who taught at the local university or who worked for the department of water and forests. Ampoza was a place that we were keen to visit. The site had been worked in the 1920s by Errol White, a paleontologist from the British Museum, who had made a fine collection of extinct giant fossil lemurs, hippopotamuses, and tortoises. We knew the site was near the town of Ankazoabo in the southwest of the island, so Ike flew directly there.

It was there that we met Libio. Before we arrived we had seen the blur of a white airplane—a crop duster—flash by underneath us. After we landed at the small grass strip near Ankazoabo and the noise of our engine died down, we heard the sound of another engine and watched as the white airplane sideslipped onto the strip and slid to a stop. The pilot was clambering out when we walked over. He wore white coveralls and announced, "Je suis Libio!" He had seen Ike's airplane and had wondered who we were in this out-of-the-way place. When we explained where we were trying to go, he immediately told us that we could get closer, by flying to another strip he knew that was on a farm owned by a man called Leferbvre. He offered to guide us there in his airplane.

Libio had little English and I was the only one in our group who spoke much French. So Ike had me sit next to him in the copilot's seat so I could translate what I heard from Libio over the radio speaker. We flew for 10 or 15 minutes following Libio, who in crop-duster fashion flew just above the tree-tops. Libio called out to say that the farmhouse strip was in sight and to watch out for the "peep" over the runway. I had no idea what this meant, and so I told Ike that we had to be careful when we landed. As Ike made his approach it became evident what the problem was—a large horizontal water pipe swung out from a tall water tower. Airplanes had to land under it! Libio had taken it upon himself to use the English word "pipe" instead of the French "tuyau". Ike took it all in stride and followed Libio in for a landing under the pipe.

The farmer, Monsieur Leferbvre, took us in for the night and volunteered to get us to Ampoza the next day. His wife gave us a meal of chicken followed with dark brown honey that we ate with spoons. That night we slept on mats on the floor of the farmhouse. The next day we all piled into M. Leferbvre's World War II Willys Jeep and drove, sometimes cross-country, to Ampoza. The jeep was so old we had to keep wandering off the road and driving into streams to cool the engine.

One of the most important sites we visited was Andrahomana, a shore-line cave not far from Toalanaro (then called Ft. Dauphin), near the very southeastern tip of the island. A professional collector named Sikora had been there at the turn of the century, but no one else since then. Sikora had sent many good specimens to natural history museums in Vienna and London, including type specimens of new species of lemurs. To get to the cave, we flew from Toliara on the southwest coast directly toward Toalanaro because we did not know exactly where the site was. Swinging along the coast near Toalanaro a few hundred feet above the ocean breakers, we could easily see the large cave, its roof collapsed and open in several places. The cave faced directly south towards Antarctica. There was nowhere nearby to land, so Ike swung back to the northwest where he had spotted a dried-up lake bed. He made a touch-and-go landing and then flew by the spot to inspect the wheel tracks to see if it was going to be safe for a real landing. He decided that it was, and so we set down on Lake Erombo.

The dry lake was just under four miles from the cave. Paul and I walked on a compass bearing to the cave, carrying a two-way radio to keep contact with Ike and Jean while they stayed with the plane. We did not, of course, have too much time to spend in the cave. But it was enough to collect bones for radiocarbon dating, which might make a vital link between the arrival of humans and the extinction of the giant lemurs. We also found a finger and part of a shoulder bone of one of the biggest of the extinct giant lemurs, *Megaladapis edwardsi*. My analysis of *Megaladapis* suggested that this animal was a koala mimic that probably weighed about 175 lbs. There were also the remains of the carapace and plastron of a huge extinct tortoise that had tumbled over the edge of the roof, smashing itself on a piece of roof-fall below.

Paul and I were hot and tired by the time we got back to the plane, but it was only a short flight on to Toalanaro, where we paid a visit to the de Heaulme family. This family of plantation owners had been in this far-flung place for many years. In addition to growing sisal, they kept a forest reserve with several species of lemurs living in it. We were put up with gracious hospitality in their guest house. In the reserve we followed and filmed the ring-tailed lemurs as they raced along the ground and the sifakas as they made their enormous leaps through the trees. The de Heaulmes also had an egg in their house of the giant elephant bird *Aepyornis*, an ostrich-like bird that stood 10 feet tall. Their eggs can still be found in sand dunes around the south and east of the island. These birds, like the giant lemurs, became extinct after humans arrived on the island.

We had made the acquaintance early on of Georges Randrianasolo, a wonderful Malgache man who worked for ORSTOM, the French overseas research group. He knew a little bit about some of the fossil sites but he knew an awful lot about living lemurs, for he was responsible for the well-being of the lemurs in the little Tsimbazaza Zoo in Antananarivo. A few years earlier, Georges had helped Sir David Attenborough on his filming trip through Madagascar. He knew only two words of English, probably picked up from Attenborough's British crew. These were, "Fucking French!"

With Georges we took a trip to a fossil site called Ampasambazimba in the central highlands of the island, a short distance to the west of the capital. This was one of the first fossil sites to have been discovered, and it was excavated early in the 1900s by a British missionary named Herbert Standing. Standing had a peculiar excavation strategy—he diverted a stream so that it ran through the deposits, and then he caught the bones in chicken wire as they washed out of the sediments! He reported that some of the leaves in the deposit were so fresh that they were still green, and that some of the skulls of the extinct lemurs still had whitish stuff (the remnants of brains) inside their braincases. Both observations suggested that the extinct animals at the site survived until quite recently.

When we eventually got to the site we found it covered with the usual paddy fields, for rice paddies are spread over the wetter parts of the island. We located the residence of the local headman and stood under his verandah in pouring rain, watching him eat a large plate of purple-colored rice, while Georges negotiated with him for permission to walk along the banks of the paddies. This was so we could see if any fossils had been thrown up by the farmers' hoes. Permission granted, we slogged along and did indeed find some pieces good enough for radiocarbon dating. Standing had published very serviceable maps and sections, and it was fairly easy to find our way around. It was clear even from our short visit that there were still lots of ancient fossiliferous lake deposits that had not been excavated. I thought that spectacular specimens might be recovered with more modern methods than those used by Standing.

On another trip with Georges we went to Lake Alaotra, a large lake some 130 miles north of Antananarivo that was mostly covered with extensive reed beds. These reed beds were the habitat of a subspecies of lemur, *Hapalemur griseus alaotrensis*, the Alaotran gentle lemur. Locals paddled us around the reeds in a dugout canoe while we looked for lemurs. These lemurs never come to dry land, living instead on the floating clumps of papyrus and sedge. Their diet is the softer parts of these plants.

In the nearby town of Andreba, Georges found that one of the villagers had one of these lemurs in a small pen, either for a pet or for the pot. As keeping lemurs was illegal, Georges gave the person a sermon about conservation and confiscated the animal. Later he arranged the official permissions for me to take it back to Kampala for study. And so this animal, together with a ringtailed lemur from the south of the island that had also been confiscated from illegal captivity, flew back with the Russells and me to Uganda.

Sadly, our trip to Madagascar finally came to a close. Paul departed for home from Antananarivo on a commercial airliner. Ike and Jean and I, along with the two lemurs, returned to Africa via the Comoro Islands. We had no intention of risking our freedom with another unfriendly encounter in Mozambique!

... **PICTURES**

Ike, his mother Editha, and the
twins Gordon and David, mid-1920s.
Courtesy of Jean Russell.

Ike the Easterner, late 1920s.
Courtesy of Jean Russell.

The Tucson golden years of Ike's youth, early 1930s. Courtesy of Jean Russell.

Ike and Jean as newlyweds in Jean's '38 Ford convertible, 1939. Courtesy of Jean Russell.

Opposite, top: Ike (with steering wheel) hamming it up with friends at the University of Arizona, about 1935. Courtesy of Jean Russell.

Opposite, bottom: Ike and his mother Editha at the Bird Yoas Ranch near Amado, Arizona, 1939. A traditional Easterner, Editha always dressed "properly." Courtesy of Jean Russell.

Ike competing in the calf roping event at the rodeo in Redington, Arizona, about 1943. Courtesy of Jean Russell.

The Russell ranch house near Cascabel, Arizona, with a new roof and an added room on the left, about 1941. Courtesy of Jean Russell.

Ike (under the left wing) and the rented Taylorcraft on the outskirts of Desemboque, Sonora, during the ill-fated trip to Yécora with Bill Swan, October 1953. Photo by Bill Swan, courtesy of Randolph and Julia Jenks.

Bad day at Yécora, Sonora, October 5, 1953. Ike (on the right) confers with local residents about the rented Taylorcraft he just wrecked. Photo by Bill Swan, courtesy of Randolph and Julia Jenks.

Ike's Aeronca Sedan on Tiburón Island, 1967. Courtesy of Jean Russell.

Ike's Cessna 185 at Ryan Field, Tucson, 1970s. Courtesy of Jean Russell.

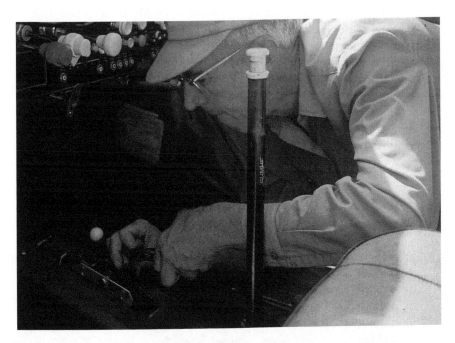

Field repairs in southern Mexico, January 1971. Photo by William T. Starmer.

At the airstrip at Desemboque, Sonora, December 1958. Behind the Seri children, left to right: Ed Moser, Ike, unidentified man, Bill Smith, and Bob Thomas. Photo by Mary Beck Moser.

Cathy, Becky, and Ed Moser at home in Desemboque, Sonora, January 1976. Photo by Thomas Bowen.

Dinner time at the Mosers' house in Desemboque, Sonora, March 1978. Clockwise from the left: Susan Randolph, Ike, Richard Felger and Becky Moser (working together on Seri ethnobotany notes), Jean Russell, and Doris Potwin. Courtesy of Mary Beck Moser.

Soft ground at Bahía Vaporeta,
Tiburón Island, January 1976.
Photo by Thomas Bowen.

Ike's Cessna 185 struggling to take off from Bahía Vaporeta, Tiburón Island, January 1976. Photo by Thomas Bowen.

Out of gas at Rancho Nuevo, Sonora, March 1967. Ike, gas can in hand, prepares to walk to the ranch house to buy a few liters of Pemex. Photo by Thomas Bowen.

Merv Larson and desert bighorn lamb.

Picnic in Baja California, 1970s. Jean Russell, Sarah Heed, and Ike. Photo by Bill Heed.

Ike, Tita Braniff, and Richard Felger in Sonora, May 1975.
Photo by Bernard L. Fontana.

Ike's airplane on the wrong mesa at Cucurpe, Sonora, May 1975. Photo by Bernard L. Fontana.

The day after the Tarahumara Epiphany celebration. Bunny Fontana, Ike, and Jean wait for a ride from Panaláchi to Sisoguíchi, Chihuahua, January 1977. Photo by Helga Teiwes, courtesy of the Arizona State Museum (No. 44181).

Ike relaxing in Bacoachi, Sonora, with
his tea satchel on his lap, May 1975.
Photo by Bernard L. Fontana.

Sharing a pasture at Bob Russell's farm near
Marcola, Oregon, summer 1972. Photo by Ken
McVicar, courtesy of Bob Russell.

*Ike's Cessna 185 after the ground loop at Madera, Chihuahua, November 1979.
Courtesy of Jean Russell.*

XB CUS after the crash on Ángel de la Guarda Island, August 1977.
Courtesy of Jean Russell.

Bunny Fontana takes a turn with the shovel as (left to right) Dave Russell,
Bob Russell, Alex Russell (Luke's son), Richard Felger, and Ward Davidson stand by.
Courtesy of Jean Russell.

South America

PARQUE NACIONAL
HENRI PITTIER
Maracaibo
Caracas
Barcelona
Barquisimeto
VENEZUELA
Bogotá
ANGEL FALLS
Santa Elena
Cali
Boa Vista
COLOMBIA
ECUADOR
Equator
Manaus
Belém
Talara
Amazon   *River*
ANDES
CHAN-CHAN
PERU
BRAZIL
Lima
Ayacucho
NAZCA
VALLEY
La Paz
BOLIVIA
Arica
MOUNTAINS
Belo Horizonte
PACIFIC
OCEAN
Rio de Janiero
ATLANTIC
OCEAN
CHILE
Mendoza
Santiago
Buenos Aires
San Rafael
La Plata
ARGENTINA
Viedma
Chiloé
Island
Chiloé
Island

| 0 | | 500 | | 1000 Miles |
| 0 | 500 | 1000 | | 1500 Km |

Puerto Natales
Punta Arenas
Río Gallegos
Tierra
del Fuego
Ushuaia

Río Gallegos
Puerto Natales
Punta Arenas
Strait of Magellan
Tierra
del Fuego
Ushuaia
Beagle
Channel

IV... SOUTHERN MEXICO AND SOUTH AMERICA

Occasionally, Ike and Jean flew to destinations
farther south in Mexico than the Gulf of
California and the mountain country that
straddles Sonora and Chihuahua. One trip was
to collect fruit flies for University of Arizona
geneticist Bill Heed; another was to support
pianist Ron Jacobowitz's Mexican concert tour.
And four times they flew through southern
Mexico on their way to South America. In
November 1968 Ike, Jean, and Jean's niece
Barbara Straub set out on a nearly eight-month
tour of South America that would take them all
the way to Tierra del Fuego. Three years later
they flew biologists Tom Starmer and Barney
Ward to Venezuela to collect fruit flies, returning
with Jean's niece Patty Thomas and her husband
Jay, who had been living there for the past year.
In December 1972 paleoecologist Paul Martin
joined them for an extended research trip down
the spine of the Andes to Tierra del Fuego and
back up the east coast through Brazil and
Venezuela. And in April and May of 1975
Ike, Jean, their son David and his wife Susan
Randolph flew south on a vacation trip to
Colombia, Ecuador, and Peru.

20

Lights Out in Ixtepec

WILLIAM T. STARMER

Ike Russell seemed to have solutions to problems, big or small, and I usually felt secure and confident whenever I flew with him. But I didn't always know for certain if his solutions were real or not. One time while we were flying over the Gulf of California he pointed to a beach on a small island and told me that he had once landed there. The beach runway was so short and the sand so soft that he knew that getting the plane off the ground was going to be a real problem. The solution, he explained, was to deflate the tires. Since then, he said, he always carried a tire pump so the tires could be reinflated before the next landing. Naturally, I wondered who was expected to pump up the tires *before* that next landing—me?

I always liked Ike's wit and ability to string people along. He was fun to be with, even when you were on the end of the string.

•••

My very first trip with Ike and Jean was in the winter of 1971. They were planning a trip from Tucson to central Venezuela to pick up Jay and Patty Thomas, who were returning to the U.S. after a year there managing a dairy farm. They had two empty seats in Ike's Cessna for the trip down, and Barney Ward and I were invited to join them to collect Drosophila fruit flies for Bill Heed's research group at the University of Arizona. Ike and Jean knew all about Bill's research because Jean had been working part-time in his lab for the last 10 years. Bill had a great interest in cactus-breeding drosophilids, and at that time there were reports of a unique Mexican species (*Drosophila acanthoptera*) being found far to the south in northern Venezuela. This was certainly possible because no one had really studied cactus-breeding drosophilids in South America, and there were plenty of cacti there. Barney was one of Bill's graduate students who worked on this fly, so he was keen to hitch a ride with Ike and Jean on their trip south. I was convinced to take the fourth seat and join them for my first field trip as a Drosophila biologist.

We gathered early one morning at Ryan Field near Tucson and stacked our gear outside a hanger in preparation for loading the airplane. I was used to traveling light and had brought my usual hiking gear and change of clothes, about 30 pounds worth, that I would normally carry on my back.

Barney had our collecting nets, jars, fly food, aspirators, bags, etc., for a one-month collecting trip. We were all set to load everything in the plane until Ike said, "Cut it in half, leave half behind, and let's go." So we did.

Off we went across Sonora, with a pleasant lunch stop along the coast, eventually arriving and staying the night in Culiacán, Sinaloa. I had flown a number of times before in small planes and knew right away that Ike was a good pilot, dependable and knowledgeable. I was confident that our trip would be interesting and full of adventure. Walking the streets of Culiacán that evening, it was clear that my traveling companions were an easygoing bunch. Ike was obviously culturally attuned to Mexico and in his element. His presence gave you a secure feeling. Jean was a delight and always had a positive view of things. Barney was unassuming, down to earth, and easy to travel with.

The next day was a long one. We hugged the west coast of Mexico, flying low over the water, late into the day. Ike told us we would be landing sometime after dark at a new airstrip in Ixtepec, Oaxaca, about 100 miles southeast of Oaxaca City. He told me that most airstrips in Mexico did not have lighted runways and so it was not usually possible to land after dark. But this new one had lights—at least that was what his new book on Mexican airports said.

Indeed it was dark when we approached the city of Ixtepec. Although we picked up the radio beacon at the airport, there were no lights and no visible runway. Ike flew toward, over, and around the beacon several times, ultimately asking us to look out of the windows to locate the runway. We did look out of the windows on both sides but nobody could see a runway in the dark. After several passes, people in the city started coming out of their houses and flashed their flashlights at us. We continued to fly low over the city looking for the landing strip that was supposed to be lighted. No voice radio contact, no lights, no runway, nowhere to land. Jean took out her tequila bottle and passed it to Barney and me.

Ike said he probably had enough fuel to fly back to Mexico City, maybe three more hours air time, but he was too tired to attempt that. So he decided that an unlighted highway might be a possible landing site in the dark, as long as we had no power lines to contend with. The plan was to fly low over a highway running north. We, the passengers, were to look out of the windows for those troublesome power lines. We banked left after passing over the airport radio beacon for a look at the highway. All of a sudden lights began coming on at the airport. They were car headlights. People of the city of Ixtepec had lined up their cars along the runway and were showing it to us. Jean put away the tequila bottle.

Ike didn't hesitate. He circled the plane and lined it up to set down on the lighted runway. The middle of the runway was now visible, but unfortunately the people of Ixtepec weren't really showing us where it started and where it ended. So when Ike touched down we were a bit short of the runway, and the plane took a BIG bump before settling again, this time on the tarmac. After a short taxi we were mobbed by the people who had "saved" us. They were all around the plane, herding us to waiting cars, then to a hotel and good food. Apparently, we were now their responsibility. The newspaper people who came to interview us wanted to know, "How did you feel?" I felt fine before and after the landing, thanks to Jean.

The next morning we made two discoveries. The first was that the big bump was caused by hitting a curb before the runway. The second was that we had not seen the landing strip in the dark because we had expected a typical small, narrow runway. The Ixtepec runway turned out to be a new military installation and was much too wide to recognize in the dark.

After we were airborne again, Ike made a third discovery—we had developed a mechanical problem. He said he could not control the airplane's pitch without constantly holding onto the controls. The elevator trim needed some repairs, so after about an hour of flying toward the coast, he put down on a dirt road that had some old buildings nearby. Our instructions were to find some straight metal bits, such as nails, brads, screws, and other "old airplane parts" along the road or by the buildings. Ike sorted through our collection until he found the appropriate piece. This he cut and filed until a makeshift rivet was ready to repair the elevator controls.

With the problem fixed we took off again, stopping for lunch in Tapachula, Chiapas, on the Guatemalan border. After lunch we crossed Guatemala and flew over west-central Nicaragua where we encountered an active volcano. Ike flew the plane right along side it, close enough for some nice photographs of the smoke billowing out. But he didn't warn Barney or me to keep our seat belts tight, and we both ended up on the roof when the plane fell a nice distance in a sudden downdraft.

Landing in Managua was uneventful, except that the mechanics there hooked up the battery charger incorrectly and blew out the plane's electrical system. It took three days to fix it. One thing I learned in Managua was what the constant honking horns of the cars in the streets meant. Apparently, the first one to honk had the right-of-way at the intersection—at least that is what Ike told me our taxi driver had said.

From Managua we flew over Costa Rica and directly over the Panama Canal to Bogotá, Colombia, where we spent the night. Barney had a good meal and then a very rough night. He was up sick all night, and then in the morning he was faced with the prospect of flying in turbulent air for the next several hours. I filled a prescription (written by him) but we needed to leave soon—we did not have the option of laying over for Barney's benefit. I was in the seat behind Ike next to Barney, who was ghostly pale. My concern was what Barney was going to do when it got really turbulent. Ike turned and gave me one of his sly smiles—he knew that my lap would be a target if Barney got sick again. Where were the little paper bags? Fortunately, Barney was pretty empty by this time and the Lomotil was doing its job, so he and I watched the scenery from high altitude and played rummy.

With the Andes to starboard, we headed for Maracaibo, Venezuela, where we landed. Unexpectedly, Barney (now largely recovered) and I caught our first drosophilid flies on some cactus right by the airport while we waited for Ike to take care of some official business. To fill the time we were strolling around the fenced perimeter of the airport when Barney spotted a suitable cactus on the other side of the fence. This is what we came for, so Barney boosted me up, I gave him a pull, and we climbed the fence to get to the cactus on the other side. Eureka!—we found flies! We aspirated them into our vials, got ourselves back over the fence, and felt we were off to a good start. In fact these were the very first Drosophila flies I had ever caught in the wild, and they turned out to be an undescribed species. It was a grand introduction to Drosophila biology.

The paperwork completed, we got back into the plane and took off. At the end of the day we arrived at the dairy farm where Jay and Patty worked. Waiting for us there was a newly bladed runway in a field with "IKE" white-washed across it. On landing we were greeted by a mule that was to carry our things up the mountain. We spent the night in the Thomas's most unique two-story house, made of bamboo and palm fronds, sitting on the very top of the mountain. I saw the southern cross low in the southern sky early the next morning and knew we had arrived.

Ike flew Barney and me to Barquisimeto the next day. Here we parted ways, and Barney and I began our field work. Our work was fairly extensive. We had plenty of help from various people at the Universidad de Barquisimeto and Parque Nacional Henri Pittier. We collected in dry areas, coastal regions, domestic habitats, and cloud forest. We concentrated on cactus flies and eventually brought specimens back to Tucson. Barney and I returned through Caracas, Miami, and Houston, using commercial airlines. By comparison with the trip down, the return trip was uneventful. Other than the frog Barney was bringing back getting loose and sticking to the cabin window between Miami and Houston, nothing much happened.

During the field work itself, we did not know what fly species we were really finding, only that they were different and probably new. In fact, we had uncovered a number of new species that would be described by Marvin Wasserman and his colleagues. Since that time, many others have used these insects as model systems. Most notably, Antonio Fontdevila and his associates and students have studied and published a number of papers on the genet-ics, ecology, systematics, and evolution of the "*Drosophila mulleri* complex in South America." If it weren't for Ike and Jean Russell's interest in Bill Heed's science, who knows how long it would have been before this group of interesting species would have been discovered. Ironically, we never did find the Mexican cactus fly (*D. acanthoptera*) that had originally enticed us to make this trip.

•••

It seems that southern Mexico always has its perils. Five years later, in February 1976, I was invited once again to fly south with Ike and Jean to collect drosophilids. This time it was going to be a short trip to Oaxaca. Bob Mangan, another graduate student in Bill Heed's laboratory, joined us at Ryan Field for a 9:30 a.m. departure.

There was heavy overcast that day so we flew low under the weather. I found this kind of flying interesting, like a one-way trip through a deep narrow cave with the tunnel getting narrower, the water level rising, and no scuba gear. We went under the clouds and through the valleys, with mountains looming all around. Fortunately Ike knew the way. We flew past Hermosillo, then headed on to Acaponeta, about 75 miles southeast of Mazatlán. After landing, we hitched a ride into Acaponeta for dinner and a hotel for the night.

The next day started in a routine manner with an 8:30 a.m. departure. We flew inland, paralleling Mexico's west coast. We landed in Tepic for fuel, flew over Colima, had lunch in Apatzingán, Michoacán, and stopped for more fuel in Chilpancingo, a city about 50 miles north of Acapulco. Soon after taking off from Chilpancingo, Ike decided we had better stop for the night rather than fly on to Oaxaca, since it might get dark before we found an airstrip there. He reminded me of the night the lights were out in Ixtepec and our troubles landing there in 1971. So we landed in the mountain village of Tlapa, Guerrero, about 60 miles east of Chilpancingo.

I am still not clear about what exactly happened after we landed at Tlapa, but we were met at the small airport by some officials who quickly escorted Ike and Jean away. Ike told Bob and me to wait at the airstrip and someone would take care of us. We waited some time speculating about what was going on. More officials finally arrived, wanting to look at our passports and other documents, and asking questions about our reason for being in Tlapa at this time. Normally, I would not have worried much. But Ike, our security, was away and there was an unusual number of people coming down the mountain toward the village. I thought there might be a bit of trouble.

Eventually, Bob and I were taken into town to join Ike and Jean at a very busy hotel. During dinner, Ike explained that we had landed at an inappropriate moment in the political history of Tlapa. We were not aware that the political aspirant for the presidency of Mexico, José López Portillo, was scheduled to arrive the following day. The officials wanted to know what four gringos were doing in this place, at this time. I must admit that, with a high profile political figure due shortly, we did not choose the best time to show up, especially unannounced, in a small airplane with a load of unusual equipment.

I still vividly remember that night. We were given separate rooms in the hotel. Mine was about six feet by six feet, with a dirt floor, a very high ceiling, and one small square window at the top. This window was well out of reach and was barred. The door had an inside hook to keep it closed, and all during the night someone would shake it trying to get in. Several times I peered out into the hallway to see it lined with sleeping people. This overflow crowd of folks that had come to see soon-to-be Presidente López Portillo was so thick that to get down the hall one would have to walk on top of them. I stayed put and waited.

Early the next morning, a bell started to toll and the hallway crowd dispersed. I found Bob, then we caught up with Ike and Jean, who said it was important to leave soon after breakfast. We did. As we walked toward the airport we were overtaken by several Mexican Army vehicles. The *comandante* had orders to escort us to the airport.

Everything seemed fine when we arrived and our departure seemed imminent when Ike said something to the commander, something that I believe was overheard by the soldiers accompanying him, something that caused the *comandante* to change his tune. We were quickly surrounded by about 12 to 15 soldiers—young boys, actually—with submachine guns, or at least big menacing-looking rifles with big bullets. They ordered us to unload everything from the airplane. Ike said to do what they asked and to unpack things slowly. Good advice—you never know what a dissecting microscope might look like to a nervous soldier when it is swiftly taken from its box! This unloading process took some time, during which there was a conversation between Ike and the *comandante*. I didn't pay much attention to that conversation—I was trying my best to seem harmless in the eyes of the boys who could barely hold up their weapons. As a consequence, I did not hear what was said between Ike and the commander, but we were finally allowed to reload the airplane and leave.

I was later led to understand that whatever Ike had said when we first arrived at the airport had undermined the *comandante's* stature in front of his men, and that Ike had to somehow rectify this mistake without being too obvious. In my estimation, only someone with Ike's experience and know-how would even have recognized the blunder, much less known how to recover from it. Without his savvy, I might still be in a Mexican jail.

As to science, the reason for flying to Oaxaca in the first place, we had two notable accomplishments. One was the capture of the elusive Mexican fruit fly *D. acanthoptera* and several related species. The other was the collection of a number of microorganisms (yeasts) growing in close association with the cactus and flies we were studying. The collection of yeasts became a significant part of my growing interest in wild yeasts found in cactus and ultimately contributed to the description of many new species and genera of yeasts by H. J. Phaff, Andre Lachance, and their associates. In fact, the work that followed this and other field trips with Ike and Jean led to establishment of one of the best known yeast habitats in the world and has served as a model biological system for the study of microbial ecology. Ike made the path to these discoveries easier and almost always more interesting and memorable.

21

A Magical Musical Tour of Mexico

MARY MCWHORTER

I buckled my seat belt, looked around the small airplane cabin crowded with people, luggage, and excitement. We were four in number—Ike and Jean Russell, Susan Randolph (a soon-to-be daughter-in-law of the Russells), and me.

It was a clear day in May 1974, and we were off to be musical ambassadors to Mexico. Or maybe a more accurate term would be stage managers/ cheerleaders for Tucson's pianist Ronald Jacobowitz (hereafter referred to as Ronnie) and his concert tour of four cities in central Mexico.

When I think of Ike, I see a tall, slender, dignified ex-rancher who carried himself with the ease and sureness of someone who knew where he was going and what he was going to do once he got there. Whether in the air or on the ground, he was a man who was up for anything. This morning, sitting in the pilot's seat in his Levis, tan work shirt, and his Charles Lindbergh boots, he was about to fly us south to Mexico and music.

Ike listened for directions from the tower at Tucson's Ryan Airfield. We taxied slowly out onto the runway. In my naivete I thought we would go clear to the end of the runway, turn around, and roll its whole length before lifting off. That was not the way Ike piloted his special plane. Halfway down the runway, he revved the engine and we catapulted up and over Baboquivari Peak.

Then we turned south toward Nogales and beyond. When the thrill of the takeoff subsided, I leveled off in my seat and was soon caught up in gazing down on familiar terrain—roads and landmarks I knew well from many trips to Sonora by car. We were off on our adventure.

As we made our way southward, I looked around at my traveling companions and thought of the dozen years of friendship that had passed since 1962, when we met at a piano recital given by Ronnie in the Russells' home. Music was an enduring thread that ran through these years of friendship. And music was one of the reasons I had been invited on this trip, for at the time I was chairperson of the Tucson Chamber Music Co-op, one of the sponsors of Ronnie's outreach tour to Mexico.

I knew of Ike's fame as a bush pilot, of course, but this was my first flight with him, and I was excited. Memories of this trip run like a movie through my mind—the short and dramatic takeoffs and landings, the hours of soaring over new and changing landscapes, the kaleidoscope of interesting people we met, and of course the sheer pleasure of Ronnie's concerts.

Our first destination was a lunch stop at Desemboque, Sonora, on the shores of the Gulf of California. We landed on a narrow dirt strip right next to the beach. Besides being the main village of the Seri Indians, Desemboque was home to Ed and Becky Moser, good friends of Jean and Ike. Becky served us a tasty seafood lunch practically on the seashore itself, and then led us to a simple concrete-block house in the desert. Here we met one of the Seri artisans who, with only a few simple hand tools and a piece of ironwood, created incredibly beautiful carvings of the animals of this area.

After leaving Desemboque we flew down the coast, stopping in Culiacán for the night. We landed at the ranch of Alejandro Canelos, one of the largest producers of tomatoes and cucumbers for Mexico and the United States. We were met by the ranch's research scientist, Dr. Ellsworth Shaw, our host and a long-time friend of Ike and Jean. He and his wife Elizabeth had been boosters and sponsors of Ronnie's musical career in Tucson and Mexico. Ike was as much at home discussing agricultural research with Dr. Shaw as he had been examining the crafts of the Seri artisans.

We left Culiacán the next morning for Aguascalientes, the capital city of the state of Aguascalientes and our first concert stop. Ike had invited me to join him up front in the copilot's seat. With a quick grin he handed me a map and asked if I'd like to be his navigator. "Sure," I replied. The land below soon became a blur of canyons with rivers in their bottoms crisscrossing the landscape. The ground was moving past faster than my ability to follow along on the maps. After five minutes as navigator, I declared, "Ike, I'm lost!"

"Well, I get the oxygen if we have to fly over these mountains!" he replied, with just a hint of a smile on his face. Of course, he knew exactly where we were, having flown over this country many times and personally explored it on the ground. This was the land of his heart, and not even a poor navigator could cause him to lose his humor, much less lose his way.

We arrived in Aguascalientes and found that the region looked much like the familiar Sonoran landscape. Here we met up with Ronnie, who had flown down commercially, and his music agent for Mexico, Luis Martínez. We had arrived with plenty of time before the evening's concert, so we all decided to take in the local market, with Ike as our enthusiastic guide. His friendly demeanor and excellent Spanish naturally drew people to him. Ike was especially keen on the varied textiles and arts and crafts of the area. Susan, the bride-to-be, was looking for items for her future home. We moved on to the vegetable market where we sipped freshly squeezed orange juice and tasted ripe mangoes and fragrant papayas.

That evening was one of contentment as we took in Ronnie's performance of Beethoven, Schubert, Schumann, and Medtner. The Mexican audience was as thrilled as we were, and they expressed their appreciation with warm and prolonged applause. After the concert, we were welcomed with an elegant and gracious reception, accompanied by sumptuous food.

Next morning we flew to our next stop, Lagos de Moreno, in northeastern Jalisco. Though only 40 miles south of Aguascalientes, we discovered that we had entered a different world. We were now in the heart of what was once Colonial New Spain, and our amazed and delighted eyes took in the incredible local architecture of eighteenth-century Europe, appearing as though magically transported from Spain and France to Mexico. One of these stately old buildings was the concert hall, a beautiful architectural jewel where Ronnie would be performing. But first we had to find someone to open the door so we could get the piano positioned on stage and so Ronnie, who always carried a tuning hammer in his pocket, could do a last-minute tuning.

A helpful young woman named Laura finally located the man who could let us in. The keys to the building were huge and a century or more old. There was some concern that the piano, on its heavy metal support, might fall through the ancient floor boards if we rolled it out onto the slanting stage. So Laura had six or eight men physically lift and carry it into position. Fortunately, the floor held!

Early that evening we readied ourselves for beautiful music in a romantic setting. It was to be a gala night for us all. Attired in our long, formal dresses, we anticipated greeting the guests coming to hear Ronnie. Jean wore a flowing skirt with a top of off-white Mexican cotton, Susan looked young and beautiful, and I was in a long red dress with lace collars and cuffs. Even Ike was wearing a sport jacket!

The atmosphere of the concert hall was especially alluring that evening. The electricity was off from a storm the day before, so Jean, Susan, and I had acted as efficient stage managers and found candles to provide light all across the stage and on a lectern behind the pianist. We were pleased with our ingenuity and the romantic result.

As Ronnie waited in the wings for his cue to start the concert, we noticed a group of men with violins, trumpets, guitars, and a guitarrón making their way through the darkened hall along the side aisle, headed for backstage. We knew instinctively that we had better not start the concert until we found out what their entrance portended. We soon realized that the mariachis were also scheduled to play—the hall had been double-booked for that night!

After some hasty negotiations, the mariachis graciously agreed to move to the Plaza de Armas and leave the hall to the visiting foreign pianist. Alas, when they left, they took all but about 30 members of the audience with them! But we forged ahead. And then, just as Ronnie began to play, the electricity was restored and the house lights came on, revealing a beautiful old concert hall with a piteously sparse audience.

That night, Ike sat as usual in the second row, listening intently. He was a man who enjoyed his music, and he also wished to enjoy these concerts even after they were over. Near his foot lay Jean's large Mexican purse, propped open. Ike had hidden a tape recorder inside the purse and was secretly taping Ronnie's concert. Later, as everyone met for dinner and drinks to discuss the finer points of the evening's performance, a sly smile would occasionally appear on Ike's face as he glanced casually at the now-closed bag containing his bootlegged concert recording. I think he savored these postconcert critique sessions because he and his accomplice, Jean, were the only ones who could actually replay the moments of the concert being discussed.

Next morning we reshuffled our rides a little so that Ronnie, also a private pilot, could do some flying with Ike. And so with part of our group in Ike's airplane and the rest in Luis's car we headed 80 miles southeast to San Miguel de Allende, Guanajuato, for Concert No. 3.

When we arrived we were once again awed at the splendor of the old Colonial architecture—golden cathedral domes and church spires gleaming in the spring sunlight, and opulent mansions. Ronnie, viewing this city, said, "It is so beautiful—it brings tears to the eyes." Ike, always the consummate tour guide, filled us in with a wealth of historical and cultural information as we explored the city.

San Miguel de Allende is also a sophisticated city where concert-goers know the difference between a mediocre concert and an inspired performance. That evening Ronnie gave the audience an inspired performance, and the audience gave Ronnie a standing ovation. And they gave us a marvelous catered reception afterward. The audience's sophisticated manners stood in sharp contrast to what we had experienced the night before in Lagos de Moreno, when most of the people deserted Ronnie's concert to follow the mariachis.

For the final concert we flew north to San Luis Potosí. Here too we felt as though we were in Spain, with the spires of ancient churches poking up every-where. The remarkable concert hall, which dated from the early 1700s, was adorned with crystal chandeliers, ruby-red velvet curtains, and shining golden balconies. As in San Miguel de Allende, the audience was sophisticated and discerning, and they too rewarded Ronnie's exquisite performance with a standing ovation. And again we all got to share in an elegant catered reception. The next morning was Sunday, and we awoke as church bells chimed over the whole city.

The tour was now complete, and everyone agreed that it had been a great success. Once again it was time to split up. We thanked Luis Martínez for all his help and said good-bye. Ronnie was scheduled to fly back to Tucson commercially, and the rest of us prepared to climb into Ike's plane. Another short and dramatic takeoff, and we were headed back to Tucson.

On the flight back, Ike veered off course to give us all one last treat—a view of the beautiful Basaseachic waterfall in the Sierra Madre of western Chihuahua. As we looked down, he said, "I've hiked down there." I couldn't imagine anyone hiking in that rugged, steep, seemingly inaccessible canyon. I would like to have shared that experience, but I was content to look down on those majestic falls from above—as only the eagles, ravens, and violet green swallows can do—or the people in Ike's airplane.

Soon we were back in Tucson. It was hard to believe that in just a few short days we had taken in a Seri village, a Mexican ranch, four glorious concerts in four Mexican cities, and a spectacular waterfall, all in the company of wonderful traveling companions. For Ike, who took jaunts like this all the time, it may not have been much out of the ordinary, but for me it had been a magical trip.

22

Corners of the Earth: South America

PAUL S. MARTIN

It might be said that my 1972–1973 trip to South America with Ike and Jean Russell was three years in the making. In 1969, I started field work in the Grand Canyon with the help of Austin Long, Tom Van Devender, and several University of Arizona graduate students. We were collecting and dating fossil dung from caves inhabited during the late Pleistocene by the extinct Shasta ground sloth. Dating this material would help us estimate when they became extinct. That information, in turn, would help us address the overarching question of *why* they became extinct. Good dates would provide a basis for determining whether the arrival of humans in the New World coincided with ground sloth extinction, and thus whether humans could have been the cause of their demise.

Ground sloth caves harboring stratified dung deposits are very rare. One of the best is found within the Grand Canyon at a place called Rampart Cave. News of our findings there gained sufficient notoriety that author James Michener heard of them and asked if he could visit the cave. We were happy to oblige him, but for us it would entail a time-consuming trip from Tucson. To reduce the travel time, I asked Ike if he would fly Austin, Tom, and me from Tucson to Lake Mead. There we could meet Michener and representatives of the National Park Service, who would take us all by boat to the site.

Ike agreed, and he added that there would be enough room to squeeze in Tom Martin, my six-foot six-inch son, who wanted to join us. Even that turned out not to be the full passenger list, because Ike showed up at the airport with Weni, Jean's Great Pyrenees. Weni was an experienced air traveler, having made many trips with Ike and Jean to San Carlos Bay on the Sonora coast. With some heavy lifting, Ike loaded the huge amiable dog into its familiar airborne kennel, the baggage compartment in the back of the Cessna. Tom clambered over the back seat to join Weni. We were five adult males and an enormous dog in a four-seat airplane. When we reached Lake Mead more than two hours later, Tom emerged from the baggage compartment smelling mighty doggish. But he claimed that Weni had been a great companion by softening his ride.

As planned, we met Michener and the Park Service people, and we had a smooth boat trip to Rampart Cave. Michener seemed duly impressed with the fossil sloth dung and its implications for the animal's extinction, and he wrote about it in the *Reader's Digest*.

Fossil sloth dung continued to be a promising means of studying the relationship between the arrival of humans and the extinction of large Pleistocene animals. Moreover, South America was becoming important as a source of information on several extinct southern species of ground sloth. In Argentina, Humberto "Tito" Lagiglia, Director of the Museo Nacional in San Rafael, had radiocarbon dates for fossil sloth dung from a nearby rock shelter at Gruta del Indio (Indian Grotto). Lagiglia's results were very close to or younger than the dates Austin and I had recovered on Shasta ground sloth dung from the Grand Canyon caves. Another locality I yearned to visit was located near Puerto Natales in southern Chile. It is the Cueva de Milodón (Mylodon Cave), named for the extinct form of ground sloth found there. This was the first South American cave discovered to harbor sloth dung—called *boñegas* (dung balls) in this part of the world. Before the development of radiocarbon dating, no one imagined how valuable they would be to both ecologists and students of Pleistocene extinction.

It would be very helpful to visit these and other South American sites so that Austin and I could compare them with the Grand Canyon caves and other North American counterparts. Three years after the trip with Michener, I was eligible for a sabbatical leave from the university. Supported with a National Science Foundation grant, I decided to spend a few months visiting various Pleistocene fossil localities. The question was how to get to South American caves and other fossil sites. Could I persuade Ike and Jean to fly me there?

Ike, Jean, and Jean's niece Barbara Straub had flown all the way to Tierra del Fuego three years before. At my urging, Ike and Jean decided it would be fun to go again. In addition to the ground sloth caves, I would be able to visit half a dozen other late Pleistocene fossil sites of extinct large mammals in as many countries. Jean talked up Carnival in Rio de Janeiro, something she had long wanted to experience. Carnival in Rio also appealed to my wife Marianne, who decided to join us later in Brazil for the event. And the Russells' old college friend Bill Swan wanted to come along as far as the Canal Zone in Panama and fly back from there.

On December 19, 1972, Ike and Jean and Bill and I somehow managed to stuff ourselves and all our baggage into Ike's Cessna, and our families saw us off from Tucson. We crossed the border into Mexico, landed at Hermosillo to clear Mexican customs, and flew on to spend our first night in Mazatlán. The next night we were in Pátzcuaro, Michoacán. We stayed with an old friend that we'd first met in Nairobi seven years earlier, geographer-turned-Buddhist-philosopher Ken McVicar, and his wife Donna.

We left Pátzcuaro, refueled in Morelia, and reached Mitla, Oaxaca, before nightfall. Ike and Jean's friend, the artist John Houser, had arranged accommodations for us at a *pension*. On the flat roof above the courtyard lived a half-wild guard dog, an attack animal guaranteed to deter any robbers attempting to reach the patio from above. Its owners fed their guard dog by tossing food up from below. Rains would flush down old bones and dog dung.

In a few days we resumed our journey. Ike decided we had enough gas to make it to Tapachula on the Guatemala border and we did, barely. Right behind us came a Lear Jet chartered by a TV crew from Mexico City. It refueled in a hurry and left quickly, the first hint we had of the severe earthquake that had leveled much of Managua a few hours earlier, killing 18,000 people. We left in early afternoon, changing our flight plan from Managua to San Salvador.

In Panama we parted company with Bill Swan, who returned home as planned. Anthropologists Tony Ranere and Olga Linares helped us locate the giant ground sloth (*Eremotherium*) fossil locality at Oco outside Panama City. They even located Joaquín Carrizo who had assisted in the original excavation. We also inspected some ground sloth bones on display in a historic *posada* (inn) being remodeled by the Panamanian government.

From Panama we flew to Cali, Colombia, for the night, continuing on the next day across Ecuador to Talara, in northern Peru. There we met archaeologist Allison Heaps de Peña, who took us to visit the famous Talara tar pits, surrounded by oil fields. Ground sloths and other Pleistocene megafauna were trapped here many thousands of years ago, and their bones are now being exposed in fresh excavations. The situation is similar to the tar pits at Rancho La Brea in Los Angeles, California, but I found Talara much more impressive.

We celebrated New Years Day of 1973 by flying down the coast from Talara to Lima. At intervals, the sterile desert slopes are transformed by rivers gushing out of the Andes. These ribbons of water are bordered by rich riparian habitat, with cultivated fields irrigated with water pumped by windmills. On the way we flew over Chan-Chan, an enormous archaeological site which features more than 10 adobe-walled compounds, each containing streets, houses, public buildings, and reservoirs. It is the largest pre-Columbian city in the New World, covering more than six square miles.

In Lima, we went to see the world-famous Moche ("Mochica") pottery at the Museo Rafael Larco Herrera. Moche ware is remarkably realistic and lifelike, and the ancient potters portrayed nearly every conceivable aspect of their lives and culture. Like most visitors, we especially admired the so-called erotic pot collection. All major coital positions are neatly modeled, and there are representations of oral sex and copulations with animals. In Ike's words, "They knew it all." Oddly, facial expressions are quite solemn—the Moche folk depicted in the pottery didn't seem to find sex very much fun.

We traveled to Ayacucho from Lima, crossing the Andes by train and *collectivo* (taxi). Ike was unhappy that Peruvian Air Control disallowed trans-Andean flights by single-engine aircraft like ours. The high point on the railroad pass lies at an elevation of around 15,800 feet. Ike knew he could coax his Cessna higher than 18,000 feet.

Near Ayacucho I visited Pikimachay Cave, guided by Freddie Ferrua from the local college. The cave had been excavated by a long-time friend, archaeologist Richard "Scotty" MacNeish, who claimed to have found evidence that people had actually butchered a ground sloth here more than 12,000 years ago. However, there was not much left in the cave to see, for most of the contents had already been removed. From Ayacucho we returned to Lima on a commercial flight and prepared to head south.

•••

International flying in a light plane bears little resemblance to taking a commercial jetliner. On our way south from Tucson as far as Lima, Peru, we made 10 stops. Many of these were at airports of entry—required stops to enter or exit a country, where one must deal with immigration and customs officials. For us, these included Hermosillo and Tapachula in Mexico, San Salvador in El Salvador, Bocas del Toro and Panama City in Panama, Cali in Colombia, and Talara and Lima in Peru. And roughly as many more on our return.

Each of these airport stops entailed a whirlwind of bureaucratic details. As owner and pilot of our airplane (and the only thoroughly competent speaker of Spanish among us), Ike naturally bore the brunt of this. For example, to leave Lima, after packing up and checking out of our downtown hotel, finding a taxi for the airport, and mailing packages and letters at the post office along the way, Ike was confronted with the following, not necessarily in any particular order: (1) finding the radioman to pay for repairs; (2) settling our parking fee; (3) checking weather reports; (4) filing our flight plan to Arica, Chile, with Lima air control; (5) finding the gas truck and paying for gas after filling the wing tanks; (6) clearing customs and immigration, with an exit stamp on each of our passports; (7) trying to make the money come out right (we were warned that at the time Peruvian currency was of no value outside the country); (8) consulting maps and local pilots regarding flying conditions to be expected in unfamiliar country ahead; and, (9) not least, getting something to eat, because Ike suffered badly if he missed a meal.

It took us over three hours to get all these things done so we could exit Lima's airport. Not all the officials who had to be consulted could be located easily—inevitably, some were on breaks. Ike grumbled that air control officers rarely did any piloting themselves. We did not manage to take off for Chile until 2:15 p.m. for a flight Ike estimated would take us four and one-half hours. Ideally, one flies early in the day when weather is more likely to be favorable, the pilot is fresh, and when unexpected delays don't mean reaching one's destination after dark. On this trip, that rarely happened.

When we finally left Lima, we flew southward down the arid Peruvian coast and over the mysterious lines of the Nazca Valley. These marvelous figures, constructed long before the time of the Incas, were built at such a large scale that they can scarcely be appreciated from the ground. Just before dark we arrived in Arica for our bout with Chilean immigration and customs officials.

• • •

Tito Lagiglia had all but given us up for lost when we finally reached San Rafael, Argentina, on January 13, over a week late. Situated in Mendoza Province at the foot of the Andes, San Rafael is a beautiful small city of 100,000 people. It is surrounded by vineyards and olive groves, irrigated by ditches and lined with tall, stately Lombardy poplars. Everything depends on the Río Atuel and its staircase of reservoirs fed by snowmelt high in the Andes. The surrounding desert is rich in shrubs reminiscent of the Sonoran or eastern Mojave Desert, including mesquite and creosote bush. We felt right at home.

Tito, his wife Margarita, and their two young daughters extended us every conceivable hospitality in their modest second-story flat. Hector D'Antoni, a palynologist from the Museo de La Plata who was studying the pollen at Gruta del Indio, drove his family across Argentina to meet us in San Rafael. Anthropologist Liliana Mamoni and her school teacher friend Berta Rissi had come from Quilmes, a suburb of Buenos Aires, to join the party.

During the next couple of days we visited Tito's museum. Then he took us all on an ecological field trip up the Atuel valley, culminating in a visit to a sulfur mine high in the Andes. On the way there we stopped for several days in a zone of rich grasslands. We camped in an abandoned and vandalized old hotel. The windows were all broken out, and at night the winds sweeping up or down valley blew dust in our faces and into our food. But on the positive side, the hotel was next to some *termales* (hot mineral springs) which provided us with the luxury of unlimited soaks.

Gauchos passed by our camp as they took their herds to higher elevations. Tito introduced us to a gaucho he knew from previous trips and we all shared a cup of *maté* tea. For $4.50 (U.S. equivalent), Tito purchased a goat, and that afternoon we enjoyed the traditional *asada* (barbecue). Besides the meat and chunks of small intestine, which I found very tasty, the menu included salad, fresh-baked bread, a nice light torte, ripe melons, and bottles of San Rafael wine. Ever the carnivore, Ike not only enjoyed the *asada* that afternoon, but in many subsequent meals he gnawed the leftovers.

Summer in the Andes is, of course, the very best time for flowering plants. Tito furiously collected whatever was in flower and spent the evenings pressing them. Although green and productive at an elevation of 5,000 feet and above, the natural vegetation on the east side of the Andes at this latitude (35 to 36 degrees South) was entirely lacking in native tree species. From the foot of the mountains to the alpine zone there was nothing comparable to the pinyon-juniper woodlands or bristlecone pine forests at an equivalent latitude in the Great Basin of the western United States. Tito said parts of the valley receive six to 10 feet of snow in winter, more than enough moisture for trees, I thought. But the tallest native species Tito showed us was an *Adesmia*, a tall shrub with yellow flowers that is a member of the pea family.

When we returned to San Rafael, Tito and Hector took us to inspect the ground sloth site at Gruta del Indio. The site turned out to be a basalt overhang that sheltered a ledge from the elements. Unfortunately, we could not be sure which kinds of sloths had lived there. There are a dozen different genera of extinct ground sloths in the Pleistocene fossil record of South America. The dung balls at Gruta del Indio were about half the size of those at Rampart Cave, smaller than any that Austin Long and I had seen in the United States, and much smaller than the specimens Tito and I would see later at the Cueva de Milodón in Chile. The species that deposited them may eventually be determined by DNA analysis. This method has recently been perfected for identifying Shasta ground sloth dung as well as the plants these animals ate.

At a final grand party, an *asada* on the roof of Tito's father's house attended by all our new friends and many others, Tito's dad asked Ike and me to sing. Any pair of Latin American men could have sung for hours, but we were stumped. I suggested *I've Been Workin' on the Railroad*. Ike countered with *Carcel de Cananea*. Neither of us knew the words of the other's choice, and we wound up not singing at all.

Jean, Ike, and I began preparing for the next leg of our journey—a flight to Mendoza, over the Andes to Santiago, and then on to Punta Arenas, just across the Strait of Magellan from Tierra del Fuego. Punta Arenas was to be the base of operations for our flights to Puerto Natales, where we could get ground transportation to the Cueva de Milodón. Tito planned to fly with us as far as Mendoza, where he was going to visit relatives, and from there return home to San Rafael.

To us it seemed a shame to lose Tito's company. We thought he should fly on with us to see the mylodon cave in Chile. After all, Tito had discovered the first ground sloth cave in Argentina and dated its dung, so he deserved a chance to see what the Chilean cave, the type example so to speak, looked like. Besides, we loved his infectious enthusiasm. Tito was all for it, but he'd promised Margarita that he would not be gone long.

So a telephone call went out to Margarita. The main burden of persuasion fell on Jean. Tito knew what the sticking points with Margarita would be, and after a little rehearsing with Tito, Jean did a beautiful job of winning her over. Margarita decided she could spare him. Tito beamed and gave Jean an *abrazo*— a big Latin hug.

With Tito now on board, we flew over the Andes to Santiago, where we visited archaeologist friends of Tito, and then headed southward, over magnificent scenic mountains that became extensively glaciated as we neared our destination of Punta Arenas.

Cueva de Milodón is a huge cavern facing out across the Ultima Esperanza Sound toward distant glaciers of the southern Andes. It shelters a sizable deposit of sloth dung, more than I've seen in any other cave. The site also contains much more hair than we have found in Shasta ground sloth caves in the United States. Radiocarbon dates of various samples, including many we collected on this trip, ranged between 10,500 and 13,000 years in age. This is remarkably close to the younger dates from Rampart Cave and to samples from Gruta del Indio dated by Austin Long, and it constituted an important discovery in geochronology.

Cueva de Milodón became famous more than a century ago, thanks to the discovery of a mylodon hide and the recent-looking dung. The fresh appear-ance of the remains, fueled by local legends, triggered a hunt for living animals. None could be found. Recently, Harvard-trained zoologist David Orem has opened another search, this time in the Upper Amazon in Brazil, based on reports from natives of a small ground sloth there. However, the consistency of radiocarbon dates on ground sloth dung from both hemispheres suggests to me that David Orem has begun his hunt 10,000 years too late. Nevertheless, one can only wish him well.

On one of our flights from Puerto Natales back to Punta Arenas, the low overcast turned squally, and Ike decided it might be prudent to land while we could still see the ground. I suspect the real reason was that it was past lunch time and we were all ravenous. Ike spotted the headquarters of a sheep ranch at the end of a narrow road. There was no sign of traffic. The road surface looked good. The wind was right. Ike landed.

Unfortunately, none of us had seen the line of small homemade telephone poles that ran across a field to converge on the side of the road just in front of us. There was no room to maneuver. Braking as hard as he could, Ike still could not stop in time. Fortunately, the wood we struck was rotten, and on impact the sturdy-looking pole flew into pieces, leaving nothing more than a cup-shaped dent in the leading edge of our wing.

By the time all had been explained to a gang of curious sheepherders from the station, we were truly hungry and we happily accepted their hospitality—steaming bowls of hearty mutton soup and mounds of tasty fresh-baked bread. That afternoon the weather improved, and after negotiating the cost of minor damages to the phone line we resumed our flight to Punta Arenas.

Back in Punta Arenas we prepared for the final leg of our southward journey and our return to Argentina. We took off and flew southeast over the ice fields toward the Beagle Channel and Ushuaia, the southernmost town in the world. But the weather turned foul, so instead we swung east and north across Tierra del Fuego, with its many herds of guanacos. We crossed the Strait of Magellan and headed up the east coast of Patagonia. At the town of Río Gallegos, on the Patagonian plain, we stopped for the night. Out here away from the mountains the winds were howling. At 52 degrees South, we were in the grip of the Furious Fifties. The tiny trees around the airport were protected behind wooden wind screens. Next to the runway we spotted a Cessna 172 upside down. It was not a good sign. It took us an hour out in the gale to find some steel stakes and a mallet to drive them into the ground so we could rig a secure tie-down for our Cessna.

Wind and Río Gallegos are synonymous to those of us devoted to Antoine de Saint-Exupéry's *Wind, Sand and Stars*. Here, sand and stars take a distant second place. Saint-Exupéry was a young French aviator and mystic who pioneered air mail routes in South America. Once as he approached Río Gallegos from the sea he was so overpowered by gale force winds that he could barely make it to the coast, only 600 feet away. Another time, also flying into the wind, he could still see the Río Gallegos airport behind him an hour after he had left it.

Fortunately for us, we had more power in our Cessna than Saint-Exupéry had in his airplanes 40 years earlier. And the gale subsided during the night, so the next morning we were able to take off from Río Gallegos without incident.

We continued north up the Argentine coast, flying over sea lion and elephant seal rookeries. At the town of Viedma we stopped to visit paleontologist Rodolfo Casamiquela, a friend of Tito's. When we landed at La Plata airport, 30 miles southeast of Buenos Aires, Hector and Susana D'Antoni, along with our friends Liliana and Berta, all gave us warm *abrazos*. We stayed with Hector and Susana at their home in nearby Ensenada and were treated to a magnificent *asada* at the *estancia* (cattle ranch) of Susana's parents.

At this point Tito left our expedition and caught a train home to San Rafael and his wife Margarita. After we saw him off, Hector took us to his lab at the Museo de La Plata. In his office, we enjoyed a visit with the famous vertebrate paleontologist Resendo Pascual and his skilled professional colleagues. The museum building itself incorporates magnificent circular exhibit halls, designed by the pioneer of vertebrate paleontology in South America, Florentine Ameghino. We especially admired the exhibit comparing sloth dung balls from the Cueva de Milodón in Chile with the dung of elephants. The elephant dung is smaller.

On the outside of the museum, the walls were covered with political slogans of the liberal left. We had come to Argentina during troubled times, and the fist of the reactionary right was about to descend. When I returned to Argentina the following year, I would see mothers of the disappeared youth parading in the plaza in Buenos Aires with pictures of their missing children. Three years after that, Hector, Susana, and their young son would be Argentine expatriates, living in Tucson.

After a week in La Plata we continued on our way to Brazil—and Carnival. As planned, my wife Marianne flew down from Tucson. Rio was jammed. We learned that to keep Carnival under control, the police had jailed some 400 trouble-making "agitators." During the parade, we witnessed blue-helmeted riot police routing political protesters who were trying to distribute leaflets, introducing another sour note into the festivities. Brazil was a police state, we were told, controlled by the iron fist of President Vargas.

Before dark Marianne and I found our way to our seats in the stands lining President Vargas avenue. The wooden stands looked fragile, threatening to snap if overloaded. At dusk, a long quiet period ended with distant flashes, like heat lightning, and the distant movement of dancers coming toward us down Vargas avenue. The whirling, leaping figures drew nearer, pulsing to the growing throb of samba drums, a gathering storm. Dancers, hundreds, swirled closer, leaders whistling, a transvestite prancing to cheers and jeers, nubile dancers in bikinis or less strutting, stopping to bump and grind, all the pelvic action needed to burlesque human copulation. Men in gym suits standing on their hands engaged in mock feet fights. Queens of both sexes and various colors swept past. The dancing intensified as the thunder of steel drums burst upon us. Infected by the energies we rose in our seats, pounded our feet (forget the rickety stands!), clapped our hands over our heads, and did bumps and grinds of our own. Black and white costumed members of a samba school—an organization that prepares all year for this event—left the avenue to infiltrate the stands, dance with us, and trade garb with spectators. The thunder died down as the drums pounded on down the avenue and the dancers melted away into crowded side streets. All was relatively quiet again. But this was only the first wave of an endless night of samba schools which swept down Vargas avenue (police permitting) until well after dawn.

Long after midnight we made our exit, too tired to care about missing the rest of the night's show. On the bus to their hotel, Jean and Ike found themselves gripping their seats as their driver began swinging his vehicle from one side of the road to the other, using his bus to cavort to the rhythm of a samba band inside, the other passengers drumming on the sides of the bus itself.

There was also a down side to our Carnival experience. Ike had his pocket picked when he and Jean entered a narrow street packed with wildly celebrating revelers on their way to the main pavilion. In the mad crush of bodies Ike and Jean suddenly discovered that their arms were pinned. Someone behind him with a free hand boldly reached over Ike's shoulder to extract his wallet from his inner coat pocket. He could not escape the brazen robbery.

Nor was that Ike's only misfortune. Swimming in the ocean at Copacabana beach a few days later, Ike was tossed in the air by heavy surf, tearing ligaments in his foot when he landed. He found himself in a cast and on crutches. How would he manage to fly, we wondered, momentarily forgetting that this was Ike Russell. He managed.

Outside São Paulo we visited the famous game and livestock ranch of Paulo Noguiera-Neto, the author of the first book on exotic animal introduction in the Americas. We were especially impressed with the success of water buffalo as milk producers in Brazil's climate. At Belo Horizonte we examined a famous fossil locality where at least 30 gomphotheres (extinct elephants) had been entombed in the mineral springs. These days the healing waters mostly attract human visitors.

The time had come for Marianne to return home. Even when she arrived in Los Angeles, she found that the adventure was not quite over. U.S. Customs agents turned hinky when they found Marianne in possession of a box of *maté* tea, the national drink of Argentina. Having found this suspect substance, they subjected her to a full body search. Fortunately, they missed the live fruit flies she was bringing to the University of Arizona Drosophila lab for geneticist Bill Heed.

Meanwhile, Ike and Jean and I gradually worked our way northward through Brazil. From Belém we cut west toward Manaus, flying low over the Amazon rain forest to get a sense of its vastness. Except for waterways, the dense canopy of trees extended unbroken as far as the eye could see. I asked Ike what he would do if we had to make an emergency landing. He replied that a light plane such as ours might be able to pancake slowly into the foliage, and that with some luck the passengers might survive a treetop landing. Of course, getting down to the ground from the canopy, more than a hundred feet up, would be another matter, as would finding one's way out to civilization. Ike recommended being extra sure of the quality of your gas when an emergency is to be avoided at all cost. Apparently, our gas was good.

From Manaus we turned north and flew over the new road being constructed up to Boa Vista, near the border with Venezuela. Boa Vista's population had recently soared from 5,000 to 30,000, and the airport sported a brand new terminal as large as Tucson's. Unfortunately, construction had outpaced services, and we found no gas and no immigration officials to clear us for Venezuela. The brand new international airport at Boa Vista was virtually empty.

Venezuela proved even more refractory than Brazil. The airport of entry was Santa Elena. We circled a radio beacon that our map identified as Santa Elena, but there was no airport to be found. Finally, Ike landed, roughly, in a field to ask directions from a friendly farmer. He told us to try a nearby town called Luepa.

Although Luepa proved to be a military airport, we were low on gas and had no choice but to land there. An army officer, Lt. Romero, took pity on us and kindly opened a 55-gallon drum of aviation fuel. This gave us enough gas to detour past Angel Falls, whose drop of 3,212 feet makes it the world's longest waterfall. Unfortunately, this was the dry season, and there was nothing more than a wisp of spray.

We flew on through dry season smoke and fires to Barcelona on the Venezuelan coast. We arrived with gas gauges reading empty and without the papers that we knew would be demanded by officialdom. We had no visas for Venezuela, no exit stamp from Brazil, and no flight plan from the dysfunctional Boa Vista airport. In our favor, Ike had a certified copy of a telegram he sent from Manaus outlining our plans. Despite the irregularities, the Venezuelan customs and immigration officials treated us kindly. Their baggage search took only 15 minutes, not bad under the circumstances, and the next morning we got our visas. Our reception was certainly much more accommodating than the threat of imprisonment we faced during our Africa trip seven years earlier, when we arrived in Nampula, Mozambique, without visas.

In Caracas I parted company with Ike and Jean. I had friends at a Venezuelan research station who would take me to see the important fossil locality at Taima-Taima. Ike and Jean flew on home by way of the West Indies. The trip had been a wonderful odyssey. In terms of my research, it had been highly rewarding, verifying what I had learned about the timing of ground sloth extinction in Arizona and adjacent states. The following year I returned to San Rafael for another field season with Austin Long, Tom Martin, and Tom Van Devender. My findings eventually found their way into two papers in *Science*, one on sloth extinctions and human entry into the New World, and the other on climate and ground sloth extinction at Cueva de Milodón, Chile.

•••

I'd hoped to make one more survey of fossil sites with Ike and Jean, this time to Australia and New Guinea, lands ideally suited for exploration by light aircraft. But by 1979, the year of my next sabbatical, Ike's health was failing rapidly.

In July of 1980, Ike died at home and was buried in his own backyard.

Numerous friends and neighbors joined with family, and a growing party lingered all that long afternoon. The gathering turning into a wake and celebration lasting far into the night. There were many stories to trade because each of us, whether or not we had flown with Ike, nursed our own private collection of rich experiences.

It seemed a miracle that despite nearly 30 years of bush piloting in rough country, including some plane wrecks, neither Ike nor any of his passengers had died or been seriously hurt. That night in July we recalled the old refrain of conventional wisdom one hears around airports large and small:

There are old pilots, and bold pilots, but no old bold pilots.

Naaah. No way. We knew the exception. We'd flown with Ike Russell.

23

You Don't Need to Be Relatives to Make a Family

HECTOR D'ANTONI

With his red and white Cessna 185, Ike Russell flew paleontologist Paul Martin to San Rafael, the second city in Argentina's western province of Mendoza. Some 530 miles due west of Buenos Aires, San Rafael is a calm, provincial town that was brought to Paul's attention because of the archeological work of my former classmate, Humberto "Tito" Lagiglia. Tito brought all the excitement of science to San Rafael by creating a museum of natural science and carrying out studies in archeology and botany. He corresponded with top-level scientists around the world to stay abreast of current research, and one of his contacts was Paul. Paul was a friend of Jean and Ike, so it was natural that Ike would fly him to South America. Yet San Rafael is at 34 degrees South and Tucson is at 32 degrees North. No ordinary pilot would make such a trip in a small plane, but Ike was no ordinary pilot.

It took my wife Susana less than a minute to accept my invitation to join them. Crossing Argentina from our home in Ensenada, just outside the city of La Plata, to San Rafael in the Andean foothills, was an appealing adventure. Our 11-month-old son Pablo was to come along too. So on a torrid day in January, the three of us jumped on board our new, large, white, and beautiful FIAT 1600 and took off. After two days of sweltering across pampa and desert, we finally began to climb into the cooler air of the Andean foothills as we neared San Rafael.

We rang the bell of No. 129 Avenida San Martín, and our host Tito welcomed us with open arms. There were Margarita, his devoted wife, and their two sweet girls. Tito told us, "The Americans are not here yet," so we took a short nap to recover from our long trip. Our sleep was interrupted by voices coming from the other room. There they were—two tall men and a beautiful woman with nice blue eyes that reflected both intelligence and kindness, much the way my wife's eyes do. Jean and Susana became friends instantly.

That evening we were joined by anthropologist Liliana Mamoni and her friend Berta Rissi, who had driven over from Buenos Aires. Dinner gave us all a chance to get acquainted. We were enchanted by Jean's natural grace and Paul's kindness and modesty, despite his scientific prestige. Ike had a presence that was captivating. His eyes had a strong expression of *picardía* (mischievousness) that his thick glasses couldn't hide. He began speaking in English, but only Susana and I knew enough of the language to carry on a conversation. Then, to my surprise, he launched into perfect Spanish with a remarkable Mexican accent, telling us wonderful stories and anecdotes. A copious Argentine dinner with beef from the Pampa, wine from Mendoza, lots of conversation across the table, and the gracious hospitality of our hosts made this first meeting a memorable one.

Next morning at breakfast we learned that the jeeps for our field trips were not yet available, so we had a full day to do whatever we pleased. Ike suggested flying over the region to reconnoiter it. In an hour we were all at San Rafael airport. The tiny Cessna was anchored on the apron at the side of the runway. It was Sunday, and many local pilots and aircraft enthusiasts had gathered in the airport's cafeteria to plan their flights or just to be closer to the machines that so much resembled the dreams of the great man from Florence. Ike greeted everyone politely and we walked out to the tiny Cessna.

The first group to fly would be Liliana, Berta, my Susana, and little Pablo. Jean, the two girls, and I would be next. Ike taxied the Cessna to the edge of the runway and stopped there to run a full test of rudder and ailerons. Then he moved out onto the runway, but he didn't taxi to either end. He stayed in the middle and ran another test of the controls. I was standing next to one of the local experts so I asked him what was going on. He replied, "Something must be wrong. He will come back and . . . ." Ike revved the engine and the little Cessna began to move. Bewildered, my companion asked, "What is he doing?" His face reflected sudden concern. "He cannot take off from there. The gringo is crazy! He cannot do it. . . . He did it!" The red and white bird lifted off smoothly through the calm morning air into a deep blue sky. When I recovered, I noticed that my advisor was sweating in the cool morning air. "I can't believe it," he said.

In an hour or so, Ike and the first group landed safely. Susana was exultant. "We have seen lakes, rivers, and snow-capped mountains. It is so beautiful!" Little Pablo liked it too, and so did Liliana and Berta.

When my turn came, I sat in the front seat and chatted with Ike. I told him about the concern of his colleagues at the airport and he laughed. "I knew it," he said. "I've installed a couple of modifications to the wings that are hard to see, but they create more lift, and taking off is much quicker. These modifications are new, so I guess they haven't reached the Latin American market yet." We flew over valleys and mountains, and on a white lake we made out the pink silhouettes of flamingos. Ike flew down close to them and they came up to join our adventure in the air.

After we landed, we left Ike's *avioneta* (he used this old-fashioned Spanish word in a funny way) tied down at the airport and returned to San Rafael for more conversation and a delectable late lunch.

Once the jeeps became available, we left for our ecology field trip into the valley of the Río Atuel. By the time the jeeps and our FIAT made it to 4,000 feet, the roads had become dirt or coarse gravel, but an unbelievable landscape in the upper Atuel valley opened up to us. Tito and I collected plants and flowers for the herbarium and the pollen study that Vera Markgraf and I published five years later as a book called *Pollen Flora of Argentina*. Paul was interested in the glacial features of the landscape while Jean and Ike took in everything. Susana and Pablo stayed with them and had a great time in their first visit to the Cordillera.

As night was descending we decided it was time to camp. Because of the wind, Tito discouraged us from setting up our large tent in the open. Instead, the whole group camped on the ground floor of the once luxurious international Hotel El Sosneado, now in ruins. From the main window of what was once the living room, we could see the magnificent peak of Cerro Sosneado (17,025 feet). Close by were the pools of the thermal springs that skiers in the 1930s used to enjoy after a day of winter sports. The ruins were now pathetic. Only the concrete and stone walls of the magnificent earthquake-resistant building were still standing. The tile and wooden roofs, mosaic and wooden floors, doors and windows, were all gone. The fine freshwater system was dead. It was so sad to see such a unique resort in ruins.

During the night we woke suddenly to a terrifying scream. A hen that was pecking the ground for food got sidetracked by the perfume Liliana was wearing. When it began to peck Liliana's head it woke her and startled her so badly that she screamed in terror. The hen ran away over our sleeping bags and disappeared into the darkness.

As we found out, the hen was not wild but lived there. The ruins of this once upper-class hotel now attract campers, and when we arrived, another family was occupying the two "best" rooms. Hens and chickens were commodities that provided fresh eggs and white meat and we, the newcomers, had camped right where the chickens lived!

Tito had been right about the wind, but he was wrong about the protection that the walls would provide. Even with high-mountain-grade sleeping bags, the cold and noisy wind and the screams of terror provoked by our feathered company added up to a fairly bad sleep. Sometime during the night, Susana and I decided that we had had enough. We set up our tent outside the hotel and slept a few hours in its quiet and warmth. Little Pablo slept between mom and dad.

Next morning, Jean and Ike joined us for breakfast and we laughed about the events of the night. Ike pulled out his small notebook and wrote, "We spent the night at Hotel de los Cuatro Vientos" (Four Winds Hotel).

The morning was cold and beautiful. We continued our field trip up the valley to Volcán Overo (15,634 feet), which has a thick layer of sulfur on the top. A mine was operating near the summit, and there were housing facilities for the workers in the foothills below. The foreman in charge agreed to let us stay in the miners' quarters, in heated rooms. We went by car nearly to the top of the mountain, a fascinating trip up a zigzag road that cuts across a glacier. The road is used by the trucks that bring the sulfur down to be shipped to its final destination. At the top, a beautiful spotless sheet of fresh snow covered everything. We walked around and somebody started a snowball fight. We laughed and enjoyed the beauty of that Andean summit. In the highlands we saw large fields of *penitentes*, erosional features of the ice that make small towers, some reaching up to three feet high. They are named after the penitents in a religious procession that they resemble.

When we stopped by Hotel El Sosneado on our return trip, Martín, one of Tito's helpers, pointed out a sad bit of history. There, across the Atuel valley, one could see a tributary valley called the Valle de las Lágrimas (Valley of Tears). It connects with the place where the airplane carrying the Uruguayan rugby team crashed, where many of the players and their family members died. Ike said something about the fate of his colleagues, the pilots. The rest of our trip down to San Rafael was full of fascinating things to look at and explore, but Ike remained quiet in the front seat, absorbed in his own thoughts.

• • •

After our field work in San Rafael, Jean, Ike, Paul, and Tito left for Chile and we returned home to Ensenada. The three Americans and Tito flew all the way down to Tierra del Fuego, at the southern tip of South America, and then back north along the Atlantic coast of Argentina. When they landed at La Plata Provincial Airport they called us and we went to pick them up.

Paul, Jean, and Ike liked our classic Spanish home in Ensenada with its doors and windows of red cedar, its clear and glossy mosaic floors, and the garden that used to be the pride of my father and mother. We cut the best rose (a Talisman rainbow) for Jean—killing a flower is a curious albeit customary way to honor a guest. Susana, of course, had prepared dinner for our guests. We talked and talked—in English to give our American guests a break after their two weeks of pure Spanish.

I turned on the lights in the living room when I saw Jean standing in front of Susana's painting of a large bird stealing an egg from the nest of another bird and flying away. The empty nest was in the dark, surrounded by little flowers, small plants, and even pollen grains on a black background. The robber spread his beautiful wings on a clean blue sky. Jean whispered, "I can't believe it." Susana had painted the picture because little Pablo was afraid of the dark and she wanted to tell him of all the wonderful things that are hidden there.

It was nine in the evening when Susana asked me, "Do you think I should serve dinner now?"

"No," I said, while looking for agreement from our guests. "It is too early yet." Our American guests were starving but no one said a word, and we started dinner punctually at 10 p.m. Obviously, we were unaware of the American schedule for meals. Even today, Jean remembers how hungry they were, more so with the smell of Susana's food pervading the house.

Next day, Ike asked me to go to the airport with him because he needed to find a mechanic that could service his plane. A man in impeccable blue overalls came to help us. He was in his late 40s, balding with deep black hair on the sides of his head and inquiring eyes. "What can I do for you, gentlemen?" he asked. Ike said the plane needed service and gave the details. The mechanic was displaying increasing irritation as Ike talked. I was puzzled. Finally I realized that Ike was addressing the mechanic with the familiar *tu* instead of the more formal *usted* which, according to Argentine standards, would have been more appropriate for talking with a mature man.

I broke in, "Excuse me, I want to let you know that my friend here was born in Rochester, New York, and he speaks Spanish the way they do in Mexico. That's why he is calling you '*tu*' instead of '*usted*.'"

The mechanic gave us a broad smile, patted Ike's shoulder and said, "Let's go see that babe of yours." They walked to the plane, and a few minutes later Ike and I were on our way back to Ensenada.

We enjoyed life with our new-old friends for the next few days. We had given Jean and Ike the main bedroom on the second floor overlooking the Plaza San Martín. Paul used my bachelor's bedroom; Susana, Pablo, and I occupied my sister's bedroom. Paul loved my father's office with bookshelves from floor to ceiling, one window looking out at the church tower and the other into the garden. He spent long hours writing his notes and reading there in the cool and calm house, with the church bell beautifully marking the passage of time. Jean and Susana worked, talked, and played with little Pablo as life-long bonds were being built.

I guess it was Sunday morning and I had just come back from the bakery with some *facturas*, the irresistible Argentine pastry. I climbed the stairs to bring an assortment of croissants and other delicacies to Ike and Jean. Ike had told me he was not feeling well and that he would need some rest before flying back to the U.S., so he was spending a couple of days in bed. He was sitting with a pile of pillows behind him. Jean was sitting at his bedside. He was sharing with Jean some passages from *Martín Fierro*, the poem about the gaucho written by José Hernández, an Argentine icon. I was happy that Ike was enjoying the book we had given him, which was a special edition by the Universidad de Buenos Aires press, with splendid etching illustrations by Juan Carlos Castagnino. But I was flabbergasted as I walked in. Ike was explaining to Jean the part where Viejo Vizcacha killed his wife "*de un palo*" because she gave him a cold *maté* tea. "*De*" means "of," not "with," so Viejo Vizcacha killed his wife not just *with* a stick, but with a single blow of the stick. The preposition "*de*" makes the noun "*palo*" become an action—a blow with a stick. "The author was emphasizing the anger of Viejo Vizcacha," Ike was explaining, "not the mere weapon, otherwise he would have said '*con un palo*'—with a stick." Ike's mastery of Spanish amazed me, for even today I struggle unsuccessfully with the use of prepositions in English.

Ike paid special attention to my conversations with Susana, and often he pulled a small notebook from his shirt pocket and took notes while we were talking. He did that not only with us but with whomever he captured in a casual conversation. What was he writing? The answer came to me one morning at breakfast. Ike sat down at the table and Susana came to kiss him good morning. He pulled out his notebook, searched for a second or two, and read, "Me diste beso y una sonrisa como el sol naciente" (You gave me a kiss and a smile like the sunrise).

Our eyes were wet and our souls hurt when we had to say good-bye, but Ike managed to cheer the moment with an appropriate observation, "'Adios' means 'Vaya usted con Dios'—May God be with you—I guess." As our American friends left our home that day 27 years ago, Susana and I recalled what a mathematician friend once remarked about our parental friendship with his young cousin. "You don't need to be relatives to make a family," he said.

• • •

If one loves cool weather, arriving in Tucson in early June is not the best choice. It was 1975. My mother had just passed away after a long and painful ailment and I had been awarded a Guggenheim fellowship to develop my fossil pollen studies. I chose the Laboratory of Paleoenvironmental Studies at the University of Arizona, then under the direction of Paul Martin. So there we were, landing at Tucson's airport. Paul, Jean, and Ike were waiting for us. The air was impossibly hot. Jean and Ike took Susana and Pablo with them, and I drove with Paul in his beautiful 1956 Buick. We traveled across town and arrived at a real oasis, with trees and vines and flowers everywhere. That was the house of Jean and Ike. "La Casa del Pueblo," Ike liked to call it, referring to the many visitors who dropped by for a cool beer, a chat, some advice, a good swim, a hard-to-find tool, or a piano concert. We loved that house—its living room with large windows, the piano and the library, the other living room with the fireplace, the grandfather clock, and those sofas.

We spent many delightful hours in that house that came to feel very much like home. Ike would tell stories of his trips, ask me questions about the fine details of the Spanish language, show me how a small apparatus works. Those were hours of friendship spent in a world of intelligence and kindness that resembled my parents' home. Susana is an artist but one who was born with insufficient time to do all she needs to do; therefore she is always in a hurry. Jean loves her expeditious way of doing things, and the two ladies always have some joint endeavor to attend to. Ike and I enjoyed the sight of that friendship in action. David, Ike and Jean's youngest son and our dear friend, nicknamed Susana "La Cometa" (The Kite) because of her sudden and unpredictable movements. In summer we spent delightful weekends in their cabin up in the Santa Catalina mountains, enjoying the cool air, the smell of pine, long walks on the mountain, and long talks by the fireplace. Time moved in a slow and most enjoyable fashion, and life could be summarized as the pleasure of being together with those whom one respects and loves.

We wanted to visit Grand Canyon so we bought a small trailer. But it was still too big for our Volkswagen to pull it. Ike lent me his blue Matador. I installed the trailer hitch but had problems finding the cables for the lights. I called Ike and asked for advice; he told me to wait for him. In 10 minutes my friend, a man who by strict profession was not under other peoples' cars, was beside me lying on the pavement of our parking lot putting cables together and using a tester to verify connections. And, of course, telling me some story of his beloved Mexico.

In spring of 1976 we flew to Mexico to join Ed and Becky Moser at their house in the Seri Indian village of Desemboque. Ike had visited them many times and the Indians knew him. We flew over to Tiburón Island in the Gulf of California and Ike made an unbelievable landing on the beach. We explored a prehistoric archaeological site and the remains of a historic Seri camp where the house structures were made with ocotillo branches that have remained in

place ever since. On the return trip we landed on a hill in Sonoita, at the risk
of upsetting some neighbors, for the pleasure of sharing a few hours with
Marjorie Denney, a most dear friend. We did so many unforgettable things
with these friends-parents of our second homeland.

We were treated as guests in the United States because of my status as
a visiting scholar at the University of Arizona. But this delightful condition
soon changed to that of exiles. During that year General Videla toppled the
government of Argentine President Isabel Perón and established his regime
of terror and murder. In October, the national research council of Argentina
ordered me to go back home. I had a tenure-track position in Argentina and I
was undecided whether to give it up. When I mentioned returning to Argentina, Jean and Ike persuaded me to leave Susana and Pablo with them and go
by myself to see how things were down there.

In La Plata, there was a rental house for students where I had spent many
of my student days visiting a girl friend or preparing for final exams with
classmates and friends. I loved that house, and it brought back memories of
delightful times during my youthful days. Now, in October 1976, a tank was
demolishing it because it was rumored that students living there might be
subversives. Academia was under attack, too. My boss and dear professor was
fired following vague accusations, and many of my students were among the
desaparecidos—the "disappeared ones". It took me a long time to get together
an academic committee for my dissertation. Some of the prestigious professors
who were vocal during democracy were now silently and obediently dancing
to the tune of the times. These were just some of the many strange reactions
of a society in terror. A couple of times I was followed by police in much the
same way they did to capture guerrilla leaders. My dissertation was approved
the same day a paramilitary squad murdered the eldest daughter of my advisor. These incidents convinced me to go back to Tucson.

Though I left my native country, I had the feeling of returning home, a
feeling that became more intense as I flew from Los Angeles to Tucson. Tucson
was home. Susana and Pablo were there, I had a job, and the three of us had
Jean and Ike. They gave me a welcoming party and all our friends were there.
Life started again.

Two years later, after publishing a number of papers and two books, my
family and I left for Germany for my postdoctoral studies. Then in 1988, I was
back in Argentina as a professor at the Universidad de Mar del Plata and as an
advisor to the national research council, trying to do my part to help President
Alfonsín rebuild democracy in Argentina. That winter I came to the United
States to visit a colleague at the University of Colorado. My family joined me
later and we all made a trip to Tucson. This was a much-desired visit to our
dear friends. Ike had passed away, but Jean was as wonderful as ever, and the

beloved house was the oasis that we had known in earlier times. David and his wife Susan Randolph were there with their beautiful daughters Garnett and Alexandra. Jean's niece Barbara Straub was a new, delightful addition to the oasis. But I just couldn't get used to my dear friend's absence.

I was standing in front of Ike's grave and slow tears were rolling down my face. It was painful not to have him around. I had so many stories of Europe and Argentina to share with him. My youngest son, Leonardo, saw me there and came to join me. He noticed my tears and offered me his support. "He was your dad, right?" I couldn't answer. At that time I wasn't sure.

V... Learning and Teaching

For Ike, learning and its reciprocal, teaching, were an essential part of what life was all about, and in one way or another he spent much of his life doing both. As for flying, he learned the rudiments of how an airplane works from his neighbor Cecil Ramsey and flight instructor Skeet Taylor. But he really learned the art and skill of flying from a variety of sources, not the least of which were other pilots, continual practice, and his own mistakes. Ike readily passed on his expertise as a pilot to others, sometimes by informal instruction, more often by setting up challenges or by his own example in the air.

But learning and teaching were not confined just to the realm of flying. Ike absorbed knowledge, perspectives, ideas, and values from many sources, including almost everyone he came in contact with. And from Ike, others learned about living a worthwhile life. This was not something Ike taught in any formal sense. For many people, simply the way he conducted his own life—and even his death—was an example that not only instructed, but inspired.

24

First Flight

PAUL DAYTON

My first flight with Ike Russell was in the summer of 1947. I had just turned six and the big world was coming into focus. I had become aware that my father worked in a deep gold mine and was tired much of the time, and that my mother was struggling with a new baby. We lived on the outskirts of Oracle, north of Tucson, in a small two-room house. Jean and Ike were very close friends of my parents, and I recall their frequent visits.

Ike's acquisition of an airplane was a much-discussed event. The adults dreamed up an adventure in which Ike would fly his plane to Oracle and give rides. The lack of an accepted airport in Oracle was not a problem for Ike—he would just land on the road (that is why God made roads, and trails, and other almost flat places). There was some discussion about whether this was legal, but such fine points of flying were rarely of concern to Ike.

The only planes I knew about were the four-engine B-24 bombers that had flown over an earlier home we had at the head of Pima Canyon, so in my mind Ike was going to put one of those monsters down on the narrow road to Oracle. Clearly, this was going to be a big event, one that would utterly dominate the mind of any just-turned-six kid.

Before Ike brought his plane to Oracle, we all drove around the flanks of the Santa Catalina mountains searching out emergency landing places—usually alfalfa farms. It was agreed that the ranchers would not mind this so long as we did not drive in their fields. In each field Ike tied a white bandanna (selected after much discussion about which would be more visible, red or white) to a pole he had brought for that purpose. As we bounced along in the old 1934 Ford there was another discussion about whether it was worth coming back afterwards to get the bandannas. After a fair bit of bouncing it was concluded that they could be left there, although Ike would have preferred to keep those poles, which he quite liked.

As the big day approached, the opportunity to ride in the airplane was a constant topic of discussion in our little house. A list of people was drawn up, and I sat there on my dynamite box dreaming of a ride in a B-24 and how scary it would be. To my amazement, my parents announced that since I had just turned six, I was old enough to appreciate a plane ride. I was not so sure about that, but in time the excitement turned to anticipation and the ride dominated every second of my day.

Finally the big day arrived, and Jean came out to meet our family by the little stone church. We drove both her car and ours out the Oracle highway toward Oracle Junction until we found a straight stretch of highway. Then we placed the two cars at a measured distance apart from each other. The cars were backed off the road perpendicular to the highway so that they could be pulled across the little road to block it from other cars that might interfere with the use of the road as a landing strip. Adults with red bandannas were placed at each end of this strip of road to make sure there were no cars on it when Ike landed or took off. It seemed as though we waited forever for Ike to arrive, and the adults were wondering which alfalfa field to check in case he had been forced down.

Finally Ike flew over, and I was really disappointed that the plane was not a B-24. In the air his plane seemed so small and fragile. Meanwhile, the adults were tying a windsock to a post on a fence beside the road. Ike flew over it and could see it hanging limp in the early morning desert air. There was an acute awareness and some continuing discussion about the possibility that the use of the highway as a landing strip might not be legal. This stuck in my mind, and a lump developed in my throat as I imagined my arrest and the rest of my childhood spent in the small stone Oracle jail, populated by drunken miners. There had been discussion that the windsock was essential to Ike, but it also was the only evidence that his landings there were planned with every intention of flaunting the law, as opposed to ordinary emergencies! Hence as soon as he was down, the windsock had to be hidden in the car. It became my job to hide the windsock, then get it out again before each landing so Ike would not crash. This was an awesome responsibility which I took very seriously.

Finally, after flying long distances over the road looking for traffic, Ike brought his little yellow tail-dragger down. It was wonderfully exciting and everybody was awestruck by this great opportunity to fly. On the ground the plane seemed much bigger, and I got over my disappointment that it was not a B-24. I looked at the wings carefully because Ike had told us that they were covered with cloth, and it was true! And as any responsible six-year-old would do, I worried a great deal about the police coming and putting us in jail even though I had hidden the windsock. But they never did come. In fact, I recall no cars the entire morning. Ike began taking adults for rides and I fulfilled my windsock responsibility with the passion that only a kid can bring to such a chore.

As the morning turned into a hot day, tempered only with a jug of lemonade my mother had brought, my ride seemed forgotten. Then I heard the adults announce that Ike was already giving the last ride of the day! When the plane landed I faithfully hid the windsock and tugged on my mother's shirt, tears in my eyes. Ike saw me and figured out what had happened. He reckoned that he had just enough gas for one more ride and that in return for such good windsock work perhaps I would be interested! I was—Oh God, was I ever interested—I could have kissed him! I reminded my mother where I had hidden the windsock and rushed to the plane. Ike and my father helped me into the seat and commented that I was so small that I was likely to be squirted out of the seat belt like a hotdog in a bun. Somebody made an analogy to a greased pig, and there was some laughter I did not share.

Ike taxied the plane back to the car, turned it around, and with a "Hang on" he gunned the little thing down the highway toward Oracle Junction. The tail lifted, and I knew real fear as the little plane bumped off the highway into the air. The heat of the day had produced thermals that threw the plane around even as we were gaining altitude. I looked out at the wing that now looked mighty small and I recalled the discussion of it being made of cloth that could rip and blow away! Ike finally tipped the plane over on its side so I could see the alfalfa field (I recall not being able to see the bandanna) and the plane lurched. At this point, loaded with lemonade and blinded with fear, I lost bladder control. I was overwhelmed with helpless fear and concern for the wing, and now that there was additional justification for the lubrication and greased pig analogy, I worried that I might slide out of the seat belt and fall into the field. Ike straightened the plane out and said he was going to show me my house, and I gagged something into the window, which had turned slimy with tears of shame and fear. I kept watching the wing to be sure that it did not start shredding or even fall off. I never took my eyes off the wing.

Ike flew the bouncing plane over the little house and banked again so that I could get a good look at my father's tiny garden and the outhouse (the house itself being hidden beneath an oak tree). By now my breakfast had been relocated, with most of it tucked into the bib of my overalls to join the rest of my mess. The stench had gotten to Ike, who opened a little flap for air. I do not recall the landing because I had even given up watching the wing and now had my eyes tightly shut. After they got the door open I tried to stand up, but the seat belt pulled me back down, rearranging my mess. When I finally did stand up, the mess relocated a last time and leaked out the legs of my overalls. I remember my father grimly trying to clean up Ike's plane with his shirt! I must have gotten Ike a little too, for although he was looking very brave and stoic, he changed his shirt.

Over the years Ike took me flying many times. My fear was soon replaced by great confidence in Ike's skill as a pilot, but my susceptibility to motion sickness remained strong as ever. I think the very fact that Ike continued inviting me to fly with him is ample testimony to his compassion and courage!

25

The Old Pilot and a Young Stud

DRUM HADLEY

In 1967 everyone in Tucson seems to know Ike
    I am 29 and he is 51
He likes to fly with two wings
    I like to fly with two wheels

My Triumph Bonneville has 650 ccs of power
    Dual carbs and having just won the Bonneville Salt Flats Speed Trials
A sticker across the gas tank that says World's Fastest Motorcycle
    I load Ike onto the back of the seat and rev the engine

I twist the throttle wide on the right side handlebar and pop the clutch
    The suspension in the front forks reaches its limit
Lifts the front wheel off the ground
    We rev to 9,000 rpms and head north up Cottonwood Lane

I grab the clutch on the left handlebar
    Jerk the left foot up into second gear
I can feel the acceleration in my whole body
    The roots of my hair being pulled in the wind

What do you think about this old man Ike I ask myself
    He brings his mouth around close to my right ear
Drum he says If you can't get this thing to go any faster
    I don't think we are ever going to get off the ground

26

Wearing the Wings

KEN MCVICAR

At the great Paleolithic shrine in the French cavern of Lascaux, there is a painting of a man wearing a bird mask. According to many traditional belief systems, putting on a mask and costume enables a person who is properly trained to absorb the qualities and energy of the creature represented by the mask and garment. The airplane was Ike Russell's costume, and few have worn it so well. There seemed to be a bird-like quality about Ike anyway. Like a stork, he had a certain awkward grace on the ground that became fluid elegance when he put on his wings. And with his wings came freedom—not only the freedom of the birds from the constraints of gravity, but a means of transcending the limitations of his frail physical form. Ike never seemed more contented or at peace with himself than when he was floating through the sky at the controls of his airplane.

In Ike's pragmatic philosophy, the mechanical airplane was a perfectly fine substitute for the feathered wings of Icarus, as long as he could use it to fulfill his own desires and benefit others. Although the product of human engineering and technology, in Ike's hands the airplane was not a machine that isolated him from nature, but a vehicle that brought him into greater contact with it. Antoine de Saint-Exupéry, one of the few flying poets, said it in *Wind, Sand and Stars*, a favorite book of Ike's:

It is not with metal that the pilot is in contact. . . . It is thanks to the metal, and by virtue of it, that the pilot rediscovers nature.

I first learned how Ike used his airplane to rediscover nature in 1965. At that time, I was lecturing in geography at University College Nairobi. Ike, his wife Jean, and Paul Martin had stopped off in Nairobi on their ambitious aerial tour of East Africa. Though we had just met, they invited me to join them on a flight into northern Kenya to see the great herds of giraffes, gazelles, and wildebeests there.

As we flew northward, I wondered what sort of person would take on the enormous responsibility of flying his wife and friends into this unforgiving corner of Africa. Not only that, but to fly low and slow over the huge herds, where any sort of engine trouble would leave only seconds to make the many decisions required for a safe landing. It was obvious that Ike had complete faith in the technology he had mastered, but even more importantly, he clearly had total confidence in his own resourcefulness. He seemed to know he would be able to get everybody out safely in the event of an emergency. His vast experience flying in remote places must have contributed a great deal to the sense of freedom from limitations that he exuded.

Not only would he fly low over the ancient places where the great herds roamed and our own distant ancestors had wandered so long ago, he would *land* there just to get a closer look. More than anything else, Ike's bush landings showed his ability to use the airplane as a means of experiencing nature, as Saint-Exupéry had written. I was astounded by his concentration and awareness of the surroundings that enabled him to make an instant analysis of the complex variables necessary for a successful bush landing. All the factors—terrain, grass thickness and height, probability of hidden obstacles, wind speed and direction, problems for takeoff—he would work out during his first pass. He would make another low-level sweep just to be sure everything still looked good. Then came the landing, always a thing of beauty. If the landing space was short he would come in slowly, nose high, just on the edge of a stall, but with enough power to create airflow over the wings so he could control the airplane. Often he would drop the wing on the approach, and with the controls crossed he would slip the airplane sideways to lose altitude quickly without gaining speed, straightening it out at the last moment—wheels touching, controls back, full brakes. His landings were invariably a fusion of clear judgement and perfect reflexes.

After that first trip into northern Kenya, we made another flight to Lamu Island, in the Indian Ocean just off the northeast coast of Kenya. This was the first opportunity I had to see Ike relate to Africans and Arabs. I was deeply impressed by how comfortable he was in the presence of people from other cultures, and his relaxed manner put everyone at ease. He was polite without showing deference, and his interest in alien customs was neither contrived nor affected. At that time, Lamu had little tourism, and its livelihood consisted mostly of ship repair, fishing, making charcoal, and exporting mangrove poles to the south Arabian peninsula. We befriended a young skipper from Aden, who took us in a dinghy out to his dhow, which was loading poles off shore. I remember Ike sitting on an ornate cushion on the fantail, his long legs crossed, eating a lunch of almonds and dried fruit from casks that were lashed to the deck. He was studying the dhow's compass, which consisted of a magnetized needle attached to a piece of cardboard floating in a bath of kerosene. Despite the language barrier, the crew sensed his interest in their lives and their livelihood, and we all got along wonderfully.

As a boy I had lived and breathed aviation, but until those flights in Kenya with Ike, I had never really understood how a small airplane could be used as a means of exploring the world. A few years later, when I actually decided to learn to fly, Ike, without being asked, began to provide guidance and instruction out of concern for my safety and the excitement of sharing his skills.

In the early 1970s my wife Donna and I, on Ike's advice, bought a 1946 Stinson. It was a tail-dragger, the kind of airplane Ike always favored for bush flying. We had been inspired by Ike and Jean's trips to South America, so we decided to take our own trip south and fly at least as far as Colombia, farther if we could. This would be the perfect test of the concentrated training exercises Ike had given us in bush flying—short-field landings, crash landing and emergency techniques, mountain flying, reading the weather, and so forth—all problems and techniques with which Ike was on intimate terms. The threats we would face would no longer be hypothetical but would likely be the ones for which Ike had prepared us. But the most appealing prospect was that flying to South America might give us a chance to share in the sense of freedom that was so fundamental to Ike's love of flight, for at that time Latin America was still relatively unencumbered with bureaucratic restrictions.

In 1972, we began our long rambling trip to Colombia. We decided to stop off for a few months in Pátzcuaro, Michoacán, and that's where we were living when Ike, Jean, Paul Martin, and Bill Swan dropped by for a visit. They had set out in Ike's new Cessna 185 on yet another of their great aerial expeditions to South America. They landed in the pasture north of town where we had our Stinson tied down. The pasture was over 7,000 feet in elevation and was tucked between a lake and a low volcano. With characteristic generosity, Ike pretended it was a difficult landing strip to make Donna and me feel more competent about our backcountry flying abilities.

During the several days they stayed in Pátzcuaro, Ike wandered around town, eating in local restaurants and chatting with local people. Mexico was familiar territory to Ike, but we saw in his interactions with people the same relaxed manner and unaffected concern for others that had impressed me so greatly in Africa. For Ike, all people were human beings and to be valued wherever they lived.

In Africa, I had been exhilarated by flying low with Ike without knowing exactly what kind of heightened awareness was required. Now, in Mexico, where regulations governing altitude were generally not enforced, I was free to fly for hours at treetop level, experiencing for myself the type of concentration and mind-body coordination that were necessary. The underlying message of Ike's example and training was, "Pay attention," and this implied a focused, yet panoramic awareness of one's surroundings that encompassed the next potential landing site, the vibrations of the engine and airframe, the colors and patterns of clouds, the instrument readings, and a host of other variables. But beyond all the practical skills which served us so well on countless occasions was the enjoyment and playful exhilaration Ike embodied in his flying. He had neither a cavalier attitude toward danger, nor was he burdened by the grave consequences of a failure of machine or concentration, and this example of sheer delight at every nuance of flight was far more important than the lessons any other master of bush flying could have transmitted.

Before they took off to continue their journey south, I went out with Ike to walk the strip. This was his ceremony of integration in which he absorbed the essence of the place and ritually removed all obstacles that might hinder his departure. As we silently walked between lake and volcano, I reflected on how I would never have trusted myself to fly among these mountains without Ike's inspiration and careful instruction. Through his example, he showed me how one can use a machine to overcome one's innermost fears and outward limitations.

27

Lessons from the Master

PETER MARSHALL

As a youngster growing up in Tucson in the 1950s, I always dreamed of flying my own airplane. I would ride my bicycle out to Ryan Field, a small airport west of town, or down Park Avenue to the edge of the big Tucson International Airport to watch the airplanes land and take off. Once in the tenth grade I heard that the beautiful war surplus P-51s that I could see lined up for miles behind a stout chain link fence at Tucson International could be bought for a mere $500. I was all set to try to figure out how to find the money when my father pointed out to me that just filling the gas tanks of one of those beauties would cost more than my whole allowance. My first chance to actually fly in a private plane came 10 years later when I met Ike Russell, a man who had a special gift for helping young people realize their dreams.

Ike invited me to accompany him on three flights into northern Mexico. One trip was to Guaymas to check on a fishing boat he was building there. Another was a flight to San Esteban Island in the middle of the Gulf of California to provision graduate students doing research there. By far the most exciting trip was one we took to Ike's mine in the high Sierra Madre Occidental of western Chihuahua, northeast of Navojoa, Sonora.

Ike kept his powerful Cessna 185 at Ryan Field. We drove out there together early one morning in 1968, loaded up his plane (which I remember looking a little beat up) and took off toward Mexico.

It was a beautiful day with unlimited visibility. We followed the course of the Santa Cruz River, and I could see geographic features of the land below that I had never seen from the ground. As we continued south the land gently rose to meet us, and at the same time as it was rising it was becoming deeply fissured by the great rivers of Sonora—among them the Río Bavispe and the Río Yaqui. This is the privilege of perspective given to pilots alone—the great sweep of the landscape of an entire portion of a continent that can only be appreciated from the air.

Finally, we were approaching the immense tangle of the western slope of the Sierra Madre itself. There in the deep labyrinth of canyons and ridges was a tiny patch of bare ground. "That's our runway," Ike said.

We were far above it, probably 5,000 feet or more, because we had just cleared some of the high ridges of the Sierra. To get down into that deep canyon we had to burn off altitude quickly, so Ike put the Cessna into a radical slip, and we dropped almost as if we were parachuting down to the airstrip. Moments later we were approaching the end of the runway, and I could see that it sloped steeply uphill. At the last instant, Ike added a quick burst of power to convert our rapid descent into a climb in order to match the slope of the tilted runway. Suddenly there was a bone-jarring bump that felt like a controlled crash. We were down.

As we got out of the plane, we were immediately surrounded by Tarahumara Indians—slightly built dark-skinned people wearing thick wool blankets like those I had seen at Ike and Jean's house in Tucson. We stayed at the mine for several hours while Ike gathered ore samples and had lengthy conversations in Spanish with several of the Indians, whom I took to be his managers at the mine.

Later in the afternoon, as we prepared to take off, I noticed that a stiff wind had come up and that it was blowing downhill. Since I knew that takeoffs are usually made into the wind, I asked Ike what direction we should be heading for ours. "You always want to take off downhill," he replied. "If it's blowing too hard to take off downhill with the wind, then you need to wait until the wind changes. You don't ever want to take off uphill!" Ike revved the engine and we began to roll downhill and downwind. Then we were airborne.

We were just beginning to climb out of the deep canyon when a terrible noise and vibration suddenly shook the engine compartment. "Look out your side and see if there's any oil coming from the engine," yelled Ike over the ear-splitting racket. I looked and didn't see any, just a vibration against the cowl cover. Ike seemed satisfied with this news and throttled back the power, reducing our airspeed and rate of climb and, at least to some extent, the awful noise from the engine. I was not so confident. I looked back at the rapidly disappearing airstrip below us and shouted at Ike over the noise, asking if we should turn back. He flashed me a reassuring grin and shouted back, "No need to give up if the prop is turning and there's no oil leakage. My plan is to fly on to Navojoa, where I know some pilots. We may be able to find a mechanic there and fix this thing today."

We flew on, silenced by the nerve-wracking din from the engine—still deafening despite the lowered engine rpms. In about 20 minutes we landed in Navojoa and rolled to a stop. Ike found a pilot and spoke to him for a few minutes. He was directed to another pilot with whom he spoke briefly also. The second man then left in his truck and returned a few minutes later with a mechanic. In the meantime, a small crowd of pilots and others had gathered, and we all worked together to remove the cowling. There we discovered the problem—the exhaust pipe had separated from the manifold on one of the cylinders. The terrible noise had been caused by the loose end of the exhaust pipe hitting against the cylinder. The engine was otherwise in fine shape. The mechanic welded in a new piece for the exhaust and bolted it together. In less than an hour we were as good as new.

There were a few minutes of good-natured banter and hangar talk in Spanish as Ike offered to pay for the work and the help that everyone had provided. But everyone, including the mechanic, refused payment for their services. I was tremendously impressed by the old-fashioned camaraderie and courtesy that these men accorded Ike Russell—a fellow pilot whom they all clearly knew and respected.

It was late in the afternoon when we finally began the uneventful flight home. I amused myself by reading the *Airman's Information Manual* that was tucked in the seat pocket of the plane. The part about clearing U.S. Customs looked awfully complicated.

"Ike, what are we going to do about customs," I asked. Our trip thus far had been blissfully free of any type of governmental interference.

"We just land at Nogales, Arizona," he replied. "They can send a customs agent out to the airport if they want to."

"It says here that we have to give them exactly 30 minutes notice of our landing time," I said.

Ike shrugged, and with his impish grin said, "People on the ground are always telling us pilots what to do. The truth is that the pilot has a lot of responsibility just making a safe flight. We have a duty to inform the people down there of our intentions, but it's their job to accommodate us."

As we approached the Nogales airport, Ike keyed his mike and radioed customs. They were waiting for us when we landed, but they politely cleared us with only a perfunctory look at our gear. Ike seemed everywhere to command respect. I couldn't help recalling when I last crossed the border at Nogales, with my beard and ratty Volkswagen beetle. The customs agents had completely torn apart my vehicle, even the tires, and then walked off leaving me to somehow reassemble it.

It was quite dark when we lined up on the lights of Ryan Field. As we drove back to Tucson I thought to myself that this was a day I would always remember—so many sights, places, and adventures compressed into a single day!

I have now been a pilot for nearly 20 years, and I've had the privilege of flying into small strips in wild country in Alaska and Canada not unlike those of northern Mexico in the 1960s. I am still thrilled by the feeling of mastery in the air that I first experienced flying with Ike—the view of the mountains and rivers, the tilt of the land—things that can only be imagined by looking at a map but that are real and filled with meaning when viewed from aloft. I also remember the kindness and wisdom of Ike Russell who welcomed me into his world of flying. There, for the first time, I experienced the brotherhood of pilots. And there I learned three important lessons that have stayed with me to this day—always take off downhill, always have a plan, and never let the people on the ground make decisions for you!

28

Saved

RONALD JACOBOWITZ

It was Ike Russell, having first taken me up in a battered Aeronca Sedan and later in his Cessna 180, who got me sufficiently interested in flying to begin lessons after I had moved away from Tucson.

Once a student pilot solos successfully, he is expected to practice by himself to accumulate a certain number of hours and attain a certain amount of experience before he can take the exam for his private pilot's license, which permits him to risk the lives of passengers as well as his own. One of the maneuvers he typically practices is the stall.

A slight digression here into physics. The *stalling* of an airplane has nothing to do with its engine, but rather is the situation in which the airplane has stopped flying under control and begins falling like a dropped object. To fly at all, a plane must reach a certain minimum forward speed—thus the takeoff run—to utilize the greater curve of the upper surface of its wing as opposed to the lower surface. This brings into play the so-called Bernoulli principle, named after the work of eighteenth-century Swiss physicist Daniel Bernoulli, who discovered that streamlines of air (or any other fluid) exert less pressure on an object as their speed increases. In the case of an airplane, a stream of air rushing over the curved, and hence longer, upper wing surface must move faster to keep up with the adjacent stream moving along the flatter and shorter lower surface. It is the resulting difference in pressure between the top and bottom surfaces (caused by the difference in speed, so says Bernoulli), that provides the lift necessary for flight.

So far so good, but now geometry complicates the situation. The direction in which an airplane is flying is not necessarily the same as the direction in which it is *pointing*, and the angle between these two directions is called the *angle of attack*. Furthermore, it can be shown that the greater the angle of attack, the greater the minimum speed needed for flight. Thus it stands to reason that if the angle of attack increases while the speed does not, the plane will eventually stall and begin falling. Any pilot in an unfamiliar airplane, and anyone studying to be a pilot, should want to test out the stall characteristics of the plane he is flying so as to get a feel for the danger point.

So in 1968, when I came back to Tucson for a visit in the middle of my pilot training, I felt it imperative to invite Ike to come for a flight to see how well his protégé was doing. We rode out to Ryan Field in his old rattletrap pickup, or it may have been in Jean's red and white Nash Metropolitan, or perhaps the Model T in which Jean thrilled my two young daughters by taking them for a short drive when she first came to visit us. At any rate, we rented a Cessna 150 and I proudly climbed into the pilot's seat. I shouted "Clear!" just as Ike had taught me to do, glancing surreptitiously over at the right seat to gauge my copilot's reaction. Ike just sat there, deadpan as usual. "Okay, I'll show him," I thought as I taxied to the runway, eased the throttle forward, and lifted off. And how to impress him? Well, I supposed a cleanly executed stall or two should do it.

So when we reached an altitude sufficient for recovery, I advised him to prepare himself for a stall. He nodded his approval—after all, he was the licensed pilot of the two of us, he had officially rented the plane, and he was legally responsible for whatever occurred during our flight. I pulled up on the nose to slow the plane. And then all hell broke loose. The earth began to spin around outside my window and approach more rapidly than it had ever done before. "Help!" I shouted.

"Just let go the controls," Ike answered calmly, and immediately corrected the situation. Then he explained what he had done, that is to say, what I should have done, and offered to supervise a few more stalls or even spins. But I was sufficiently shaken by the experience to call it a day. Not surprisingly, the drive back to town didn't have the same lighthearted spirit as the trip out to the airport.

So what went wrong? Just this—the preceding discussion of the stall assumes that the wings are level. But if the wing on one side dips lower than the other, as is the case when the pilot is turning or is careless, the angles of attack of the left wing and right wing will differ, and one of them will require a different minimum speed than the other in order to fly. Do you know what can happen then? If the actual speed of the airplane falls right between these two minimums, one wing will continue to fly but the other refuses. The plane begins to act like those maple seed pods that spin down to the ground. That is what a *spin* is all about, and that's what I got into.

Needless to say, when I returned home, I demanded that my flight instruc-tor teach me spin recovery, a technique for some reason missing from the private pilot curriculum. Also, needless to say, if the spin had happened when Ike Russell was not sitting beside me, you would not be reading this memoir because I would not be here to have written it.

29

Because It's There

BOB RUSSELL

When my wife Nancy and I moved from Tucson to Oregon early in 1971, we didn't know we would soon be witnessing yet another example of Ike's piloting expertise and chutzpah. After we first arrived in Oregon we visited my Uncle Bob and Aunt Pat, who showed us the farm they had recently bought west of Salem. This wonderful retreat included a farmhouse and fields that were surrounded by forest and completely isolated from all traces of civilization. Inspired by this, over the course of the summer Nancy and I searched for a property in the Eugene area with the same openness and isolation. My cousin's wife showed us a ranch they had been looking at on the Mohawk Loop north of Marcola, and we fell in love with it at first sight. Forest surrounded some 50 acres of open fields, and a small river flowed along the north edge. There were a couple of existing houses and barns.

We bought the place and moved in during the spring of 1972. It was a grand enterprise for us, and we jumped into ranch life right away. We remodeled the house, renovated pastures, and bought a dozen chickens and five head of rather scruffy cattle.

Ike almost immediately wanted to come and visit. He wanted to check out how it differed from the ranch he had owned in the San Pedro Valley, east of Tucson, and to find out what I planned to do with it. I mentioned to Ike that the fields in the center of the property were of sufficient length to provide a landing strip for a small airplane. Unfortunately, though, most were studded with old tree stumps, and a power line crossed through the middle of the ranch alongside a road. Even so, I could tell that he was intrigued with the idea.

He waited until summer to check the place out for himself. He and Jean flew his Cessna 185 from Tucson to the Springfield airport, outside Eugene, and Nancy and I drove into town to pick them up. We had hardly gotten back to the ranch and out of the car when Ike started eyeing the field across from the house. It was smooth and level and almost a quarter of a mile long, north to south. But the obstacles were daunting indeed. A stand of fir trees 80 feet tall lined the north end and the east side of the field, and a stock fence ran diagonally across the middle. A drainage ditch angled across the south end and Bunker Hill, a rocky headland and local landmark, rose some 500 feet high another quarter of a mile beyond. And that power line ran the entire length of the field along the west edge. At least there were no stumps here. Ike and I walked out into the field with some stakes and flagging material and paced this way and walked that way for a couple of hours. He put down two lines of flagged stakes where he thought the best landing place would be. We measured the trees and spoke disparagingly of the fence and that power line.

Early the next day Ike said to me, "Let's go do some flying." We jumped into my pickup and headed for Springfield, with the idea of flying up the valley and around the ranch. The landscape always shrinks dramatically when you look at it from the air, and when we flew over the ranch it seemed to have shrunk with a vengeance. I looked down at that incredibly long field—which had taken five minutes to walk end to end—and it seemed to have shrivelled into a little patch of brown grass with towering trees and power poles in every direction. And we couldn't even see the fence!

We flew around and around, spooking the neighbor's cattle and scaring my chickens. I was enjoying the great view of the Mohawk Valley, but I wondered how Ike was going to land on that postage stamp of a field.

Finally Ike said, "Let's try it." We lined up on the flagged stakes and headed down. He pulled the flaps down to about half, throttled back to about 30 percent power, and started descending through a gap in the trees at the north end of the field, regulating the rate of descent with the engine. We dropped below the trees and now we could see the fence. A little more power to clear it, then Ike cut the throttle and we quickly settled and hit the ground some 50 feet past the fence. The instant we touched Ike let off the flaps, putting the full weight of the airplane onto the wheels, and at the same time he pulled the yoke back and stood on the brakes. We came to a stop in a small cloud of dust at least several dozen feet short of the drainage ditch.

The reception committee came out immediately—Nancy and Jean, my brother-in-law Jay, every one of my five heifers, and Jean's Pyrenees Mountain dog. But no chickens. We stood around, admiring the craziness we had just pulled off, and then went in the house and had some tea.

The next morning, after more tea, Ike decided to look around the area from the air some more. Invitations went out to Nancy and Jean to go for a ride. No takers ("Are you kidding?" they asked). So he and I went back out to the field and the airplane, parked there with cows standing and lying under the wings. The dust had settled from yesterday and the air was still cool and dense, though it would be much hotter later on. We got in, Ike fired up the engine, ran through the checklist (magnetos, set altimeter, trim for climb-out). Then I braced for the takeoff toward that fence, looking so much closer now, and those evergreen trees just beyond, looming like a shower curtain at the end of the tub. Ike revved the engine up to full power, adjusted the mixture for optimum fuel ratio at our elevation, gripped the flaps lever, and let the brakes go. The power of 300 horses shook the airplane in a deafening roar and pushed me back into the seat as we bounced along through cow pies and over gopher mounds. Ike, peering intently ahead, watched the approaching fence and waited for the last possible moment to pull the flaps. We ballooned over the fence and into a climb that took us so high over the trees that I hardly even saw them. After we levelled out he looked over at me, saw me shaking my head in disbelief, and smiled.

30

Landing a Butterfly

CHUCK HANSON

Once during the mid-1970s, Ike was flying a colleague and me from the Arizona-Sonora Desert Museum to Alamos, Sonora, to pick up some specimens. Ike had recently had a STOL conversion kit installed on his Cessna 185, which made the plane perform much better for getting in and out of very short landing fields. We left Ryan Field, near Tucson, and headed south toward Nogales, Sonora, where we had to land to clear Mexican customs. Shortly after takeoff my colleague, who was in the back seat, nodded off, while Ike became engrossed in pointing out to me interesting features of the landscape below. As we approached Nogales Ike suddenly realized that we were still several thousand feet above the ground, way too high to make a normal approach and land. So he asked me if I had seen what the airplane would do in a stall with the new STOL conversion in place. Of course I hadn't, and with that Ike casually pulled back on the yoke. The plane rose, stalled, and pitched down, and as Ike again pulled back on the yoke, we rose, stalled, and pitched down again. We stalled again and again, floating downward like a falling leaf. Ike had apparently forgotten all about the man in the back seat, who had been sound asleep when this maneuver began. But he wasn't asleep for long! He woke instantly and, not knowing what was going on, began screaming, certain that we were falling to our deaths.

Ike stalled the airplane nearly all the way to the runway, to the delight of the Nogales airport officials, who knew Ike well and were watching the show from the ground. They were still laughing when we parked the airplane, and they told us that the descent had been very impressive. The plane, they said, looked like a *mariposa*—a butterfly fluttering down to land.

31

Grace

DAVID RUSSELL

When people get together and tell about their experiences flying with Ike, there are always a lot of tales about close calls in which he and his passengers barely escaped disaster. In these stories everything seems to come out all right. The impression they create is that Ike often called it close, but he never made any mistakes. The truth is that Ike *did* make errors, and he was very honest about admitting it. One of his favorite sayings was, "If you don't ever do anything, you'll never make any mistakes." Then he'd add, "But if you do things, you're *always* going to make mistakes." Ike didn't try to cover up his errors, but he didn't often talk about them either. It's just that they never particularly bothered him so he didn't dwell on them. Sometimes they taught him a valuable lesson, but after they happened he just went on with his life.

Although Ike sometimes made mistakes while he was flying, he was a good enough pilot that most of the time he really *was* able to correct the situation so that he came out of it unscathed. But there were a few times he didn't. As best I can recall, Ike was involved in eight crashes that damaged his airplane badly enough to have to get it repaired before it would fly again. I happened to be along on four of these. And the fact is that I, not Ike, was responsible for two of these wrecks.

The first time Ike had a mishap flying was in late 1947, when we lived on the ranch in the San Pedro Valley. He was flying the Piper J-3 Cub that he owned with our neighbor Cecil Ramsey. The crankshaft suddenly broke, the plane lost power, and Ike landed dead-stick in an arroyo. The plane was fine other than the crankshaft, and so was Ike. This was just a forced landing caused by a mechanical failure, so it really doesn't count as a crash. During his flying career Ike made a lot of forced landings that did no damage to himself or his airplane.

A few months later Ike really did crash, and that time I was along. It was early 1948 and I was only about five years old. He took me out to the strip he and Ramsey had built on another neighbor's place. That little J-3 had only two seats, one in back of the other, and usually the pilot sat in the back. But you don't sit in the back if you're Ike—for some reason he put me in the back seat and he sat in the front. We flew around for a while and then we came in for a landing. We touched down and suddenly the airplane was blown to the left off the runway. We were careening through some enormous rocks and the airplane started coming apart. I began beating on the seat in front of me with my fists because I was really scared and I was angry at Ike for going through those big rocks.

When we came to a standstill, he turned around and laughed and asked, "Why are you beating on my seat so hard?"

I said, "Because I'm mad at you! Why did you go through these rocks?"

And he replied, "Well, I'm sorry, I didn't mean to scare you, but the wind picked us up and got under our right wing and shifted us, and we went off the runway."

The plane was pretty badly beaten up, but neither one of us was hurt. We drove home and he didn't say any more about it. I think he told Jean, but otherwise he must have kept quiet about it, because neither of my brothers remembers this crash.

I don't think the airplane ever got fixed. Ike hardly flew at all for the next couple of years after that, until we moved to Tucson.

Ike crashed again in October 1953, at Yécora, which is a little mountain town in the Sierra Madre in eastern Sonora. This incident became famous because both Paul Martin and Randolph "Pat" Jenks wrote about it, though not entirely correctly. I was not along, but Ike told me about it. He had gone there with his friend Bill Swan. At the time, the airstrip was nothing more than one of the streets leading into town. He and Bill landed there and stayed overnight, and in the morning Ike decided he'd go flying and maybe make a couple of practice landings. So he took off and flew around a little, and then he made his approach. But once you get up in the air the landmarks all change, and nothing looks the same as it does on the ground. He told me later that it was only after he actually touched down that he realized he was in the wrong street. But then it was too late, and he couldn't get back out. The street was too short and the plane plowed right into a woman's house. Amazingly, no one was hurt, but the plane was totaled, and all he could salvage was the engine.

When I asked Ike what went wrong, he just said, "I got the wrong street." And that's it. There was nothing fouling the controls, as one version tells it. Ike just made a mistake. I think if it hadn't been for Yécora, he would eventually have killed himself. Yécora gave him a chance to wreck an airplane because of inadequate attention to detail and walk away from it. And I think he realized how fatal that kind of inattention could be, and he took it to heart. Of course, this is a deduction on my part because Ike just never talked about how that kind of thing affected him, with me or with anybody else, as far as I know.

Ike also had a minor accident when he and Jean and Paul Martin were in East Africa in 1965. One of his brakes had failed and they weren't anywhere he could get it fixed. The next time they took off Ike had to brake suddenly before they got into the air. With only one brake working they ground-looped, which destroyed the landing gear and did some other damage to the airplane. But once again, no one was hurt.

One time, probably in the early 1970s, Ike misjudged his landing at Jean's brother's farm outside Salem, Oregon. His landing place was a field that ran downhill, with a low approach over trees to the west, and high trees at the far end. It wasn't particularly short, and he'd gone in there a lot, but it was still a hard place to land. One day he flew in there and was still 30 or 40 feet above the ground when he realized that he had overshot the field. There wasn't room enough to get out. When Ike told me about it I asked him, "What did you do?"

He said, "Well, there wasn't anything I *could* do. I just had to drop the airplane. I just had to drop it in." That meant he stalled it—he cut the power and pulled the nose up so the airplane quit flying. It fell about 15 or 20 feet.

It hit the ground pretty hard and completely bent up the propeller. But it didn't really bother him any. He just took the propeller off, went to a prop shop in Salem, got another one, and put it on. He took the bent one home to Tucson and got it straightened out there.

For Ike, that was just a minor mishap and he really didn't think anything of it, but it's the kind of thing that might have killed somebody else. Another pilot might have panicked and pulled back on the yoke to try to get over the trees, and he would have either hit the trees or stalled the airplane at a fatal altitude.

Ike's maneuver worked but maybe it wasn't the best. I told this story to Walt Douglas, the pilot who gave me formal flight instruction, and Walt asked, "Well, why didn't he slip it in?" because that's what you'd normally do.

And I said, "I don't know why." Slipping is when you turn an airplane sideways and fly it down the runway sideways, which lets you lose altitude very fast, and then just as the wheels touch, you kick it back around so the nose is pointing forward again. And I knew that Ike knew how to slip a plane because he did it one day when I was with him. Walt would probably have slipped it and not hurt anything, because he was *really* good—he had thousands of hours, taught aerobatics, and had trained fighter pilots in World War II. Ike may have had a reason not to slip it. Or maybe he just didn't want to. Or maybe he just didn't think of it—who knows?

The next crash, in August 1974, was my fault. Ike was teaching me to fly. Most pilots will let the person sitting in the right seat take over the controls once they are in the air, and I did a lot of that kind of flying with Ike. But he was teaching me to do a lot more than just that. He was teaching me to fly the way he did, including takeoffs and landings in fields and other places with no prepared runway. Of course it was not legal for him to be doing this because he did not have an instructor's license, but Ike didn't worry much about those kinds of regulations.

We usually flew the Stinson that Ken and Donna McVicar had flown to South America and left with Ike out at Ryan Field. Ike kept the plane tied down outside so we built a gust lock for the rudder, which kept it from flopping around in the wind. The Stinson was a tail-dragger, and Ike liked the idea of a person learning to fly in a tail-dragger because there's a lot more to think about than in planes with a nose wheel. Mostly we flew around out in the Avra Valley. We had a course of about eight places to go where we'd practice landings. Some of the landing places were pretty difficult. One was at a dump, and the runway was pretty short and only about eight feet wide. At one end of it were bushes, and at the other end was a power line. We were landing there one day, and didn't even see the power line until after we got on the ground. I looked up and I said, "Ike, did you see that power line?"

He said, "No, I didn't. Good thing you didn't hit it." His attitude of not getting upset about mistakes was pretty contagious. It was easy to view these incidents as calmly as he did when I was flying with him.

One day we were out flying around our course in the Stinson, and I landed out in a big field. After we rolled to a stop Ike decided, in his unique way, that I should fly around alone—that I was ready to solo. So he got out of the airplane. As I taxied out, he ran after me and yelled, "Stop! We left the gust lock on—we've been flying the plane with the gust lock."

I realized right then that I had actually been bending the rudder to turn the airplane. I was used to steering it with the lock on, and once he took it off I knew I would badly over-control. I was really uneasy about this and I said to him, "I don't want to solo right now." So Ike took the lock off and got back into the airplane and came with me.

We took off, made a pass, and came in. When we landed, I *wasn't* able to control the airplane because it *did* handle completely differently without the gust lock on. I also didn't really understand that you can't use the brakes in a tail wheel airplane when you are landing or taking off. The brakes are on the top of the pedal, and the bottom of the pedal is the rudder. It is very important to just use the rudder, and to always keep your feet *off* the brakes. That hadn't been made as clear to me as it should have. So now we were weaving all over the field because I was overcontrolling with the rudder that no longer had the gust lock on it. If I'd just let the airplane go, nothing would have happened because there wasn't anything to hit. But I panicked and put the brakes on, and that flipped the airplane over on its back and broke both wings.

So there we were, hanging upside down, and gas was running everywhere, out of the wing tanks and down over the windows. I remember saying to Ike matter-of-factly, "Well, I guess this is it, isn't it?" because I thought that in just a couple of seconds we'd be on fire, and I knew there wasn't any way we could get out of the airplane very fast.

"Well, not necessarily," he replied. "These things don't always burn." I thought he was trying to give me a little hope.

Then I heard a rustling noise, as if a rat had gotten in, and I asked, "What's that noise?"

"It's me," he replied.

"What are you doing?"

"I'm trying to find my tools." He was digging around, trying to find his tool box.

"Don't you think we ought to try to get out of the airplane?" I asked.

"Yeah," he said, "we should probably do that too. But if this thing doesn't burn, we're going to need those tools. Anyway, I can't figure out where the door latch is."

"Well, you know, it's probably the opposite of where it ought to be, because we're upside down."

The plane didn't burn, and we did figure out how to open the door and got out. We were both fine, except that Ike had a cut on his face and another one on his hand. They had been bleeding and so there was blood all over the inside of the plane and out on the ground. He was still bleeding as we walked half a mile to a trailer house. We knocked on the door and Ike's cuts scared the woman who answered the door, but she gave us a ride back to Ryan Field. From there we just went home.

Ike didn't immediately report the crash, and so the first report came in from a pilot who was flying over and spotted the airplane. The sheriff came out to investigate and of course found the plane empty. Then the newspapers got hold of the situation and wrote it into a big story about drugs, where the pilot and copilot crawled away and died, leaving a trail of blood. And there were people who read that and believed it.

For me that flip was an interesting way to start a short flying career, because the next day I was supposed to start formal flight instruction with Walt Douglas. I went out to the air field and knocked on his door. "Come in," he said. He was reading the newspaper, and there was a picture of the flipped Stinson. He gave me sort of a penetrating look. "I don't think we have to do very much—you're already famous, you're in the papers!" Then he said, "According to this, your dad's dead. Is he okay?"

"Yeah, he's all right."

"Well, go gas up the airplane and I'll meet you out at the hangar."

I was going to try to talk him out of flying that day. I said, "Well, you know what, it might be better for me to wait a week."

"Oh, no," he replied, "you didn't drive all the way out here just to turn around and go home. Let's go."

Walt was the same kind of pilot as Ike—he didn't think a wrecked airplane should bother anybody as long as you walked away from it. He laughed and told me, "You know, you could explain what happened by saying you were flying upside down too slowly too close to the ground!"

The last thing I wanted to do right then was go up in an airplane. But I had the lesson anyway.

Since it was not legal for me to have been flying the airplane, or for Ike to have been acting as my instructor, Ike told the authorities that he had been flying the plane and had used the brakes improperly when we landed. He took the blame for my crash.

The most disturbing crash took place in August 1975, on the way back to Tucson from Plymouth, Massachusetts. Nobody is quite sure why Ike let it happen, and the entire episode is still a pretty sensitive topic for some members of our family. We had all been together at a big family reunion on an island in Plymouth Harbor, but it ended on a sour note. On the boat trip back to the mainland Ike became the focus of a serious dispute. It upset him deeply and it may have threatened his self-esteem. But we needed to leave, so when we got to shore Jean and Ike and my wife Susan Randolph and I went out to the airport, got in Ike's plane, and took off for home.

The reason we crashed is that we didn't have enough gas for the long first leg of the trip Ike planned to fly that day. The day before he had taken his sister Alice flying all around Cape Cod to show her the sights, and now it looked like we were about to take off for home without gassing up. We were taxiing out and I asked Ike if he was going to get gas on the way out. He said he didn't think he would.

Some of the family believe Ike was so distraught that he just forgot about the flight with his sister and thought he had full tanks. But I think these are things pilots don't just forget. I was pretty sure Ike knew right from the start that he didn't have enough gas to get to where he wanted to go. So I mentioned to him casually, "I guess there's a gas station somewhere out there, and we can stop on the way."

He said, "I think that's probably the best way to deal with it." He didn't seem to have a gas stop clearly in mind. It was just somewhere down the line.

After we had been flying for a while I knew for sure we weren't going to make it to our destination. Two hours into the flight we were nearing Cleveland and the gas gauges were on red. I thought to myself, "This is one of those days. From here on we're just going to have to take it minute by minute." Then I saw we were over water. According to our flight plan we weren't supposed to be over water.

I asked Ike, "What are we doing? Why are we flying over Lake Erie?"

I understood what was happening when he replied, "It's a good place to land. Better to land on the shore than the middle of a city."

He knew what he was doing—Ike *always* knew what he was doing—he was one of the most aware people I've ever been around. When he said that, I got rather angry because I knew he was just going to fly the airplane until it quit, and then land somewhere. But the only way I could ever deal with Ike was to be cooler than he was, because any other approach just made him resistant.

So I looked at him and said, "You know, we don't have a lot of leeway, do we? We have only 1,200 feet. Those gauges have been on red for a while. You're probably not going to make your destination." And he looked at me in a way that seemed to acknowledge that we weren't going to make it. Then I remember thinking, "Oh, well, it's probably going to be all right. If we don't make it, we'll figure out something." And I was reasonably content with that. It was almost as if this scenario had to be played out, and Ike was just going to have to play his role.

Then we turned away from the lake and headed southwest, and he said something very revealing. He said, "Well, I guess we'd better head to the country."

I looked at him and said, "Huh? What do you mean?"

"Well," he replied, "it's just an old expression, but a country boy, when things get bad, always heads for the country."

"Oh, you mean it'd be easier to set down somewhere if we weren't over the city of Cleveland?" It was pretty clear that we both knew there wasn't going to be any gas left pretty soon.

"Yeah," he said, "I think it's better to go to the country."

Of course there were airports all around the area, so I asked, "What would you think of going to Cleveland International Airport?"

"Well, there's no need to do that," he countered. The thing was, you couldn't *make* Ike do anything.

About 10 or 15 minutes later, as we were passing over the town of Elyria, the engine quit. I turned to him and said, "All right, *now* what are you going to do?" knowing full well what he was going to do. And he did—he pushed the auxiliary pump, which is a device that pumps gas out of the tanks into the fuel injectors and can enable an airplane to run another 10 or 12 minutes. It *can* do that, but this time it didn't. He pushed the auxiliary pump and nothing happened.

Everything was silent. We all started looking for a place to land. Ike thought he saw a place below us, and he pulled full flaps and made a short left turn to start a circle to land. But a moment later he realized that there were power lines in the way that were some 800 or 900 feet high. *I* didn't see them, but *he* did. About a second after that he muttered, "Well, that was a big mistake," and he let the flaps off. The airplane lofted back up.

It was pretty congested below, and there just weren't many places to set an airplane down. I suggested the freeway, but he said, "No, that's no good, there's just too much traffic." Ike kept gliding around looking. Susan and Jean, in the back seat, were pretty collected about the situation, and they were looking for a place to land, too. Finally we saw a field that looked okay, and Ike headed toward it. I was really angry at this point and I started cussing Ike out for getting us in this predicament. He said nothing for a while; he just let me work him over. Then he said very quietly, "You'll have to quit now, Dave, because I need to concentrate on getting this airplane down."

He made his approach over a low fence. About a second before we touched we crossed a ditch about eight feet deep that none of us had seen until we were right over it. Then he touched down in a flawless three-point landing. But the airplane rolled for several hundred feet, and it didn't stop until we ran into the trees at the far end. The impact completely knocked out the right landing gear and tore up the leading edge of the right wing. Another pilot might have done something stupid like apply too much brake and flipped the airplane over or ground-looped it, which might have done even more damage. But Ike didn't. He just let it roll until we hit the trees.

None of us was hurt at all, but I scrambled for the door latch and Susan and Jean and I started rushing to get out. Ike, cool as always, said, "There's no need to hurry—there's no gas left in the airplane to catch on fire." Even in this crazy situation he never lost his sense of humor. And we found out later that we had crashed right next door to a wheelchair factory!

We were all quite pissed off at Ike for a long time after that crash, but he even weathered that pretty well. The plane had to be taken apart to get it out of there so it could be repaired. The inspector who investigated the crash said about Ike, "That guy made a perfect landing—he sure is cool as a cucumber!" But Ike had to recertify with the FAA before he could fly again. Running out of gas in Ohio is not like running out of gas in northern Mexico.

The last two crashes happened in 1977 and 1979. In 1977 he was starting to get sick, and by 1979 he was really in pretty bad shape, and that probably had a lot to do with these incidents, directly or indirectly.

The first one occurred in August on Ángel de la Guarda Island, in the Gulf of California. Ike was ferrying people and supplies between two bad strips there, and he damaged his tail wheel landing. Rather than risk landing again and getting stranded, he came to Tucson for another plane, and flew it back to the island. This time he overshot the runway and crashed in the arroyo at the end. Since Susan Randolph describes this affair in her story, I won't say any more about it here.

The last incident took place in November at Madera, Chihuahua, up in the Sierra Madre. It was really my crash, not Ike's. To fully appreciate what went wrong, it's worth relating how Ike happened to buy the airplane I wrecked. That airplane was a Cessna 185, with a monster 300 horsepower Continental engine that delivered a frightful amount of power. It was one of the features Ike loved about it. The guy he bought it from was John Donaldson, who owned and ran the Empire Ranch. One day in 1967 Ike was out at Ryan Field just sitting in Fred Grissom's office. John, who was tall and lanky and wore boots and a cowboy hat, walked in, completely pale, and said, "That goddamn sonofabitchin' airplane!"

"You want to sell it?" asked Ike.

"If you want to buy it, I'll sell it to you right now," John growled.

So Ike took out his checkbook. "How much do you want?"

"Aren't you even interested in asking why I want to sell it?" asked John.

"Well, I thought you'd get around to telling me that," Ike replied, "but I'll write you a check first." And Ike wrote him a check right on the spot.

So Ike bought the airplane, and John told him what had happened. While he was taking off from his ranch, the pin that held the pilot's seat in place failed and the seat suddenly slid all the way back. So there was John sitting way at the back of the cabin trying to get the plane into the air and just about unable to reach the controls. He got it into the air somehow and managed to keep it there, and he flew around for 10 minutes trying to get the seat back in position so he could actually control it. He was pretty badly shaken up, so he headed straight to Ryan, and that's when he sold it to Ike.

The problem with the pin wasn't just a quirk of John's airplane—it was a design flaw of several models of Cessnas, and eventually Cessna got sued for it. Anyway, Ike knew about that flaw with the seat pin right from the start, and he was always careful to check that it was in place before he took off.

So in November 1979 Ike and I flew in his 185 up to the mountains of Chihuahua, first to Madera, then over to Huisopa. By then Ike was so sick he may have thought he might not make it back. But he probably figured it would be all right to go because I had a license and he would have me fly the airplane if he couldn't. This might have seemed okay to him, but it was really not a very good idea because I had never been checked out in that airplane. Although I had ridden in it much of my life, I had never really flown it. I had never sat on the left and had never made a takeoff or landing with it. But none of this was an issue for the trip down. Ike flew the plane to Huisopa, where we spent three days at a ranch, and then he flew it back to Madera. Oddly, before we left for Madera, I asked him, "Have you checked your seat?" He just looked at me and said, "Yeah, I have," and we took off. We spent that night in Madera.

The next morning Ike felt so bad that he asked me to sit in the left seat and fly. I didn't want to do it, especially because we had passengers—two adults and a kid. But Ike was really sick, so I said okay. I was pretty preoccupied when we taxied to the end of the runway. I pushed the throttle in for takeoff. The airplane with its big engine lunged forward, and my seat promptly slid all the way back. In my preoccupation with other things I had forgotten to check the pin.

I tried to pull myself forward with the yoke but there was just no way I could get to the pedals. Ike reached over and pulled the throttle, which cut the power, but without the rudder pedals I couldn't steer the airplane. I was thinking as all this was happening that Ike had a full set of controls on the right and that he would just take care of the airplane. But he didn't. It all happened very fast, and his condition was so bad that he just wasn't really very sharp. So we veered off the runway and ground-looped in the dirt. No one was hurt, but it tore out one side of the landing gear and caused some other damage. I had to take the wings off the airplane and remove the engine, and put it all in a big cattle truck to haul it to Tucson.

When I told Walt Douglas about the wreck, he said, "You really shouldn't feel bad about that. Your dad should have checked you out, and gone over two or three things that were really important in that airplane." And then he added, "*I* don't feel bad that you did that." I think he said this because he didn't take wrecks any more seriously than Ike did. And Ike never made me feel bad about it. It was just one of those things that happen when you're doing something.

I *did* feel bad about that ground loop, but I also knew that what happened wouldn't even have been considered a real wreck in the old days in Mexico. I once saw Dave Coughanour, who was one of the greatest bush pilots Chihuahua ever had, do the same thing at Maicoba, another little town up in the mountains. As he was taking off one day, Ike and Jean and my wife Susan and I were standing under the wing of Ike's airplane, and the next thing we knew Dave's airplane went off the runway into some brush.

Ike walked over. "Is everything okay?" he asked.

Coughanour got out and said, "Yeah, it's okay," and he got out a hammer and started bending the strut and the damaged cowling back into shape.

Ike asked him, "Well, what happened?"

"I forgot to set the seat," he replied. Coughanour's plane was a Cessna, too.

The old timers and the pilots up in the Sierra didn't think about wrecking airplanes the way people do today. Pilots now are much more timid. Ike wrecked (without my help) four or five airplanes, but he never seriously injured himself or anyone else. He told me that Coughanour also wrecked four or five planes during his career as a bush pilot and never hurt anybody—until the last one. He was flying in his plane and had a heart attack. Two paying passengers were with him and they all went down and were killed. We were talking about that one day, and Ike said, "Well, at least those two guys got a free ride to Chihuahua."

32

Closing the Loop

DOUG PEACOCK

Ike Russell came into my life through Ed Abbey, the anarchist writer, who became, I might add, the most difficult close friend I ever had. Within the symmetry of that brotherhood, Ike Russell supplied a most satisfying chunk of ballast. These two good men propelled my young life into unforeseen realms and, in the end, taught me something about dying a good death.

Ed Abbey and I shared numerous serious interests as well as a number of nefarious adventures in defense of the wild; the most important of these were exploration and protection of wild deserts. Walking was our preferred mode of travel though we sometimes used pickups to drive to the frontiers of these wilderness areas. Of course, there were wild desert enclaves we couldn't get to by ordinary transportation. In particular, these were islands, uninhabited islands, desert islands in the Gulf of California. We'd heard about them and, naturally, we wanted to go there. This was the context in which Ike Russell's name was presented to me over an ironwood campfire. "He'll land anywhere," Ed Abbey said.

I'd heard about Ike, of course. Among my desert rat friends and associates, Ike was a bush pilot legend. Russell, Abbey said, had landed his little Cessna 185 in places no other plane had ever been. He once landed on a desert bajada on the edge of Ángel de la Guarda, one of the islands Ed and I were talking about. He'd explored a bit, then spent a few hours building a makeshift runway ending at a 50-foot vertical sea cliff so he could get back into the air.

I had heard he had also landed on Tiburón Island, the island of the Seri Indians, many times. Tiburón seemed like another place we needed to go.

The idea of flying with Ike to these islands surfaced during an especially memorable desert wilderness trip into the vast wasteland of southwestern Arizona, the Cabeza Prieta—the place where Ed would take his last walk. It now seems to me that the essence of my long and cranky friendship with Edward Abbey is contained between two trips—the one to Cabeza Prieta during which we conceived the idea of going to the islands, and my trip to Tiburón Island just weeks before Abbey's death in 1989. In between, Ed and I got to fly to Angel Island with Ike.

That trip to Cabeza Prieta took place during December of 1973. At that time, Ed and I were without families. We had spent a sniffling, lonely Christmas Eve at a topless bar in Tucson drinking whiskey. Thinking we could improve on that, we packed up and drove 150 miles west over Charlie Bell Pass into the Cabeza Prieta. We sipped beer all the way from Three Forks and were a tad plastered by the time we hit Charlie Bell Pass. We got my '66 Ford truck stuck several times creeping down the dark treacherous road to the well—hanging up the ass end of the truck, jacking it up in the dark, rocking it free, and then dropping down into the Growler Valley.

At Charlie Bell Well we got out for a piss break. We stumbled around in the dark using a flashlight until we found the Indian petroglyphs carved on basalt boulders. We knew about them. There were carvings of sheep and lots of stuff that looked like thunderheads with lightning and rain pouring down.

This was the place where the ancients waited for the first rain of the monsoon season so there would be water for their trek south to collect the sea shells they carved into their dream animals. We found one carving that looked like a thunderbird. Ed thought it was probably a turkey vulture and said that when he died he planned to come back as a buzzard.

We continued on for one more six-pack towards the north end of the Granite Mountains, where we got stuck again. We finally crawled into our sleeping bags shortly after midnight.

The next morning, we awoke and walked off our hangovers exploring the north edge of the Granites. To the north, the dark outline of the andesitic Aguilas—the "Eagle" mountains—loomed on the horizon. I had never been there. Neither had Ed. The Aguilas might have been the wildest spot out here in the Cabeza Prieta, the biggest, driest, and emptiest of deserts. Someday I'd go there. We followed Growler Wash where it bent around the north end of the Granite Mountains, then turned south. There was nothing or nobody within 50 miles of here now. The white flag of an antelope bounced towards a gap in the Bryant Mountains. "You know, you could walk straight through that pass all the way to Ajo," said Abbey.

"Yeah, it'd be clear sailing all the way to Charlie Bell. You could water up there," I answered.

"That's a hike we need to take sometime," he noted. "This driving pick-ups is for wimps."

Later, on New Year's Eve at Eagle Tank, at the foot of the eastern escarpment of the Sierra Pinta, it sleeted and snowed on us—an unusual occurrence. We sat out the rain for a day under a tarp, stoking an ironwood fire. We charted the desert islands we wanted to visit in the Gulf of California—Tiburón and Ángel de la Guarda. Guardian Angel would be the first. We'd wait for a rare thunderstorm to fill the tinajas with water, then prevail on Ike Russell, who had already landed there. I'd take a hand line to jig for spotted cabrilla and a Hawaiian sling for black sea bass.

Meanwhile, Ed scribbled notes for the book he had been writing the past couple years and now was working on full time. Ed was especially concerned with the technical credibility of this book. "I want it to read accurately to a bulldozer operator or hard rock miner," Ed said. "I'd like you to take a look at it when it's finished."

I said, "Fine, when it's done I'll do it." At that time, I didn't know it was a comic novel of environmental saboteurs. Ed had already consulted a copy of *The Blaster's Handbook*. In the back of my pickup I had a little field library of military manuals and "confidential" materials passed out at the Center for Special Warfare when I was a Special Forces medic stationed at Fort Bragg. One was a manual on improvised weapons and demolitions—a little cookbook on how to make zip-guns, napalm, and thermite using common household and hardware store materials. Ed seemed interested in its contents.

I asked him more about his idea for the book, about inspiring cells within a movement, about the book's theme of No-Compromise-in-Defense-of-the-Wilderness, and what it was he really cared about. "People," he said. "People like you and our friends and families. I would never sell out a friend for an idea. A single brave deed is worth a hundred books and this book will be no different."

Huddled around that soggy desert campfire, we drank a toast of beer. Above the granitic spires, soaring below the rare roof of heavy desert clouds, a big dark bird emerged then faded into the gloom. We toasted the golden eagle of Eagle Tank, as uncommon as the Arizona sleet and scudding clouds. We popped another beer and drank to friends, wilderness, trips to Ángel de la Guarda and Tiburón Islands, and the success of Ed's mission and his new novel.

An island trip with Ike Russell didn't unfold until 1977. In the meantime, my friendship with Abbey became increasingly rocky. It was a two-way rocky road, because for my part I was a very hard case to begin with. Hostility—generally expecting the worst from people—had been my adult lot in life since Vietnam. My inability "to reenter society," a society I saw as clearly pathological, left me a desperado sneaking around the treelines of our own culture. The waters were further muddied in 1975 by the publication of Ed's book, which he called *The Monkey Wrench Gang*. For its hero, Abbey had created the fictional personality of George Washington Hayduke, a hairy, beer-swilling, crazy ex-Green Beret, a character loosely based on an earlier Doug Peacock. The book sold half a million copies, and the character of Hayduke became famous in a lowbrow sort of way. "Hayduke Lives" was scribbled on bathroom walls in bars throughout the American West. This was hardly an endorsement of excellence, nor flattery of any variety; Hayduke was a one-dimensional dolt. As an acquaintance of both myself and Abbey remarked, "Friends don't do that to each other." He meant that in modeling Hayduke on Peacock, Ed was abusing our friendship.

Then, in the middle of our worst squabbling and a long extended silence, a miracle happened. Ed Gage, a mutual friend, insisted on dragging me down to the Poet's Cottage at the University of Arizona to reconcile with Abbey. Abbey had a magazine assignment and expenses to fly to Ángel de la Guarda. He offered to pay my way to the island. Ike Russell would fly both of us into the Gulf of California.

I wince as I write the names, the two Eds, my best desert pals ever, and Ike Russell, a more recent friend, all gone now. Ed Gage, the bastard, surprised me by curing his pain with a shotgun. With Ike and Ed Abbey it would be much better.

We all met at Ryan Field, a little airport west of Tucson. There was Abbey, an artist friend, and three other members of what was to be a five-day expedition. I shook hands with Ike, a rugged handsome man who was then about my age now. The plane could only haul a couple big men and their gear at one time, so I drove down to Caborca, Sonora, to await Russell's return trip from Guardian Angel Island.

Hours later, I soared with Ike Russell off the coast of Sonora over the Gulf of California into the gentle breeze blowing off the Baja peninsula. Ike pointed south towards Libertad where he had seen a pod of finback whales just puttering around on the surface, perhaps in some kind of social gathering. He said that the boojum trees there (a thin band of upside-down 50-foot carrots growing for about eight miles along the Sonoran coast) had probably been seeded by birds caught in storms and blown over from central Baja. There was also a colony of these rare trees, Ike said, on the leeward side of the highest peak on Ángel de la Guarda. I sat up and looked around; this man Russell knew some things.

Ángel de la Guarda loomed ahead in the late afternoon sunlight, at first appearing to float as a shape-shifting mirage on the sea, then suddenly rising out of the ocean to greet us with its sheer volcanic peaks and limonite talus slopes. Ike flew right into it. Dodging a little offshore islet and a sea cliff, he drifted down onto a barely improvised airstrip hacked out of the brittlebush and bursage, bouncing to a quick stop on the 800-foot runway, on which, I was later told, only Ike had ever landed.

We unloaded our gear on the big uninhabited and mostly unexplored island in the Gulf of California 10 miles off the Baja coast. It was February of 1977. I remember because the trip signified a milestone in my friendship with Ed, marking a rapprochement. It also came at a time when I badly needed it. Nothing serious, just the usual midthirties metaphysical doldrums, when the whines of indecision ruled—what to do, whom to be, where to go, whether to go on—all the whimperings of a subadult male who has yet to commit to anything or hold down his first job. The gas and Ike's expenses were Ed's present to me, a wild gift I never forgot.

I spent the next four days trying to get away by myself. Not that there was anything wrong with my companions, just that uninhabited islands push me towards solitude. At night, we drank rum by the campfire; all had a grand time.

When Ike returned to the island on the fifth day to pick up Ed and the others, he left me behind for 10 additional days on Angel Island. This was all Ike's idea. He said he had to drop off a herpetologist in 10 days near Puerto Refugio, at the northern end of the island. He flew me up there and left me with five gallons of water. Russell would, barring the disastrous unforeseen, be back in 10 days. He flashed me a big tooth grin as he throttled up the Cessna. He knew what this meant to me.

And for me, it was like Brer Rabbit getting thrown into the briar patch. To be abandoned on a deserted desert island, forced to camp alone in the desert by the sea was the essence of everything I loved best about Baja and desert islands, that marriage of ocean and cactus. In short, a dream come true.

I made camp behind a low dune on the northeastern tip of Ángel de la Guarda, along an immaculate white crescent of beach running from headland to headland. The biggest problem here would be water. A half gallon a day, though adequate for survival, is marginal for comfort. I wondered about tinajas. There are deep hidden arroyos draining the Cerro Ángel on the north end of the island and large palm canyons on the eastern midsection. Most people think that there is no water on the island, though in fact Ed Abbey discovered a large tank big enough to swim in (bearing in mind that it is poor desert manners to swim in another's drinking water). Maybe it dries up in years of total drought, which are not unknown on this arid island.

This tinaja was, however, too far away. Another water hole was rumored to lie high on the northern flank. The second day, I made a run for it but the decaying volcanic rock is so rotten and treacherous that slopes steeper than 40 degrees were largely unapproachable. Still, I scrambled up the volcanic talus on the northeast side of the collection of summits, which constitute the Cerro Ángel. I thought I could see through my binoculars colonies of stunted boojum trees clinging to the highest slopes.

I never located fresh water on the north end of the isle, but solved my problem instead by drinking sea water in small gulps throughout the day and using the ocean for cooking and everything else.

The other problem was food. I had survival rations but was counting on fish and shellfish for the main dish. Trouble was, I had no experience in ocean spearfishing. Two hours before slack tide, I packed up my diving gear and hiked north through the halophytes and scabrous vegetation over a low pass to the very northern tip of the main island. A few torote trees and creosote bushes overlooked a boiling channel about 250 yards wide and flowing west to east. Beyond was the smaller Mejía Island and two rocky islets occupied by roosting seabirds and small colonies of cardon cactus. One of these headlands had brown pelicans nesting on the top, a peregrine eyrie and Craveri's murrelets on the side, and fish-eating bats living in the cracks and caves. I avoided the rock because the pelicans were extremely spooky and abandoned their nests if disturbed, so I never approached closer than about 500 yards.

I scrambled down to a tiny beach and pulled on my borrowed wetsuit and flippers, then waded out backward into the channel until I was almost waist deep. I squatted and the current knocked me off my feet and swept me eastward toward a rocky headland. I was surprised by the strength of the tidal bore and the coolness of the water. I turned around and swam toward the setting sun, kicking against the tides with sufficient effort both to maintain a stationary position and generate enough body heat to stay warm. Clouds of upwelling plankton and small debris, along with a few fish, drifted by as I hovered behind a large rock, finally ambushing a small dinner-size cabrilla with the Hawaiian sling.

Fortunately, this was the time of big, low tides. My skill with the Hawaiian sling was so poor I expended at least twice the thermal energy chasing cabrilla and black sea bass as I gained from eating the occasional catch. With the big tides, however, I could pluck blue mussels off wave-washed headlands and dig clams. It took me a whole day of clamming to catch on, but once I learned how to spot the siphon holes, the clams were the easiest pickings. They were big disk *Dosinias*, lots of them, as big as your hand. Served with Mexipep, they were a great delicacy.

On the tenth day, I was getting a little workout in, running naked (not a pretty sight) back and forth on the quarter-mile crescent of sand beach when I heard an engine. Ike's Cessna roared into the adjacent cove just to the south and disappeared behind a long spine of volcanic ridge running out into the ocean. I raced back to camp and started packing up my gear. Tying everything to the big backpack, I staggered down the beach.

Ike was waiting with a smile on his face at the west end of the improbable runway he had hacked out of the brittlebush bajada. A herpetologist and his equipment stood stacked on the bajada nearby; Ike would return in a week to pluck up the scientist. We loaded up my stuff and Ike started the engine. The little aircraft bounced down the unimproved track and lurched into the air just as the surf reached up to embrace us. Ike circled and I looked back on the tiny beach that had been my home. The rift with my buddy Abbey had disappeared along with the roll of belly fat around my waist. It was another great day to be alive on earth.

Ike Russell put the plane on a northeasterly course for the Sonoran coast. Through the distant southern haze, the Sierra Seri pierced the clouds with Tiburón looming offshore. We approached the mainland near Puerto Lobos. Suddenly, Ike pulled up and banked to the north.

"Look," he said, "it must of rained hard on just that one spot." Ahead, an island of immaculate green sat surrounded by the dry browns of stark desert vegetation. An isolated thunderstorm had dumped an inch or so of rain onto this tiny garden. As if by magic, the slumbering desert resurrects itself with the vibrant blush of spring—like the bear in her den, dying the little death of winter, then re-emerging in April with the gift of bear cubs.

I didn't see much of Ike during the next three years. Then friends told me of his illness, and I took to calling Ike up every week or so. The only other person I had ever felt comfortable approaching like this was my paternal grandmother, to whom I had grown especially close in the weeks before her death. I had waited much too long to thank Ike for sharing those priceless moments, those gifts, with me.

My last talk with Ike was shortly before he died. Mostly we talked about places, trips, great desert trips, island trips, Sierra Madre trips that we could take, going on until I realized that Ike knew he'd never take them and I broke down—we both did. I'd have to take them for both of us, and for the most part I did, following his spoor deep into the barranca country of the Tarahumara, and to Tiburón Island of the Seri Indians.

I was not there when Ike Russell died. Kim Cliffton and Bunny Fontana told me about his wake and burial. There were lots of people there. Kim managed to get Ike's boots back on and Bunny prepared a pot of pinole as food for the journey to the underworld. Ike was buried in his back yard with care and ceremony by friends who loved him, who believed in the fundamental laws of respect and dignity. The sort of people I knew didn't do this. It made a deep impression on me.

• • •

Years afterward, in February of 1989, I was headed down through Nogales, Sonora, when I spotted a Cessna 185 descending from the west headed into the Nogales airport. For a moment I thought it was Ike. We had cleared customs here when he and I returned from Angel Island. Then I snapped out of it—Ike had been dead for nine years and now Ed Abbey was dying. I was on my way to Tiburón Island to close the loop for all of us.

A few weeks later, four friends took turns sitting up with old Ed during his last days. I was alone with Ed most of that final night—the last six hours of his life. The very last time Ed Abbey smiled—it was just before dawn—was when I told him he was going to be buried as he had wished, in the desert, illegally, in the outlaw spirit of old Hayduke.

• • •

The rudimentary shovel work, the sweaty labor that was the consummation of trust, finally testing the exact configuration by lying down in the freshly dug grave to check out the view—bronze patina of boulder behind limb of paloverde, turquoise sky beyond branch of torote. Then receiving a sign— seven buzzards soaring above joined by three others, now all 10 banking over the volcanic rubble and riding the thermal up the flank of the mountain, gliding out and over the distant valley.

• • •

I have traveled out here alone to Ed's grave, bearing little gifts, including a bottle of mescal and a bowl of *posole verde* I made myself, a notion partly inspired by Bunny Fontana's offering when they buried Ike. I sit quietly on the black volcanic rocks listening to the desert silence, pouring a little mescal over the grave and down my throat until the moon comes up, an hour or so before midnight. There is not a human sight or sound, only a faint desert breeze stirring the blossoms of brittlebush. I smile when I think of the small favor, the final duty, the last simple task that Ed's friends, Ike's friends, can do for one another. We should all be so lucky.

VI... FAREWELL

One day the Russells' neighbors brought over a bag of ripe tomatoes. Jean could see that there were more than they could eat before they spoiled. As they were discussing what they could do with the surplus, someone asked rhetorically, "You can't freeze tomatoes, can you?" Ike, who was just walking by, heard the question. He immediately grabbed a tomato, opened the freezer door, and put it inside. "You can if you have a freezer," he said.

33

The Grate

Luke Russell

Let me tell you about two events in the life of Ike Russell: the first, a forced landing in 1947 shortly after he had first learned to fly; the second, the last time his family and friends would see him as they buried him in his own backyard, more or less according to his careful and explicit instructions.

During his last weeks, Ike's heart was too weak to clear fluids from his lungs or body and he needed bottled oxygen to breathe. He had given up reading because lying down made breathing more difficult and he was too weak to hold his head up while he was sitting.

I had come from Philadelphia to be with him and was reading aloud to him books I thought he would like. W. B. Yeats he found "too airy," but Alan Paton's *Too Late the Phalarope* he loved. We read through it for his last five or six days, putting the book aside as different things came up that he wanted to talk about.

The rigid Presbyterianism of Paton's characters prompted sharp remarks from Ike about the equally stiff aunts and uncles in Avon and Rochester, New York, where he had been born and lived until the age of eleven, when he had been sent to Arizona for his health. Ike would raise his head and say, "I'll be damned. A battle-ax, just like Aunt Mae." Then he would rest his head again on the pillow on the table in front of him and wait to hear me read some more.

His memory was bright, hotly focused, and precise. I asked about events whose dates I couldn't remember—When had I accidentally crushed my brother's finger in a piece of farm machinery? "Summer of '44," he'd quickly reply, or "Thanksgiving '46," when I asked when he had gotten his first airplane. He explained that it was a J-3 Piper Cub that he and Cecil Ramsey, another rancher on the San Pedro River, had bought from a military surplus dealer in San Diego.

I remember that plane as canary yellow. It had a wooden propeller, two seats in tandem, and a right side door to its cabin that folded out and up. A person in either seat could, if he or she wanted, tuck in a right shoulder, lean over, and fall out. There was no radio, no lights, no electricity. Turning the propeller by hand started the four-cylinder engine.

Getting an airplane was a great idea, he and Ramsey figured. Ramsey, who'd flown in the war, would teach Ike to fly; they would build a small hanger off one of their fields and have an airplane available to check fences,

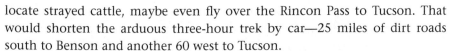

locate strayed cattle, maybe even fly over the Rincon Pass to Tucson. That would shorten the arduous three-hour trek by car—25 miles of dirt roads south to Benson and another 60 west to Tucson.

Ike never doubted the wisdom of buying the J-3, he said, even though on that first day as he and Ramsey were flying it back from San Diego, he noticed on the highway below that the cars going east were pulling ahead of them. One of them was the very Model A Ford that had taken them to pick up the plane.

My brothers, ages five and three, and I, age six, were loading firewood in our wagon from the pile in front of the ranch house when Ike and Ramsey roared over our heads. We were ecstatic. The plane banked, then settled down in the dust of a barley field nearby. We were over there like a shot.

The high-octane gas smelled funny. Our fingers drummed pleasantly against the tight lacquered fabric of the fuselage and tail. The low-pressure tires bulged out sleepily over the barley stubble. The shock absorbers looked exactly like what they were, huge bulgy rubber bands knotted together.

Ike learned to fly that winter, at first informally by Ramsey taking him up, letting him handle the plane and do "touch-and-go" landings on the barley field, and later and more formally by taking regular lessons from "Skeet" Taylor, a certified instructor who ran the Benson Airport. In 1947, the airport was a dirt strip east of town near the Southern Pacific tracks. Instruction cost four dollars an hour. That included gas and airplane.

Crop dusting was Taylor's other vocation, and some think the cause of his death—but not as one would expect. He died of insecticide poisoning at home, sitting bolt upright at dinner. From Benson, he had moved to Tucson and then on to Marana, where he had continued hurtling through the air and rising and falling between rows of windbreak cottonwoods, a sloshing tank of toxic materials strapped into the passenger's seat in front of him. Ike's excellence in short-field flying may owe an early debt to Taylor's wizardry at dusting crops and to Ramsey's having, I am told, spotted artillery from a J-3 during the war.

Ike's first accident was the spring of 1947, a time when his notes say, "Ike flew cub a lot." The one-room school my brother Bob and I attended broke for afternoon recess. We had seen the yellow Piper flying around. At day's end the school bus—a '41 Ford pickup with a rack on the back, driven by Ramsey's wife Betty—picked us up. She said, "Your dad went down. But he's okay!"

As we and two other kids whose ranches were also south of the school piled into the back of the truck, we positioned ourselves around the small window in the rear of the cab so we could look forward into the cab and then beyond at the dirt road leading to the San Pedro River. Then, as we could smell the pungent green brush that grows along the edges of dry rivers in Arizona, far in the distance, across a field of gravel and sand, we saw the smudge of yellow that was the J-3. When we drove up, Ike was standing beside it, having already taken off the cowling with tools he had borrowed from a nearby ranch. He told my brother and me to have our mom return with his truck. By then, he would have the propeller off and the engine loose so he could take the engine to Tucson and have the crankshaft replaced. The crankshaft had broken in the air and fortunately, he had shut the engine down quickly. Hence the case was okay. He had landed "dead stick" on the gravel and sand of the riverbed. The plane was fine. A week later, as my brother and I played at recess, once again we could see the yellow Cub practicing landings on the airstrip Ike and Ramsey had cleared on top of Charlie Remick's mesa near the school.

As I read aloud further into Paton's novel, Ike and I became engrossed in the plot, which revolves around a father and a son who live in the same city but who are estranged from each other. We, too, had had strong differences and had been exploring ways we might bring about a reconciliation. The father in the book attempts to bridge the gap by giving the son, an avid birder, a book that describes wild species around Johannesburg. It states that a certain phalarope, a type of wading bird, can be found in a local marshland.

"Did you get the grate yet?" Ike asked me suddenly.

"What do you mean," I asked, but his head was down again and he didn't answer. So I read on.

The son in the novel states he knows the marsh well, and he insists no such bird exists there. He flatly rejects the gift.

"Did you get the grate yet?" Ike asked again, and this time added, "It's at Pappadias' Salvage Yard on the Freeway. Take the truck, Luke. You'll need it. It's big." He didn't explain more and put his head down, so I read more. The father in the book suggests the two of them make a trip to the marsh and see if they can find the bird. They go, and for most of a day they trudge around in the marsh finding nothing—no bird, no phalarope. Discouraged, they return and continue struggling against each other for another hundred or so pages, Paton making clear what they—locked in their situation—can't see, that just by going to look for the phalarope they had found it.

"Take the truck and put the grate out in back by the storeroom where you can find it when you need it. Jean won't like it if you don't have it."

He rested a minute, then explained what I already knew—that he had arranged for a doctor to come to the house after he died, and that he would fill out the required paper work. Ike had also cleared things with the county, determining that a person could legally be buried on his own property. He had also set aside a narrow, blue, household door, stashing it on the back porch, telling my younger brother, "Now don't forget, Dave. You'll need that door to get me out of this room. A dead body is a lot heavier than a live one."

The problem in all these plans, though, was the grate. He hadn't been able to get the grate from the scrap-iron dealer. He wanted it brought right away.

The grate, he said, would allow him to be buried in a shallow grave. He didn't want to be buried too deeply, too far below the earth's natural processes.

"Now get the grate, Luke, and remember I don't want to be buried more than three feet deep."

The grate, a metal security grate for a window, he wanted laid over the top of his grave, "so the dogs won't dig me up."

As we read toward the end of the novel and as Paton's characters began to resolve their differences, so, I think, were Ike and I doing the same for ourselves. Differences except for . . .

"Just go get the grate, Luke."

So a little later, I made sure his windows along the driveway were open, got my brother's big pickup and drove it loudly and slowly up the driveway past his room and out into the back of Ike's property. After about 10 minutes, I loudly drove the truck back the other way. I then came back into the house and continued reading the novel aloud. Ike never mentioned the grate again.

It made sense that he'd want to be buried in this way. I remember Jean telling me that when she and Ike were first married, in order to learn about ranching, they had worked building fence on a ranch near Amado. One day she noticed Ike sitting on the ground not moving. When she, slightly alarmed, went up and asked if he was okay, he said nothing was wrong except he wasn't sure it was a good idea to be putting "all these holes into the earth."

Similarly, I knew that for most of the years Ike had lived in Tucson he had left unrepaired a settlement crack in a block wall of a building on the back of his property at Cottonwood Lane. A certain blue-collared lizard—about the size of a small yam—lived there, may still be there for all I know. I remember several winters, cold ones, when the lizard would be hibernating and quite stiff. Ike would reach into a particular place in the crack and gently lift him out, look at him, and then put him back. Also, I knew that Ike had given 15 or so acres in Esperero Canyon in the Santa Catalina Mountains to the Audubon Society to block development of the upper watershed and to provide living space for quail and javelina.

So the grate made sense but the story doesn't end exactly as Ike had planned. He died a few days later. Peacefully in the night. People came from Tucson, from Mexico, and from the San Pedro Valley to pay respects.

We began digging the grave under the large fig tree behind the house, and many who came wanted to help. Apparently, helping to dig is a long-standing tradition in southern Arizona and Mexican ranching communities.

People shed fancy shirts, picked up a pick or a shovel, climbed into the hole and took out dirt. When the hole got too deep to climb into easily, we found a ladder. A bucket and a rope helped remove the dirt. One excavator was Hope Islin Jones, a rancher from near Redington who had known Ike and Jean in the 1940s. She was in her nineties and a bit frail. People helped her down the ladder, and she slowly filled a bucket, saying, "I'm sad to dig a grave for Ike Russell."

Throughout that hot July day probably 30 people worked at excavating the hole. Late in the evening, we lowered Ike in. We used the blue door and we dressed him in his flying clothes—khaki shirt and pants, high-top combat-style boots, and a pair of mechanic's overalls on top. Jean brought out a cotton sheet for a shroud; Ike had ordered, "No box."

Then everyone present put the dirt back, first by slow handfuls and individual shovels full, and then in larger amounts. We left a mound under the fig tree.

And because so many had wanted to dig, we couldn't stop at two or three feet. We actually buried Ike closer to seven.

A good thing, too, that it was that deep, because we never actually had a grate.

34

Que en Paz Descanse

BERNARD L. FONTANA

It was a Sunday morning when the telephone rang. The date was July 20, 1980, two decades before I am writing these words. "Ike died last night," the voice said. "We knew you'd want to know. If you want to see him, you'd better come over to his house now. We're going to bury him today in his back yard."

"Can you do that?" I asked.

"You can if you have a shovel," was the answer.

I dropped whatever it was I'd been planning for the morning and drove right away to the Russells' house, where a large crowd was already gathering. Ike's widow Jean, their three sons Luke, Dave, and Bob, daughters-in-law, grandchildren, and assorted other relatives were there, most having been at the house in anticipation of his death even before the end. They, and friend Kim Cliffton, had been with Ike when he breathed his last.

Ike's last weeks had been spent at home. No hospitals for him. He had known his days were numbered, so he began to make all the plans. It was tough on Jean having to be an around-the-clock nurse, but they would have it no other way.

Ike had made arrangements with a physician friend, who knew the details of his condition, to fill out the necessary death certificate when the time came. Ike had also checked with city authorities to make sure it was legal to be buried on one's own property and had assured himself, at least, that it was okay.

When I got there a few minutes later, the grave was being dug in the rich, loamy soil of the ancient flood plain of the Santa Cruz River, which has its modern channel just east of the Russells' house. After briefly paying respects to Ike where he still lay on his bed, I drove home, changed into digging clothes, grabbed a couple of shovels, a Tarahumara earthenware bowl, a bag of pinole, and returned with my youngest son, Nicholas. Friends and neighbors were still arriving, as they did all day long. Most brought food and liquid refreshments, chiefly beer and soft drinks. Jean and other immediate relatives were kept busy in the kitchen and greeting the dozens of guests. Singly and in pairs, people crowded into Ike's small room for a final viewing and to bid him farewell. Kim Cliffton was massaging Ike's lower legs and bare feet to reduce the swelling that had set in so he could get Ike's high-top combat shoes on. He finally had to cut the leather sides so they would fit and Ike would not have to go to his grave barefoot or in slippers. And the clothes he was dressed in were those he'd worn piloting friends.

Outside in the back yard, under a fig tree, neighbor and friend Charley Figueroa, a former jockey, sat in his wheelchair supervising excavations. In time-honored Mexican, Yaqui, and Tohono O'odham tradition, people took turns deepening the four-foot by eight-foot hole. Less traditional was the fact that women helped with the digging.

I had my turn with a shovel, as did my son Nicholas. The digging was easy through the fertile alluvial soil. The ground that years ago had been laid down by the Santa Cruz River's flow would now be Ike's resting place.

As the hot and humid July afternoon wore on and the crowd began to swell, the feeling became more festive. Armando Maya, a biologist who had flown with Ike, was there with his guitar to play and sing Mexican music. Ike's niece, Janet Romanishon, played classical music on her flute. People ate, drank, laughed, and talked, most swapping stories about adventures they'd had with Ike or about what a wonderful friend and neighbor he had been. Jean and the rest of Ike's kin were so busy there was no time for serious mourning. This was a wake, and it was doing what wakes are meant to do—to say "good-bye" with a celebration of life rather than with morbid remorse over death.

Above all, it was an occasion of love. Love was palpable. There was an outpouring of joy for one another. There was a bonding of kindred spirits, souls joined in mutual commemoration of a beautiful life that had brought enrichment to so many others. Never before or since have I been surrounded by as much love as on that unforgettable summer day.

By midafternoon the grave had been prepared, and Jean asked me if a cleric shouldn't come over to say a few words before Ike was buried. I immediately thought of the Reverend Charles Polzer, a Jesuit priest who had been among Ike's friends and who knew Ike's record of flying historians and other scholars into remote parts of Mexico. Jean agreed he would be a good choice, so I called Charlie on the phone. When he answered I explained the situation to him.

"We're burying Ike in his back yard," I said. "And Jean would very much appreciate it if you would come by and say a few words."

"Bury him in his back yard! Can you do that?" he wanted to know.

"You can if you have a shovel," I answered. "And we have plenty of shovels."

"I'll be there as soon as I can," he said, and hung up.

True to his word, Father Polzer was at the house in less than an hour. He brought his dalmatic and stole so he would appear in his proper role when the time came. After he had had time to talk with friends and enjoy something to eat and drink, the decision was made to move Ike's body from his bed to his grave. A blanket and pillow were laid on an old door Ike had chosen for the occasion, and his body was gently lifted and placed on it, his head resting on the pillow. With skillful maneuvering, Kim Cliffton and Ike's three sons were able to get the door, held carefully horizontal, out of the bedroom, out of the house, and placed next to the hole under the fig tree.

Before Ike was laid to rest, there was more music. Ike's flutist niece played the famous solo from Christoph Gluck's *Orpheus*, a favorite of Ike's.

Family friend Mary McWhorter held a Coleman lantern next to Father Polzer in the rapidly fading daylight while he gave an impromptu talk about Ike. He began by noting that Ike was not a Catholic nor had he been a person deeply committed to any form of organized religion. He was, however, said Polzer, a deeply spiritual person. This he demonstrated by reading a couple of passages from a book written by the Jesuit priest and paleontologist, Pierre Teilhard de Chardin. They concerned exploration, discovery, flight, and matters of a cosmic nature—all themes touching at the core of Ike's being. What I remember thinking was that it was almost as if Teilhard had written the words with Ike in mind.

By the end of Charlie's brief and eloquent panegyric, twilight had turned to darkness. Ike had prepared for that eventuality as well. "Ike's Last Project," as it was worded about, had been to fashion a lamp hanger out of an iron rod. Speculating that his wake, if not his burial, would last until after dark, he had made a hanger that could be stuck in the ground with a Coleman lantern suspended from it.

With the lantern in place on its hanger, Ike's body, still on the door, was lovingly lowered into the grave and covered with a Tarahumara blanket. Botanist Richard Felger added a collection of plants; I put the Tarahumara bowl filled with pinole at his feet. Someone else placed some chocolate Hershey bars—one of Ike's favorite foods—in the grave as well.

Just as people had taken turns digging the grave, now we alternated in filling it. It started with everyone present picking up a handful of earth and one by one dropping it onto the blanketed body below. That done, others took turns with shovels, tossing in the back dirt from either side of the grave where it had been thrown earlier in the day. At one point, Luke Russell's son Arthur, who was about eight years old, bent over on top of one of the piles and used both hands to scoop the earth backwards through his legs into the grave, tears streaming down his cheeks all the while.

In a short time, the hole was filled and a mound was placed over the grave with the remainder of the back dirt. The last to handle a shovel was Joe Contreras, a Yaqui Indian neighbor. He placed the shovel in a certain way as a traditional indication that the job was finished.

Gradually, visitors began to drift off into the darkness. There was still eating, drinking, conversation, and music, but the mood was now more subdued—even if the love was not. Teilhard would have understood. "Love alone," he wrote in *The Phenomenon of Man*, "is capable of uniting living beings in such a way as to complete and fulfil them, for it alone takes them and joins them by what is deepest in themselves."

The day after Ike was buried brought still more visitors. One was Charles Lowe, a University of Arizona ecologist whom Ike had flown on many trips to Mexico. He had missed the wake, but he wanted to know where Ike was buried. Directed to the grave, he sat all day in a chair next to the low mound marking the site.

The final farewell to Ike on that day could not have been more appropriate. Dave Russell, Ike's youngest son and himself a pilot, flew Ike's plane low and slow over the grave in a last salute.

Que en paz descanse, Ike. May you ever rest in peace.

The day after Ike's burial there was one visit to the Russell house that was not so welcome. Luke Russell remembers it well because he was the one who had to deal with it. Though tired and emotionally drained, the family had spent the morning taking care of the things that still needed to be done. Then around noon someone said, "Oh my God, there's a police car out front!"

Everyone was apprehensive because even though Ike had checked, the rest of the family was not entirely convinced that it was legal to bury a person in the back yard. Burial on a ranch was one thing, but this was the City of Tucson. Had the police picked up on rumors of a dead body and wild goings-on and come to investigate? Grim fears surfaced of their all being arrested, city backhoes exhuming Ike's body, forensic specialists swarming over the grave, interrogations to determine if a crime had been committed.

Luke walked slowly toward the patrol car with Ike's caution filling his head: "Boys, always call a policeman 'Officer' and don't sass him." The policeman was a middle-aged, somewhat portly man with the easy-going manner of a good Western lawman. He introduced himself, and Luke did likewise.

*"I understand there's been a burial somewhere
here," he began. "Did someone die?"*
*"Yes, my father died yesterday," Luke replied. "He
had cancer. He was 63. He was a rancher in the
grand old style, and he wanted to be buried on his
own land. So that's what we did." Luke showed the
policeman the extent of the property, which was
quite a few acres and resembled a small ranch.
The officer looked around carefully as Luke pointed
out the boundaries. "He wanted to be buried on
his own place, huh?" he asked.*

*"Yes," said Luke, "he knew that other old
ranchers had done it, and he wouldn't have it any
other way." Then he added, "Since the property is in
Tucson, we in the family were uncertain at first
about the legality of it. But my father hired an
attorney to research the law, and he verified that it
was within his rights to be buried here." Luke gave
the policeman the attorney's phone number.*

*The officer said, "I guess this is pretty hard on
you guys."*

*Luke agreed, and explained that one of Ike's
physicians had been on hand to fill out the
Certificate of Death, and that he lived nearby
if the officer had any questions.*

*The policeman briefly removed his hat. "Just
checking," he said. Then he walked back to his
patrol car and drove away.*

*And that's exactly what happened, as Luke
himself recalls it. But a lot of folks around Tucson
will tell you that's not what really took place.
The way most people tell the story, the conversation
went a little differently:*

"Good morning, Officer," Luke began politely. "Is there something I can help you with?"

"Well, I'm here because we've had reports that someone got buried at this address. Is that right?"

"Yes, it is. My dad died yesterday, and we buried him here last night."

"Where did you bury him?"

"Back there," Luke replied, nodding vaguely toward the back yard.

There was a long pause. "You sure this is legal?"

"Yes we are, Officer," Luke answered. "We have permits from the county I can show you, and the lawyer who researched both the state and county statutes is in the house right now, if you'd like to talk to him."

Another long pause. The policeman scratched his head. "Well," he said finally, a note of resignation in his voice, "if you've checked thoroughly to make sure it's legal, I guess it's okay." He began walking slowly back to his patrol car. Suddenly he stopped and turned toward Luke, uncertain and confused.

"Aw, come on, you can't really bury someone in your back yard, can you?"

Luke suppressed a weary grin. "You can if you have a shovel," he said.

Afterword: A Few Words about Ike

Thomas Bowen

When people met Ike Russell for the first time they often didn't know quite what to make of him. What they saw was a lanky, six-foot-five lean-faced man, wearing wire-rimmed glasses and simple work clothes, looking for all the world like the cattle rancher he once was. They didn't hear much from him either, for Ike was usually a bit taciturn around people he had just met. But those who got to know him learned that this was no simple cowboy. Beneath the humble and unassuming exterior was a cosmopolitan and sophisticated man with wide interests, a quick wit, and a razor-sharp mind—to say nothing of a pilot with enormous skill in the difficult art of backcountry flying.

So who exactly was Ike Russell?

Ike was born Alexander Russell, Jr. (no middle name) on September 7, 1916, in Avon, New York. He never liked the "Jr.," so years later when his father died he dropped it and became simply Alexander Russell. As for "Ike," it was a nickname given him by his older sister Alice when he was a young boy. Although he always signed his name "Alexander," he was known to everybody as Ike.

As an adult, Ike always considered himself a country boy, but he was born into a well-established, well-educated, and very proper Eastern family. His paternal grandfather had been a highly respected Presbyterian minister in Oyster Bay, New York, on Long Island. The Reverend Russell's congregation often included Theodore Roosevelt and his family, who spent summers at their nearby Sagamore Hill estate. The two families were well acquainted, and Ike's father and his two brothers became good friends with the Roosevelt boys.

As they grew up, the lives of the three Russell brothers took somewhat different paths. Ike's uncle Gordon followed in his father's footsteps and became a Presbyterian minister. His other uncle, Henry Norris Russell, joined the faculty of Princeton University and had a distinguished career as an astronomer and director of the University's Dudley Observatory. Ike's father, Alexander Sr. (known as "Alec"), graduated from Princeton and entered the world of business. He moved upstate to the Rochester area and went to work for the Monroe County Water Authority, eventually becoming president of its board of directors.

Alec Russell married a Rochester girl by the name of Editha Brewster. She was the daughter of a local banker who had been instrumental in financing the young George Eastman's camera company. The couple set up housekeeping in the small town of Avon, about 20 miles south of Rochester. Here Editha presided over the family home and produced Ike and his four siblings.

Alec and Editha's first child was their only daughter, Alice. Their first son was Ike. After Ike came William, who died when he was a year and a half old. Last were the fraternal twins David and Gordon. Ike and Gordon were of different temperaments and were friendly but not particularly close. He hit it off well with David, and he was always especially fond of Alice.

Although the Russells expected their children to attend college and follow traditional careers, it didn't work out quite that neatly. Alice enrolled at Vassar College and took a Bachelor's degree in mathematics. Later she became a surgical nurse, and during World War Two served a grueling stint in a military hospital in Normandy. After the war she married Ward Davidson, an optical engineer who worked at the Kodak Company, became the mother of two children, and eventually settled with her family in Tucson.

Ike's brother Gordon graduated from Princeton with a degree in electrical engineering and worked for several companies before taking a faculty position with the School of Engineering at the University of Arizona. Gordon's twin brother David suffered from dyslexia and had a difficult time in school. When he graduated from high school, war in Europe was imminent, and he decided to enlist in the Army Signal Corps. He was killed during the Allied invasion of Italy.

Ike was the one who broke most completely with family tradition. Although he did attend college, he never quite graduated, nor did he pursue a career in the conventional professions. Instead, Ike became a rancher and a bush pilot.

From early childhood, Ike was plagued by poor health, and this more than anything else influenced the course of his life. He was born with a serious respiratory disorder that produced uncontrollable drainage from his sinuses. This in turn led to bronchiectasis, a chronic pulmonary condition marked by progressive damage to the lung tissue. When Ike was 11 years old, his parents were warned that he would not survive another winter in the damp cold of upstate New York. This was a time long before family mobility was respectable, so there was never any thought of the entire family moving for the benefit of Ike's health. Like many Eastern families of the period, the Russells arranged for their ailing son to relocate on his own to the warm dry climate of the Southwest. In 1928, Ike's mother took him to Tucson and settled him in with a family there.

Over the next decade, Ike would live in Tucson for most of the year, returning to New York only in the summers. Two or three times his mother and siblings made winter visits to Tucson, staying for several weeks in a rented house. Ike was quite devoted to his family and he was always glad for these opportunities to be with his parents and siblings. But these were also important formative years, and as he became attuned to the casual friendliness and easy tolerance of the Southwest, he found Eastern formality and authoritarianism to be increasingly stifling. It was something of a relief when his summers in New York were over and it was time to return to Tucson.

Ike had always been a self-confident boy who did pretty well on his own, and his parents gave him a lot of latitude to follow his own path. Living in the relaxed atmosphere of Tucson gave him an additional measure of freedom that allowed him to flourish. He soon began to think of himself as a Westerner, and he actively cultivated his growing sense of independence and self-reliance, qualities he would later value highly in both himself and in others. These ideals would later surface in his own family as frequent and not always appropriate admonitions to his sons to "use your head" and "be tough" in the face of adversity.

His second home in Tucson was with the Fairgreaves family. Captain Fairgreaves had just founded a private boarding school that catered to Eastern boys like Ike who needed the salubrious Southwestern climate for their health. It was staffed with fine teachers and named the Southern Arizona School for Boys. It was where Ike went to high school.

The school was located near Sabino Canyon, at the base of the Santa Catalina Mountains. In addition to academic subjects, the curriculum included horseback riding and each boy kept his own horse there. This could not have better suited the independent-minded Ike, for it gave him his first opportunity to explore the backcountry and taste the joys of wilderness.

High school turned out to be a wonderful time for Ike. During these years he rode his horse all through the Santa Catalina range, getting to know every nook and cranny. Years later he could still recall the precise location of many of his favorite spots and the characteristics that had made these places so special.

After graduating, Ike entered the University of Arizona. By now he had decided he wanted to become a cattle rancher, and so he enrolled in the School of Agriculture and began taking courses in animal husbandry. Though this was direct preparation for his chosen occupation, he found himself bored by formal education and turned into a rather indifferent student. Then in the spring of 1938, during his Junior year, Ike met Jean Straub, a Stanford graduate who had come to the University of Arizona to start a Master's program in anthropology. Their courtship blossomed quickly and intensified during the following fall. Ike and Jean both finished the fall semester, but not their degrees. In late December of 1938, after their final exams, they dropped out of school and were married.

After leaving the University, Ike and Jean began looking for a ranch to buy. Nothing suitable was immediately available, so the young couple decided to take temporary jobs on the Bird Yoas Ranch near Amado, south of Tucson. Ike signed on as a cowboy while Jean worked as a cook, and it was here that they learned many of the practical aspects of the ranching business. In 1940, after a few months at Amado, they heard about two small adjoining ranches on the San Pedro River, east of Tucson, that were up for sale, and Ike and Jean bought them. With their infant son Alexander, whom they nicknamed "Luke," the young couple began their life as a ranching family.

Life at the Russell ranch was isolated and primitive. The nearest settlement was the tiny village of Cascabel. Benson, where the groceries came from, was an hour's drive on washboard roads. The adobe ranch house they moved into had two rooms, a dirt floor, no electricity, and no running water. One of their few luxuries was a battery-powered record player. Ike and Jean loved music, and this device enabled them to listen to Ike's fine collection of classical recordings. But the two-room adobe was not adequate for the long term, so interspersed with the chores of mending fences and caring for 80 head of cattle, Ike designed and built a more modern ranch house with electricity and indoor plumbing. Meanwhile, the family itself was growing. Robert came along in 1941 and David was born two and a half years later.

The San Pedro Valley was a wonderful place to raise a family. All three sons began their education in the relaxed atmosphere of a one-room schoolhouse. As young boys they were constantly outside, immersed in the world of nature, and to Ike and Jean's great pleasure they developed a keen appreciation of the natural environment. By helping out with the chores they picked up many of the skills that are an essential part of life on a cattle ranch. And the boys also gained an understanding of cultural and linguistic diversity. Many of their neighbors and schoolmates were Hispanic, and the Russells' hired hand was always a Mexican cowboy who was regarded pretty much as part of the family.

But for Ike and Jean, the long-term prospects for the ranch were not promising. Running cattle in that country was a marginal business at best, and Ike was determined to do it in a way that was respectful of the environment and kind to his animals. It was an approach that turned out to be better suited to subsistence ranching than running a successful business. Moreover, Ike's health was never good. Even with hired help, he and Jean eventually realized that his chronic respiratory problems utterly sapped him of the physical strength and stamina that ranching required. Besides, they found themselves constantly driving to Tucson to seek medical attention for Ike's frail lungs. Tucson was clearly where they needed to be, so in the spring of 1948 they reluctantly decided to put the ranch up for sale.

It took nearly three years to find a buyer, but in the spring of 1951 the Russells were finally able to move to Tucson. They found some acreage on Cottonwood Lane, just south of town, in a beautiful spot between the two channels of the Santa Cruz River. Here Ike set about designing and building what was to become their permanent home.

Though ranching had been beyond Ike's physical capacity, flying was not. About four and a half years before they left the San Pedro, their neighbor, Cecil Ramsey, suggested that he and Ike buy a Piper J-3 Cub from the government surplus market. Ramsey had flown these airplanes during World War Two when he had served in the Army as a forward artillery spotter. Neither the Ramseys nor the Russells had a very good place on their ranches for takeoffs and landings, so another neighbor, Charlie Remick, let them bulldoze a dirt airstrip on his property and keep the airplane there. Before long, Ramsey and Ike were exploring the San Pedro Valley together from the air. And not long after that, Ramsey began informally teaching Ike to fly.

In many ways, Ike and airplanes were a perfect match. He was fond of machinery, and he understood intuitively how airplanes worked, not only the mechanical aspects, but the physics of flight as well. He was also quick to recognize that flying did not require much physical strength. It was an activity that took brains and a cool temperament, qualities he had in abundance. So with Ramsey's encouragement, Ike decided to become a pilot himself.

The fact that Ike had little practical use for flying was inconsequential. The important thing was that he wanted to do it, and it was something he could do. On February 26, 1947 Ike took his first formal flying lesson at the Benson airport, going aloft for half an hour in a Piper Cub with a crop-duster-turned-instructor named Neil S. "Skeet" Taylor.

When Ike decided to do something, he did not dabble. On March 31, just over a month after his first flying lesson, he soloed. Over the next several months he flew mainly around the Benson-Tucson area. Much of the time he went up in order to practice specific skills and maneuvers, sometimes with instructors, more often alone. Although he understood thoroughly the principles of flight and could calculate almost instantly what kind of action was appropriate to nearly any situation, Ike was not a "natural" pilot in the sense of having an innate "feel" for the controls. The fact is that his motor coordination was not very good, and he had to make up for his lack of natural ability with dogged practice. He performed maneuvers over and over, training his hands and feet and eyes to work in synchrony until they did so automatically. And he continued to practice periodically throughout his life. Thus Ike was not so much a *talented* pilot as a highly *skilled* pilot. And his emerging skillfulness paid off quickly, for on May 24, 1947, the crankshaft of the Cub broke and Ike had to make an emergency landing without power in a river bed.

By the end of 1947 Ike had logged 12½ hours of dual time and over 23 hours of solo time. He apparently received his pilot's license two weeks later, on January 14, 1948. Two months after that a crosswind blew his plane off the runway and into some rocks as he was landing. He and his son Dave walked away unscathed but the J-3 Cub never flew again.

Between the loss of the airplane and the closing of the ranch, Ike was left with little opportunity to fly. During the nearly four years between March 1948 and January 1952 he went up only eight times. But in January 1952, with the family resettled in Tucson, Ike resumed flying with gusto. He began renting a 65 hp Taylorcraft from a neighbor named Richard Apodaca and flew nearly every weekend. Many of these were practice flights, and for the next year and a half he flew mostly around Tucson and southern Arizona. But on May 26, 1953, with nearly 95 solo hours under his belt, Ike headed off on a cross-country flight that would forever change his flying career. Leaving Tucson with his close friend and family physician, Dr. Robert Thomas, Ike flew Apodaca's Taylorcraft south into Mexico. After landing at Nogales, Sonora to clear Mexican customs, they continued southward to Hermosillo and then northwest to the Seri Indian village of Desemboque, on the shores of the Gulf of California. Here they not only encountered the Seris, but also met Edward and Mary Beck Moser, the linguist-missionaries to the Seris who would become two of Ike and Jean's closest friends. Becky recalls that when she learned that Ike's companion on that trip was a physician, she asked him to treat Josefita Torres, a Seri woman who had been bitten by a rattlesnake. Dr. Thomas had not come prepared to treat patients, so he merely injected her with saline, but she did recover. For both Ike and Bob Thomas, there would be many medical flights to the Seris in the years to come.

After this first meeting with the Seris and the Mosers, Ike and Bob continued south, crossing several miles of open water and landing on the dirt strip at Tecomate, the remote Seri camp on fabled Tiburón Island. After a night camped under the wings of the airplane, they flew back to Tucson by way of Magdalena and Nogales. Ike's career as a bush pilot had begun.

The following October Ike again headed south in Apodaca's Taylorcraft, this time with his old college pal Bill Swan. Their destination was Maicoba, a remote village in the Sierra Madre mountains of western Chihuahua, where they planned to attend the annual feast day celebrations. This was to be a leisurely adventure, so they went by way of the Sonoran coast so they could spend a few days in Desemboque and Guaymas. From there they flew inland to Yécora, the town closest to Maicoba where they knew they could land. The airstrip was simply a dirt street between some houses at the edge of town, so that's where they set the airplane down. Then a while later Ike went up for a short practice flight. Everything was fine until he turned to land. He inadvertently lined up on the wrong street and wound up planting the airplane in the side of a house. With characteristic understatement, Ike wrote in his flight log that this landing constituted the "End of Trip."

Again, no one was hurt, but the crash totaled Apodaca's airplane, and the only part of it they were able to salvage was the engine. Even that operation was something of a challenge. There was a steep and very rough road down from Yécora, so Ike and Bill hired a local mining truck to bring the engine down. But it was an old truck that leaked brake fluid, and part way down the grade it began to lose its brakes. There was no extra brake fluid anywhere around, but Ike and Bill did notice that the man who owned the truck had some tequila with him. Figuring it was better than nothing, they poured the tequila into the reservoir, and with this surrogate brake fluid they managed to get the engine out to civilization. As for the rest of the airplane, it wound up in pieces, decorating houses on the outskirts of Yécora as yard sculpture.

During the next year Ike flew mostly around the Tucson area in another rented Taylorcraft. He made one nine-day trip into Sonora. Then in September 1955 he bought his own airplane, an Aeronca Sedan with a 145 hp engine. The added power and greater lift opened up many more possibilities, and with this new airplane Ike began making regular flights into Mexico.

As psychologically uplifting as flying was for Ike, his physical health remained poor. It was a constant struggle for him just to maintain a level of activity that most people take for granted. Living in southern Arizona had given him a reprieve, but it had not cured the underlying condition. Sinus drainage often led to blockage, and he suffered severely from sinus headaches. Far more serious, his chronic respiratory disorders were gradually destroying his lungs. In 1957, Ike learned that he had developed amyloidosis—protein deposits on the lung tissues already damaged by bronchiectasis—and that he would have to have the affected tissues removed very soon or he would not live more than another four or five years. The surgery was scheduled as two separate operations so that the first lung could heal before the procedure was performed on the second. When Ike emerged from the anesthetic for the second time, he had lost half of one lung and about a third of the other.

People who knew the extent of Ike's surgery were often amazed to discover that one of his great loves was hiking. Considering how little lung capacity he had, he showed a surprising amount of endurance, though sometimes he paid a heavy price for his hiking in pain and eventual exhaustion. His flying was largely unaffected by the operations, apart from keeping him grounded for a while to convalesce. Altitude was never a particular problem for Ike because he rarely flew high enough to have any need to breathe supplemental oxygen. Until his last few years, the only times he used it were a few flights over the Andes when he had to climb above 15,000 feet.

After 1955, Ike flew regularly, often going aloft several times a week. During many years he logged more than 200 hours of flight time, and sometimes much more. Some of his flights were local trips around the Tucson area and southern Arizona. But Ike's real passion was cross-country flying, and he enjoyed it so much that he often spent a third of the year or more away from home on trips.

Around 1960 Jean began to fly with Ike for the first time. Until then she had largely considered flying to be Ike's domain, and she herself was busy raising their three sons. Ike had often taken the boys up, but flying as an entire family was difficult, because it meant squeezing five people into a four-place airplane. But as their sons began leaving home, flying could become a family activity for the ones who remained, and now Jean began to join him on cross-country trips. During the early 1960s, they made innumerable short hops into northwestern Mexico, and several times they flew to the East Coast and to the Pacific Northwest to visit relatives.

Nor was there any reason to limit their travels to the United States and northern Mexico. In August 1962, Ike and Jean took off with their son David and flew to the Caribbean, returning a month and a half later after visits to Puerto Rico, the Virgin Islands, Haiti (a police state even then), the Dominican Republic, and Guadeloupe. In 1965 they embarked on their most ambitious venture, the nine-month research trip through East Africa and Madagascar with paleoecologist Paul Martin and primatologist Alan Walker. This was followed in 1968–1969 by an eight-month trip with Jean's niece Barbara Straub that took them through Central and South America all the way to Tierra del Fuego.

But as marvelous as these far-ranging trips were, the place Ike loved most was northwestern Mexico, and throughout the 1960s that is where he flew most often.

Like many pilots, Ike eventually quit maintaining a detailed log of his flights. He did fill out a log book for the 1960s, but the entries were all recopied from scattered notes, loose sheets of paper, and memory. As a result, the information is sometimes confused and of dubious accuracy. In the case of one flight known from other sources, his entry is off by nine years. The last complete year Ike kept a log at all was 1970. According to that year's entries, which are probably more reliable than his records for the 1960s, Ike spent 255 hours in the air. About 21 of these hours were flown locally, many of them for advanced instruction and practice. He made 28 trips outside the Tucson area and was away a total of 128 days. There were no major international trips that year, and the longest flights were to Oregon (20 days duration, 29 hours flying time) and Philadelphia (15 days duration, 31 hours flying time). Most of his cross-country trips, as always, were to Mexico. That year he flew to Mexico 18 times, spent a total of 68 days there, and logged half his flight hours on those trips. Most were flights to Sonora and Chihuahua, but twice he flew as far as Cabo San Lucas at the southern tip of Baja California.

By the end of 1970, Ike's logbook indicates that he had more than 1,900 hours of total flight time. But the true figure is at least 600 hours greater, because several years earlier he hadn't bothered to carry over his accumulated hours from one logbook to the next.

As far as can be determined, Ike continued flying at pretty much the same pace until the late 1970s. During the first half of the decade, he and Jean made three major international trips. The first was the 1971 trip to Colombia and Venezuela with geneticists Tom Starmer and Barney Ward, followed two years later by their trip to Tierra del Fuego with Paul Martin. The last major foreign flight took place in the spring of 1975, when Ike and Jean spent a month and a half touring Colombia, Ecuador, and Peru with their son David and his wife Susan Randolph. Interspersed with these ventures, Ike took every opportunity to fly to his beloved northern Mexico. As always, many of these flights were to take scientists and other scholars to remote localities to do field research. Others were visits to relatives and friends or just for the fun of it.

In the late 1970s Ike was diagnosed with myeloma—cancer of the bone marrow. This new illness and the chemotherapy to combat it, coupled with his other health problems, reduced him to a state of chronic exhaustion that even heavy medication could not mitigate. As the months passed, it became increasingly difficult for him to muster the energy and concentration he needed to fly. Often he needed to sleep immediately after a flight, and sometimes he had to rest for two or three days before he could fly again. Occasionally he was too ill to fly at all and was forced to cancel scheduled trips at the last minute.

And one of his flights ended in a crash on Ángel de la Guarda Island, leaving him injured and stranded for three days in the brutal heat of summer. The ordeal almost certainly took a heavy toll on his declining health.

During the last year of his life, Ike seldom flew. On December 10, 1979, Ike took two scientists to Kino Bay on what was probably his last flight. By then he knew he would not be able to pass another flight physical and that this would bring an end to his flying career. With that depressing prospect looming, Jean, who had never had any interest in learning to fly, began to take flight instruction. If she obtained a license, Ike could fly without one if she were along as the pilot of record. And so in early January, Jean took her first flying lesson. By mid-April she had logged about 20 hours of dual time and was ready to solo. But by then there was no point in continuing, for pulmonary edema had set in and it was clear that Ike would not live.

Ike's health had always been so fragile that he was accustomed to viewing each successive day as a bonus, and he accepted his approaching death with equanimity. When he realized that he would not recover, he calmly set about putting his affairs in order and planning the end of his life. Self-reliant as always, when he decided the time had come, he took two sleeping pills and gave himself a lethal injection. During the small hours of July 20, 1980, Ike Russell died in his sleep. He was 63 years old.

GLOSSARY

Aileron: Hinged section at the back of each wing near the tip. They are operated by turning the yoke, which raises the aileron on one wing and lowers the other, causing the wings to bank.

Crash: As used here, any contact between an airplane and the ground which requires repairs before the airplane can take off again.

Dead-stick landing: A landing with no power, usually after the engine quits.

Dual time: Flight hours a student pilot accumulates with an instructor riding along in the airplane.

Elevator: Usually a hinged section at the back of the "tail" (horizontal stabilizer), controlled from the yoke, that changes the pitch of the airplane. Pushing the yoke forward lowers the elevator, which causes the nose to drop and the airplane to dive. Pulling the yoke back raises the elevator and brings the nose up, causing the airplane to climb.

Flaps: Hinged sections at the back of the wings next to the fuselage that can be moved downward to create greater lift, enabling the airplane to fly at a slower speed without stalling.

Flip: An unintended ground maneuver in which the airplane's nose pitches forward with one of two results: either the airplane comes to rest with its nose in the ground and its tail in the air, or the tail section summersaults completely over the nose and the airplane ends up upside down. Flips occur when tail-wheel airplanes stop too fast, either from too soft a landing surface or excessive use of the brakes. They usually wreck the propeller and may cause other structural damage.

Ground loop: A usually inadvertent ground maneuver in which the airplane abruptly pivots on one of its main wheels and comes to rest pointing sideways or backwards from the direction it was traveling. Ground loops are most often caused by inattention to wind conditions, and they can result in damaged landing gear and other structural harm.

Magneto: A device that generates high-voltage electrical current for the engine's ignition system.

Mixture: The relative proportions of fuel and air brought together in the carburetor. Because air is thinner at higher altitude or when it is hot, airplanes have a control that enables the pilot to adjust the air-fuel mixture for best performance and efficiency.

No-go-around strip: An unforgiving airstrip with an obstacle (such as a high cliff) at the end so serious that once the pilot commits to a landing he cannot pull up and circle around for a second try.

Pitch: (1) The up-and-down orientation of the nose of the airplane. An airplane is diving when the nose is pitched steeply downward. (2) The angle of the propeller blades with respect to the circle it describes while turning. Variable-pitch propellers enable the pilot to match the pitch with the engine speed for a desired amount of power. When maximum power is needed, as for takeoff, the pilot will set the throttle for high engine rpms and the propeller control for minimum pitch (the equivalent of putting a car in low gear with the engine racing). Level flight requires less power, so engine rpms are reduced and propeller pitch is increased.

Rudder: Hinged surface at the back of the "fin" (vertical stabilizer) in the tail section that controls side-to-side motion (yaw) of the airplane. Moving the rudder helps the airplane turn in flight and controls its direction during take-off, after landing, and while taxiing. The rudder is controlled by two pedals at the pilot's feet.

Slip (Sideslip): A safe but often dramatic aerial maneuver in which the pilot drops the left wing and turns (yaws) the fuselage to the right, or vice versa, without changing the direction of travel. This forces the airplane to fly with the wings tilted and the fuselage pointed sideways. It is used routinely for landing in a crosswind and sometimes as a way of shedding altitude quickly, prior to landing, without gaining excessive speed. Because it can be a violent maneuver, it may be frightening to passengers who have never experienced it.

Solo time: Flight hours accumulated by a student pilot without an instructor on board.

Spin: A usually unintended aerial maneuver which occurs when one wing stalls but the other wing does not, causing the airplane to spiral downward in a corkscrew pattern. Spins have often proved fatal, and spin recovery was once a required part of flight training. Most modern airplanes have been engineered so they will not spin.

Stall: The condition that occurs when an airplane is traveling too slowly for the wings to support flight. When this happens, the controls briefly become ineffective, the nose (the heaviest part) drops, and the airplane begins to fall rather than fly. Stalls close to the ground are potentially fatal, and stall recovery is a required part of flight training.

Stall warning alarm: A device that emits an unpleasant noise to warn the pilot when his airspeed drops close to the airplane's stalling speed.

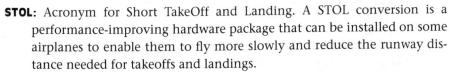

STOL: Acronym for Short TakeOff and Landing. A STOL conversion is a performance-improving hardware package that can be installed on some airplanes to enable them to fly more slowly and reduce the runway distance needed for takeoffs and landings.

Tail-dragger: An airplane with a tail wheel or skid at the back of the fuselage instead of a nose wheel at the front. Many bush pilots prefer tail-draggers because they provide greater clearance for the propeller and greater strength for landings on rough surfaces.

Throttle: The control that regulates the speed of the engine, analogous to a car's accelerator pedal. On many airplanes it is a knob on a metal shaft protruding from the instrument panel. Pushing the throttle in or pulling it out increases or decreases engine rpms, respectively.

Touch-and-go landing: A maneuver in which the pilot briefly touches the ground with the wheels and then lifts off without bringing the airplane to a stop. Student pilots perform it as a training exercise to improve landing proficiency, and bush pilots perform it to test the firmness of the ground before committing to a landing.

Yaw: Roughly, side-to-side motion which changes the compass direction toward which the nose of the airplane is pointing.

Yoke: One of the airplane's main control devices which looks something like the flattened lower half of an automotive steering wheel and serves a similar function. Turning the yoke in either direction causes the wings to bank; when pulled back or pushed forward it causes the nose of the airplane to go up or down, respectively.

ABOUT THE CONTRIBUTORS

Thomas Bowen is professor emeritus of anthropology at California State University, Fresno, and a research associate at the University of Arizona Southwest Center. His major research interest is the ethnohistory and archaeology of the Seri Indians and the Gulf of California. He can often be found prowling the Gulf islands or climbing an occasional mountain.

Dean Brooks, now retired, has been clinical professor of psychiatry at both the University of Oregon and the University of Washington Health Services Center, and for 27 years was superintendent of the Oregon State Hospital. His professional career has been directed toward eliminating the dehumanizing effects of institutional care. During his superintendency, the Academy Award-winning film *One Flew Over the Cuckoo's Nest* was shot at the Oregon State Hospital. For this production, he served as both technical advisor and actor, playing the role of Dr. Spivey. He is also a musician and was, in earlier days, an avid hiker and mountaineer.

Joy Cooper was trained as a zoologist and works as a quality assurance specialist with Fred Cooper Consulting Engineers, Inc., a civil engineering firm in Portland, Oregon that specializes in construction management and certification. She has worked as a volunteer in many capacities and currently tutors inmates for the Multnomah County Department of Corrections. She and her husband Fred are devoted kayakers.

Hector D'Antoni, now retired, was a senior research scientist at NASA's Ames Research Center in California. He has been a Guggenheim and a Humboldt Fellow, has received an award from the National Research Council, and fifteen awards from NASA. His research on the role of short-term disturbances over long-term processes of global change led to the discovery of solar UV-C radiation as an environmental factor in Tierra del Fuego. He continues working to fully explain this discovery. He lives in Spain with his wife, and he collaborates with scientists at the Research Council of Spain, the Autonomous University of Madrid, and the Institute of Conservation and Restoration of Cultural Goods in Valencia. He is investigating Argentine history, writes poetry and fiction, loves opera, and is an enthusiastic carpenter.

Paul Dayton is professor of marine biology at Scripps Institution of Oceanography in La Jolla, California. His research covers a wide array of problems in marine ecology, and he has conducted field work from Alaska to Antarctica.

Richard Stephen Felger is Adjunct Senior Research Scientist in the Department of Soil, Water, and Environmental Science at the University of Arizona, and Research Associate at the San Diego Natural History Museum. He has conducted research in deserts worldwide and has been active in Southwest and international conservation. He has more than one hundred peer-reviewed publications, in addition to books and popular works in botany, ethnobiology, and new food crops for the world.

Bernard L. Fontana, now retired, was formerly field historian at the University of Arizona Library and an ethnologist at the Arizona State Museum. His research focuses on the anthropology and history of the American Southwest and northwestern Mexico. His most recent book is *A Gift of Angels: The Art of Mission San Xavier del Bac.*

Drum Hadley is Executive Trustee of the Animas Foundation, which oversees the 500-square-mile Gray Ranch, a working wilderness along the Mexican border in southwestern New Mexico and southeastern Arizona. He is a founding member of the Malpais Borderlands Group, an organization of ranchers, environmentalists, and government personnel who use the concept of grassbanking to preserve the culture of ranching and open space landscapes. He has published three books of poetry and is working on a fourth. Ike's ghost finally got to him in 1995 when Drum became a pilot at the age of 55. He flies frequently.

Chuck Hanson is the founder and original owner of Arid Lands Greenhouses, headquartered in Tucson, which specializes in the propagation and rearing of rare succulent plants. He was formerly the curator of birds and mammals at the Arizona-Sonora Desert Museum.

Bruce Hayward is professor emeritus of biological sciences at Western New Mexico University in Silver City. He is a mammalogist with a long-standing research interest in bats. Since retiring, he has spent much time traveling and watching birds, an avocational interest he has nurtured since boyhood.

Bill Heed was professor emeritus of ecology and evolutionary biology at the University of Arizona, whose research focused on the biogeography and speciation of fruit flies. After retiring, he explored the relationship between the scientific paradigm and spiritual consciousness. He practiced Yoga, conducted classes in meditation for prison inmates throughout southern Arizona, read and wrote poetry, and enjoyed his family. Bill Heed died on September 10, 2007, at the age of 81.

Robert R. Humphrey was professor emeritus of range management at the University of Arizona. In addition to his wide-ranging studies of the boojum, he conducted research on a variety of problems in ecology, including pioneering the use of prescribed burns as a way of preventing catastrophic forest fires. Not surprisingly for an inveterate field scientist, he loved camping, fishing, and traveling. Bob Humphrey died on March 13, 2002, at the age of 97.

Ronald Jacobowitz is professor emeritus of mathematics at Arizona State University, with research interests in algebraic number theory and biomedical statistics. He has maintained a parallel career as a concert pianist and has toured widely in the United States and Mexico to critical acclaim. His repertoire includes both the standard classical literature and the works of lesser-known masters such as Charles-Valentin Alkan and Nikolai Medtner. He has held a private pilot's license since 1968, though he no longer flies regularly.

Cathy Moser Marlett works with the Summer Institute of Linguistics, illustrating literacy materials and dictionaries for minority language groups in Mexico. After spending much of her childhood in the Seri Indian village of Desemboque, Sonora, she earned a Bachelor's degree in art and biology and pursued further study in scientific illustration. She also works with watercolors and soft pastels, and many of her paintings, including her landscapes of the Seri area, have been exhibited. She works out of her home in Tucson, but travels widely with her linguist husband.

Peter Marshall is a family physician in private practice in North Pole, Alaska. After obtaining a private pilot's license in 1982, he spent five and a half years with the Public Health Service flying to Athabascan and Inuit villages throughout Alaska with his medical kit in the back of his airplane. He continues to fly regularly, and he and his wife Laura frequently head off to remote areas of northern and western Alaska, where the fishing for arctic char and grayling is glorious.

Paul S. Martin is professor emeritus of geosciences at the Desert Laboratory facility of the University of Arizona. He is a specialist in paleoecology whose research focuses on the extinction of large animals in the late Pleistocene. He has been a Guggenheim Fellow and has received the Distinguished Service Award of the American Quaternary Society.

Jaime Armando Maya, now retired, was associate professor of zoology at Eastern Illinois University in Charleston. He research interest is mammals, with special attention to bats.

Ken McVicar, now retired, was associate professor of geography at California State University, Hayward. He has held a private pilot's license since 1970, though he no longer flies.

Mary McWhorter is Oriental Studies librarian emerita at the University of Arizona Library and was a founder, facilitator and teacher of Vipassana meditation at the Tucson Community Meditation Center. From 1973 to 1983 she served as chairperson of the Tucson Chamber Music Co-op. She now lives in Logan, Utah, where she is a member of the Williamsburg Retirement Community.

Doug Peacock, wilderness advocate and conservationist, is the author of four books and many articles for such magazines as *Audubon, Outside,* and *Esquire.* After a year and a half in Vietnam as a Special Forces medic, he spent 20 years in the field studying and filming grizzly bears. A PBS film of his experiences, titled *Peacock's War,* won Grand Prizes at the Snowbird and Telluride Mountain Film festivals. A recent recipient of a Guggenheim Fellowship, he is writing a book on global warming, human colonization of the Americas, and Pleistocene extinction.

David Policansky is associate director of the Board on Environmental Studies and Toxicology at the National Research Council in Washington, D.C. His research spans many topics in ecology, fisheries, and natural resources management. He obtained his private pilot's license in 1969 but has traded flying for piloting a small power boat on Chesapeake Bay.

H. Ronald Pulliam is Regents Professor in the Institute of Ecology, University of Georgia. His research covers an array of problems in biological diversity and population dynamics of plants and animals, a field he first began to explore when he was 10 years old. He and his wife Janice now live in Arizona.

Susan Randolph teaches gifted students at Tully Elementary School in Tucson. In 1976 she obtained a private pilot's license, though like her husband, David Russell, she no longer flies regularly. Instead, she enjoys spending her leisure time horseback riding and birding.

Bob Russell is Ike and Jean Russell's middle son. He is a millwright and the owner and operator of a farm near Eugene, Oregon, where he raises sheep, hay, and timber. He owns two ultralight aircraft which he flies locally.

David Russell is Ike and Jean Russell's youngest son. He operates a Tucson-based import company that brings textiles and ceramics from Mexico to the United States. He obtained a private pilot's license in 1976, though like his wife, Susan Randolph, he no longer flies regularly.

Jean Russell was Ike Russell's wife of 40 years and the mother of their three sons. She and Ike operated a cattle ranch in the San Pedro Valley during the 1940s, and from 1960 to 1980 she worked half-time as a laboratory assistant to Bill Heed at the University of Arizona. She has maintained her home in Tucson as a small farm over the past 50 years, and during the last 20 years she has been deeply involved in neighborhood environmental issues. She continues to keep her doors open to friends, neighbors, and visitors.

Luke Russell is Ike and Jean Russell's oldest son. He is associate professor of English at the Community College of Philadelphia, where he specializes in inner city literacy and second dialect instruction. He lives in a restored Victorian house in the Tulpehocken National Historic District of Germantown, which has been cited nationally as a model community for racial integration. He is an urban farmer, raising chickens, guinea pigs, and chinchillas, and takes special pride in his roles as husband, father, and grandfather.

William T. Starmer is professor of biology at Syracuse University. His research encompasses a wide array of problems in evolutionary biology.

Alan Walker is Evan Pugh Emeritus Professor at Pennsylvania State University. He carried out research in Africa and Madagascar on primate and human evolution. He has held Guggenheim and MacArthur Fellowships and is a Fellow of the Royal Society, a Member of the National Academy of Arts and Sciences, and a Foreign Member of the National Academy of Sciences.